T0314208

Asian States, Asian Bankers

A volume in the series
CORNELL STUDIES IN POLITICAL ECONOMY
edited by Peter J. Katzenstein

A full list of titles in the series appears at the end of the book.

Asian States, Asian Bankers

Central Banking in Southeast Asia

●

Natasha Hamilton-Hart

CORNELL UNIVERSITY PRESS

ITHACA AND LONDON

First published 2002 by Cornell University Press

Library of Congress Cataloging-in-Publication Data
Hamilton-Hart, Natasha
    Asian states, Asian bankers : central banking in Southeast Asia / Natasha Hamilton-Hart.
        p. cm.
    Includes bibliographical references and index.
    ISBN 0-8014-3987-6 (cloth)
    1. Banks and banking, Central—Asia, Southeastern.   2. Finance—Asia, Southeastern.   I. Title.
HG3290.8.A7   H36   2002
332.1′1′0959—dc21   2002067731

Printed in the United States of America

Cornell University Press strives to use environmentally responsible suppliers and materials to the fullest extent possible in the publishing of its books. Such materials include vegetable-based, low-VOC inks and acid-free papers that are recycled, totally chlorine-free, or partly composed of nonwood fibers. For further information, visit our website at www.cornellpress.cornell.edu.

Cloth printing   10 9 8 7 6 5 4 3 2 1

For David

Contents

Acknowledgments

I have been lucky to have had many sources of help and inspiration over the last eight years. Most of all, I thank Benedict Anderson, Peter Katzenstein, and Takashi Shiraishi for being wonderful teachers and for guiding this project when it was still taking shape. In Peter's case, my debt has grown since. My thanks also go to other people who have provided ideas and advice at different stages, especially Jennifer Amyx, Chua Beng Huat, Milton Esman, Jomo K. S., Gregory Noble, David Pine, John Ravenhill, Garry Rodan, Wynne Russell, and Richard Stubbs. In addition, I am grateful to the readers of my manuscript for Cornell University Press for their constructive comments, to Robin Ward for expert indexing, and to Roger Haydon for his help.

Between 1996 and 1999 I made several visits to Southeast Asia to carry out research. For logistical support, access to library resources, and expertise, I thank the Institute of Strategic and International Studies in Kuala Lumpur, the Centre for Strategic and International Studies in Jakarta, and the Institute for Southeast Asian Studies in Singapore. The National University of Singapore, Bank Indonesia, Bank Negara Malaysia, the Bank of Thailand, and the Monetary Authority of Singapore kindly allowed me to use their libraries. At Cornell University the Peace Studies Program, the Mario Einaudi Center for International Studies, and the Graduate School all provided financial resources for parts of this research. A postdoctoral fellowship from the Research School of Pacific and Asian Studies at the Australian National University allowed me to write this manuscript and also funded fieldwork in 1999 and research assistance in 2000. I thank Andrew Lawler for unearthing library sources and Jennifer Hendriks for patient translation from the Dutch. Final revisions were completed at the National University of Singapore. While I appreciate the assistance given by all these organizations and individuals, they of course bear no responsibility for my results.

In Indonesia, Malaysia, and Singapore, vital help and information came from many quarters. Ruth and Peter Nichols in Jakarta and Theresa and David Taylor in Kuala Lumpur were very gracious hosts. Staff at the local offices of the *Far Eastern Economic Review* and the *Asian Wall Street Journal* very helpfully made available their newspaper clippings files. For not talking about banks, I thank Choon Heng in particular. To those who did talk about banks, central banks, and bureaucratic life, I am sincerely grateful. Most of my interviewees did not wish to be mentioned by name, so I can only thank them collectively for sharing their memories, thoughts, and time. I hope that this book does not offend any of the people who so generously helped me put together a picture of how government organizations in their country work. Since the issue of corruption runs implicitly or otherwise through much of this book, I make explicit here the difference between organizational systems and the people who work in them. Dedicated and principled people often serve in organizations that manage to produce perverse outcomes. During my research I heard of many people whose integrity and courage were all the more striking because of the adverse environments in which they worked or lived. I feel fortunate to have met some of them.

Finally, it is perhaps appropriate to end at the beginning. I do not suppose that the NZDF often gets thanked for inspiring a book on central banks but in this case such thanks are in order.

N.H.-H.

Singapore

Asian States, Asian Bankers

I.

States, Money, and Financial Governance

Money and credit are not only the lifeblood of every modern economy; they are core concerns of every modern state. An intimate connection between politics and money is universal. This book looks at central banks, governments, and private bankers in a group of Southeast Asian countries, but the problems of financial regulation it discusses are by no means peculiar to the region. The evolution of private financial institutions and government strategies to attract or influence financial flows have generally gone hand in hand, if not harmoniously. The business of sovereign lending, for example, was both the making and at times the ruin of prominent financial houses in Europe and America, from fourteenth-century Florentine financiers to the Rothschilds, Barings, and Morgans who rose to prominence in the nineteenth century. In country after country, the reciprocal engagement of political authority and private actors tended over time to generate institutions with similar missions: central banks and other agencies concerned with standardizing a country's money, regulating its banks, financing government deficits, and influencing the terms on which financial resources are used (Conant 1927; Collins 1993).

These institutions for the organization and control of finance are deeply implicated in the emergence of the modern state, understood as a system of government based on rational-legal authority and bureaucratic administration. Indeed, the rationalization of regulatory, tax, and currency systems was in many ways constitutive of the modern state. The development of these functions reflected and supported two of the state's defining projects: the standardization of instruments and objects of rule; and the transformation of the administrative role as office-holding, no longer a matter of private property and private law, acquired a distinctly public character (Silberman 1993, 4; Scott 1998). The evolution of the state along these lines in colonial Southeast Asia was in many ways similar to the transformation that took place in Europe. Incremental moves to separate private and public roles in Netherlands India (later to become independent Indonesia), for example, did not occur very much later than in the Netherlands itself. The changes, beginning in the early nineteenth century when administration of the colony passed from a failed trading company to the government, gathered pace toward the end of the century and were consolidated in the early twentieth century. Modern tax collection systems operated wholly by public officials eventually replaced privately operated revenue farms (Rush 1990; Diehl 1993). Currency rationalization started in 1828 with the establishment of a colonial bank of issue (also a commercial bank with mixed government and private ownership) and extended to vigorous, though never completely successful, attempts at purging the many nonofficial currencies still circulating in the Netherlands Indies in the early twentieth century.

Similar processes of state-building, standardization, and bureaucratic development occurred in most of Southeast Asia from the end of the nineteenth century: the expansion of state-provided infrastructure, the adoption of new governmental responsibilities (such as health, welfare, and education services), the hardening of territorial boundaries, and the rationalization of revenue systems. The broad thrust of these developments was common to both the colonized areas of Southeast Asia and nominally independent Siam (Trocki 1992; Butcher and Dick 1993). In each political unit the precursors of modern central banks, mostly currency boards or commercial banks with note-issuing privileges, had been established by the turn of the century. Their public roles centered on currency issue and maintaining foreign exchange stability. They were only minimally concerned with domestic financial development and regulation until well into the twentieth century. Thus the Java Bank, the region's oldest central bank, did not acquire the full range of modern central bank functions until after its nationalization by the Indonesian government in 1951. Central banks elsewhere in the region were established in midcentury: in Thailand in 1942, in the Philippines in 1949, in Malaya in 1959. Singapore's de facto central bank, the Monetary Authority of Singapore, began operating only in 1971, although other government agencies had shared its responsibilities earlier.

Despite these similarities in the evolution of state organizations across Southeast Asia, there were important differences among the colonial states and their post-independence incarnations in how the process of state expansion and rationalization took place. This book explores one aspect of these contrasting experiences of modern statehood: the emergence of organizations tasked with managing money and finance. Standing at the center are the central banks of Indonesia, Malaysia, and Singapore. Central banks do not exist in a political or institutional vacuum, but they are the organizations most directly involved in the implementation of monetary and financial policy in Southeast Asia. The way they implement policy tends to reflect their internal structures and routines. In turn, how they implement policy has important economic and political consequences: the stability of the financial system, the government's capacity to mobilize and control financial resources, and the viability of different strategies for governing internationally open economies.

MONEY AND FINANCE IN POLITICAL ECONOMY

Finance is an area where a government role is particularly important and virtually unavoidable. Asia's financial and currency crises of 1997 and 1998 demonstrated once again that governments need to be involved in prudential regulation and crisis management.[1] In the wake of the crises, the governments of the worst affected countries all became significantly more active in their financial systems. Their responses suggest that governments will inevitably be involved in the financial system—but in what way, and with what effects?

Currency issue, tax collection, and the compulsory mobilization of financial resources are now normally the sole province of public authorities, in Southeast Asia as elsewhere. On other issues, the roles of government and private actors have been more subject to revision in the modern era. Government regulation, government ownership of commercial banks, the ends to which financial policy has been directed, and the means selected to achieve these ends have all varied. Prudential constraints on banks and other financial institutions, however, have increased in a more or less secular fashion since the nineteenth century. Despite much-touted episodes of financial deregulation, the sheer volume of legal regulation has grown markedly—in Europe and America as well as in Southeast Asia.[2]

This long-term trend to increase prudential regulation is partly a response to perennial problems of financial instability. Periodic financial crises have been a feature of all economic systems where the use of money and credit is widespread (Kindleberger 1989). In addition, many countries tried to strengthen prudential regulation during the 1980s and 1990s, because a concurrent or slightly earlier shift toward selective liberalization had made stronger prudential regulations necessary. During the 1980s and early 1990s, financial institutions in many countries acquired greater freedom to set their own prices, develop and market new financial instruments, and compete both nationally and internationally. In the same period, competition in the financial sector was also enhanced by the partial (in some cases total) retreat of government-owned institutions from the business of banking. A series of postliberalization financial crises reinforced two lessons: financial systems are prone to failure in very costly ways, and reducing the role played by government in the financial marketplace can be a double-edged sword. In Indonesia, for example, a widely lauded financial liberalization program in the 1980s succeeded in transforming an inefficient, sluggish, and corrupt government-dominated financial sector into a dynamic, private-sector-led one. Although the scale of the currency and financial crisis that followed owed a lot to external factors, signs of instability in the financial sector *preceded* Indonesia's crisis of 1997–98. Some kind of postliberalization crisis should have been expected on both theoretical and empirical grounds (Diaz-Alejandro 1985; McKinnon and Pill 1996; Nasution 1992).

The public costs of financial crises can be very high. The fiscal costs of crises in Asia, Latin America, and Scandinavia over the last two decades of the twentieth century have frequently risen above 20 percent of GDP (gross domestic product) for the countries concerned and in some cases much higher: the fiscal cost

1. This conclusion is shared by accounts that emphasize the inherent instability of international financial markets as a factor behind the crisis and those that attribute a more causal role to such domestic factors as corruption. See Noble and Ravenhill 2000 for discussion of the different arguments.
2. See, e.g., Vogel 1996, 17–18, 93–117.

of Argentina's crisis in the early 1980s came to 55 percent of GDP, Chile's at the same time was over 40 percent; Thailand's of 1997–98, about 30 percent; and the public costs of Indonesia's recent crisis, an estimated 50 percent of GDP.[3] In these circumstances, governments almost always step in with bailouts for bank depositors, if not for distressed banks and firms as well. Frequently, insolvent private banks are taken into government ownership, at least temporarily. And over the longer term, financial crises tend to prompt increased government involvement in the financial sector in the form of revised prudential regimes.

Recurrent crises are one reason why finance, even when largely in private hands, is inevitably a public issue. This vulnerability is not the only reason. Banks (and other financial institutions) are special, as Benjamin Cohen notes (1986, 12), because "banking is a peculiarly influential industry, owing to the central role that banks play in providing, through their credit and deposit facilities, the means of payment for transactions of every kind." Banks are not like factories producing furniture or steel; they rely more than other firms on public trust. As creators and suppliers of credit they have through their operations direct, economy-wide effects on investment levels and prices; when they fail, the effects are particularly contagious, with failures often spreading not only to other financial firms but also to producers in the "real" economy. These characteristics of finance mean that, at a minimum, governments are likely to promote financial system stability and to intervene during times of crisis. Because of the economic (and therefore political) centrality of money and finance, governments intervene in the financial system also to foster private savings, to mobilize financial resources for particular purposes, to subsidize certain types of economic activity, to redistribute wealth, and to support a range of social goals.

Monetary conditions and monetary policy cannot be entirely divorced from financial policy. Monetary policy, which uses a variety of tools and proxy mechanisms to influence inflation rates and currency values, affects banking activity, asset prices, and the sustainability of many government policies. Whether disinflationary or expansionary, it also has distributional consequences for particular economic groups (Kirshner 1998). In turn, financial markets and policies can significantly affect monetary conditions. This interrelationship is reflected in the dual role that many central banks play. Until very recently, all Southeast Asian central banks were both the primary regulators of commercial banks (sometimes of other financial institutions as well) and responsible for monetary policy and currency management.

This book does not investigate the issue of central bank independence: the degree to which the central bank is empowered to pursue monetary policy goals without regard to the immediate preferences of the government. The issue

---

3. Estimated costs of financial crises from Montes 1998, 8; Claessens, Djankov, and Klingbeil 1999, 22; *Business Times*, 11 September 1999. According to Morris Goldstein, the public costs of bank bailouts in more than a dozen developing countries from 1982 to 1997 came to over 10 percent of their GDP; see *IMF Survey* 20 (10): 161 (26 May 1997).

dominates almost all contemporary discussions of central banking, but until recently it has been irrelevant in Southeast Asia. For most of the time since their formation, none of the central banks in the region could meaningfully be described as independent. They were all part of the government and subject to political control, despite the formal prerogatives or informal influence they may also have enjoyed. Most have been explicitly concerned with economic growth as well as monetary stability. It seems better to acknowledge these facts about regional central banks than to search for alternative definitions of independence to explain why they have mostly been inflation-averse organizations operating in countries that have (with a few exceptions) generally had low or moderate levels of inflation.[4] The consequences of central bank independence for economic growth, equity, and democratic accountability do appear to be significant—and not necessarily positive (Simmons 1994). Recent crisis-inspired changes in the status of some Southeast Asian central banks, therefore, warrant separate study.

GOVERNING CAPACITY

The broad differences among governments in their capacity to control the financial sector are fairly obvious. Prudential regulations in some countries are virtually ignored. Low-interest loans for national industry can be hijacked by political cronies and simply flow out of the country. Government banks are sometimes appallingly inefficient; in the absence of competition, private banks may be just as bad. Increasing competition can lead to financial instability, crisis, and public bailout. In contrast, banking regulations in some countries are rigorously enforced; financial policy can nurture internationally competitive industries; and some governments own banks that are profitable and prudent.

Singapore and Indonesia illustrate almost opposite ends of this spectrum. For forty years, Singapore has maintained a stable financial system that has not required publicly funded bailouts. It has developed steadily over time, supported an exceptionally high national savings rate, and provided financial services that have been (at the very least) of sufficient quality not to impede economic growth. While limiting price subsidies in the financial sector, the Singapore government utilized a wide array of interventionist mechanisms for both prudential and developmental purposes, including limited entry into the banking market, a substantial role for government-controlled financial institutions, compulsory savings, and targeted loan support for strategic industries. Over the same period, Indonesia's financial system suffered two severe episodes of financial instability with disastrous economy-wide effects: the first in the 1960s, the second since 1997. In the intervening years the financial sector was an almost constant drain on government

4. Maxfield 1997 argues that independence is usefully operationalized as influence and, further, that by this definition the Thai central bank has at times been independent.

resources and probably imposed significant costs on the economy as well. In the end it didn't seem to matter whether financial policy in Indonesia revolved around heavy government subsidies through a state-owned banking system or followed a much more deregulatory path; neither policy orientation produced a financial system that was both stable and efficient.

What can explain such different outcomes? Economic context is likely to be important, since regulatory tasks become more inescapably public and complex the more a financial system is developed, competitive, and internationally open. Policy choice can also matter. Unconstrained credit creation, for example, may have seen several revolutionary governments (including Indonesia's in the 1940s) through critical periods but always at the cost of inflation and disruption to the financial system. What this book shows, however, is that within a fairly wide (but not un-bounded) range of policies, policy choice is less critical to determining financial stability or economic sustainability than consistent implementation of declared financial policy. To discuss the merits of financial policies in the abstract—such as whether government-owned banks are a drag on economic growth—makes little sense when a bank owned by the Singaporean or Taiwanese government is a very different animal from a state-owned bank in the Philippines or Indonesia.

It may also make little sense—or at any rate be only the starting point for analysis—to observe that government authorities in some countries pursue self-defeating or risky policies. For example, in the decade before the onset of its financial crisis in 1997, Indonesia carried out fairly radical financial liberalization and maintained a tight monetary policy in the context of an open capital account and without any systematic means for monitoring capital flows into and out of the country. With hindsight, the policy combination can be faulted on a number of counts: for providing perverse incentives to borrowers, for failing to provide adequate information on the true extent of Indonesian foreign liabilities, and for having missequenced capital-account and financial sector liberalization. Yet these failures were not simply policy oversights. Given Indonesia's political and admin-istrative institutions, Indonesian regulators and policymakers before the crisis faced some genuine dilemmas. The absence of systematic capital-account moni-toring, for example, was a matter of concern to officials at the Indonesian central bank well before the currency crisis. Yet the central bank's own administrative capacities and the government's complex relationship with Sino-Indonesian busi-ness meant that a capital-account monitoring system was widely considered both unfeasible and counterproductive. Many officials, private investors, and analysts thought that a monitoring regime could not be administered efficiently and without bias; hence, the attempt to institute one would undermine investor confidence. In contrast, Singapore and Malaysia had intensive capital-account monitoring regimes in place before the crisis, without any apparent negative repercussions.

It is easy to say that governments like Singapore and Malaysia have, in this respect at least, governing capacity that Indonesia does not have. What is this capacity and what sustains it? Governing modern financial systems requires the government to be organized enough to carry out complex administrative tasks, to exercise self-restraint, and to impose public authority on private actors. This means that government organizations must resolve two basic problems: building effective channels through which policy is administered, and ensuring that individual opportunistic behavior is constrained. The kinds of organizations likely to resolve these problems conform to essentially traditionalist, though currently unfashionable, notions of state and bureaucracy. Thus an important factor determining governing capacity will be the extent to which the state resembles a Weberian rational-legal governing system with an organized, disciplined, and skilled bureaucratic apparatus run according to rule-based and meritocratic precepts.

A fundamental precondition for the emergence of such rationalized state structures is that the distinction between public and private must have been brought into what Bernard Silberman calls "the realm of discussion and action," thereby opening the possibility for political leaders to confront the problem of "how to exhibit the public character of the state"—a problem which, in some countries at least, the development of rationalized administration was uniquely able to resolve (1993, 418–19, 55–76). But this takes us only so far. As noted above, no Southeast Asian state had failed to go through some process of rationalization by the early twentieth century, by which time the notion of public and private as distinct categories had taken hold, conceptually if not in practice. What needs to be investigated are the different ways this dual transformation takes place and is (or is not) reproduced over time.

CAPACITY FOR WHAT?

My understanding of governing capacity is more restrictive than are many other approaches to governance or the quality of government. Very often, government quality is understood as an amalgam of institutional factors (such as the rule of law) and specific policy orientations (such as low marginal tax rates; see, e.g., La Porta et al. 1999). These conceptualizations formulate a different set of conditions for effective government because they have a different measure of performance in mind. Not all good things inevitably go together. There is very little reason to suppose that the factors that maximize economic growth, for example, are the same as those that minimize corruption or economic inequality. My focus is on the regulatory functions of government with regard to money and finance, rather than on such aspects of performance as promoting financial development or rapid industrialization.

In the first instance, I am concerned with understanding patterns of policy implementation, which can vary in a number of ways. At the most basic level, does the government implement its own declared financial policy? For example, if a government decrees that banks should allocate 20 percent of their loan portfolios to certain categories of borrowers, does this figure correspond with the banks' actual lending patterns? Another area for comparison is whether policies are implemented with reasonable consistency or whether enforcement is erratic. This is a different issue from that of whether policy itself is discriminatory. For example, policy may single out foreign banks for special treatment, but as long as *all* foreign banks are held to the same standards, then we can say that enforcement is consistent. A third question is whether policy is administered in a rule-abiding manner or whether implementation violates other government rules and standards. Often, this is not a clear-cut issue but involves the degree to which rule-following is observed in administration. Implementation may be rule-abiding but nonetheless not satisfy the conditions of "the rule of law" or adhere to highly specific, formal standards. Japanese administrative guidance, for example, or the wide discretionary authority exercised by the Monetary Authority of Singapore does not mean that policy implementation in these countries is not rule-abiding—unless it violates recognized standards of behavior. This qualification means that not all institutionalized patterns of behavior can be categorized as rule-abiding. Corrupt behavior, for example, may be routinized but, by definition, is not consistent with acknowledged rules.

Second, I wish to show that the way policy is implemented has implications for financial outcomes and can influence policy choices. These outcomes range from the fairly obvious—the failure to enforce prudential regulations governing banks will, all other things being equal, raise the chances of financial crisis or instability—to less apparent consequences. The government's ability to control and influence financial resources through an active financial policy, state-owned banks, compulsory savings schemes, or compulsory purchases of public debt is related to its ability to implement policy in a consistent, rule-abiding way. Governments that do not have much capacity in this sense may well have the political authority to nationalize commercial banks, for example, or to appropriate private savings through centralized pension funds, but they will have very little ability to run the banks or the pension funds in ways that are not vastly costly. Thus a downstream effect of governing capacity on financial sector outcomes is the greater latitude it creates for meaningful policy choice.

Governing capacity will also influence the prospects for certain kinds of international cooperation. When any activity that governments attempt to regulate is internationalized or has a significant transboundary element, effective regulation may depend on cooperation. A lack of governing capacity at the domestic level will impede cooperation, which requires a significant implementation effort. And implementation at the domestic level remains crucial to the basic model of international cooperation that is unfolding in many policy areas, from finance to environmental protection. International organizations may be focal points for the formulation of rules and the collation of information, but in most areas, certainly in finance, ultimate information-gathering and enforcement remains the province of national government authorities (Kapstein 1994). The success of new cooperative attempts to safeguard international financial stability in the wake of the series of financial crises in 1997 and 1998 will thus depend on whether national governments are able to implement international rules.

Defining governing capacity as the ability to implement policy in a consistent and rule-abiding way has the merit of disentangling, at least in part, arguments about the effects of organizational characteristics from arguments about the effects of different policies. This means, however, that a caveat is in order about the limits of such analysis. Governing capacity will not *guarantee* desirable outcomes and may even facilitate some undesirable or suboptimal ones. And what is categorized, given my definition, as governing ineffectiveness may still produce outcomes that are viable on some measures. In certain circumstances, state incapacity may open up channels of influence which sustain economic activity or allow ordinary citizens to extract a measure of security that they would otherwise not enjoy. Much will depend on the aspirations of particular governments and the political and economic circumstances in which they operate. The organizational characteristics that underlie state capacity are likely to predispose government actors toward certain goals and away from others, and thus entail public policy biases in favor of order, regularity, and the integrity of state organizations. Largely, however, the preferences and relative power of particular individuals and groups in a polity determine the substantive ends to which government is directed.

OUTLINE OF THE BOOK

Chapter 2 elaborates why we should expect a relationship between the micro-institutional attributes of state organizations, governing capacity, and outcomes in the financial sector. Organizational structures, routines, and norms that are stable, mutually consistent, and relatively formalized in their internal disciplinary systems lend themselves to consistent, rule-abiding policy implementation. This kind of governing capacity is an important determinant of financial stability and performance. Economic conditions and policy choice also affect financial sector outcomes, but they do so in ways that make governing capacity especially critical in modern financial systems that are liberalized, internationally open, and developed.

Chapters 3, 4, and 5 give an account of how state organizations and central banks developed in very different ways in Indonesia, Malaysia, and Singapore, respectively. From the emergence of modern state organizations in the colonial era to the regionwide financial crisis of 1997–98, different patterns of financial policy implementation have been associated with different types of state organization. In each case, the central bank emerged as the primary organization responsible for implementing financial policy. Anchored within the institutional framework of the broader state system, these central banks developed different organizational structures and norms that lent themselves to particular routines of interaction with government and private actors. Selective personnel recruitment, effective reward and disciplinary systems, and performance-based promotion criteria in government organizations underpinned Singapore's interventionist financial policies, providing for the government's ability to regulate private bankers and manage financial assets directly. These capacities and attributes were also present, to some extent, in Malaysia's central bank and other state organizations. Ascriptive principles, loose disciplinary systems, and a lack of differentiation between public goals and private interests in other parts of Malaysia's governing system, however, sometimes compromised the governing capacity of the central bank and often raised the costs of Malaysia's most ambitious economic policy initiatives. In Indonesia, state organizations with personalized informal hierarchies, vague disciplinary systems, and mutually inconsistent routines and norms were rarely able to implement declared financial policies in a consistent way. As a result, both interventionist and liberalized financial policies in Indonesia had high costs.

Chapter 6 considers the implications of economic openness and capital mobility for government control over the economy and financial system. Private capital in Indonesia, Malaysia, and Singapore has been significantly mobile for the entire postindependence period, in part because of long-standing personal and interfirm ties linking private actors transnationally. Mobility has had some effects on regulatory outcomes, and new forms of mobility in the 1990s brought new challenges, but again one sees significant intercountry variation in both the type of capital mobility experienced and the challenge it has posed. Because of the greater latitude for policy choice created by higher levels of governing capacity, the state's micro-institutional attributes influence what capital mobility entails. Singapore and Malaysia have had high or moderate success in either managing the terms of internationalization or developing strategic responses to their internationalized environments. Capital mobility has consistently represented a far greater challenge in Indonesia.

Chapter 7 asks whether these intercountry differences look set to endure in the wake of financial crises in 1997 and 1998, which prompted most countries in Asia to embark on programs of reconstruction and reform. Not only was the nature of the problem different in each case, however, but different national capacities lent themselves to different responses to the turmoil. Singapore reacted to the crisis by accelerating a controlled shift in financial policy toward further liberalization, combined with selective government stewardship. Malaysia responded in more heterodox fashion, with limited capital controls and a reasonably successful government-led program of domestic debt resolution and bank restructuring. In Indonesia the crisis pushed the country's institutions to breaking point, bringing about a multifaceted collapse on political, economic, and administrative fronts. Although this cleared the way for an ambitious reform agenda and genuine political change, economic and institutional reconstruction remained limited and fragile. Trends in Thailand, Taiwan, and the Philippines point to similar variation. Overall, despite the rise of an officially sanctioned "governance" agenda, the capacity to implement financial policy remains unevenly distributed across Asia.

The concluding chapter considers the implications of these ongoing differences in governing capacity for international initiatives aimed at managing open financial systems. These initiatives—both for a "new international financial architecture" at the global level and for greater regional cooperation—have been prompted by concerns that national efforts to maintain financial stability in an environment of high capital mobility are sometimes inadequate. National central banks and regulatory agencies will play key roles in any such cooperation, since they remain the primary organizations tasked with implementing financial and monetary policy, whether that policy is cooperative or entirely independent. Their characteristics and capacities will also help determine whether distinctly regional institutions and responses emerge within the wider international regime governing finance. The regulatory capacity of government organizations in countries such as Indonesia and Thailand will not make much of a dent, one way or the other, on international arrangements. At the regional level, they assume a much greater significance.

2.

State Organizations and Financial-Sector Outcomes

The German state of previous centuries casts a long shadow. There is debate over whether it or its Prussian predecessors were hierarchical, rule-based organizations that embodied a distinct "spirit of bureaucracy."[1] What has gained widespread acceptance, following Max Weber's analysis, is the idea that such attributes capture something essential about modern state bureaucracy: an impersonal, rule-based form of organization that represents rational-legal authority. This remains the starting point for many theories of bureaucratic behavior and expectations of bureaucratic autonomy. Serious scholarship can start with Michael Barnett and Martha Finnemore's assumption (1999, 707) that "rational-legal authority and control over expertise are part of what defines and constitutes any bureaucracy (a bureaucracy would not be a bureaucracy without them)."

In reality, rather than there being any one logic of bureaucracy, contemporary states are constituted in a great variety of ways.[2] The French and Japanese states, at least residually, embody Weber's ideas of bureaucracy more than was ever the case for British and American state organizations (Silberman 1993). Even so, dense webs of personal and institutional relationships linking the bureaucracy with business and political spheres in France and Japan mean that these states never enjoyed the insulation that Weber believed to characterize rationalized state systems (Kadushin 1995; Amyx 1998). Many other state bureaucracies are not remotely defined by rational-legal authority and control over expertise. The Philippines, with its politicization of public office, weak bureaucracy, and tradition of government-as-plunder, is so dissimilar to the Weberian image of rational organization that it is has been portrayed as another Weberian type, that of the patrimonial state (Hutchcroft 1998).

STATE ORGANIZATIONS AND GOVERNING CAPACITY

Talking about organizations—banks, government ministries, or "the government"—as purposive actors is more than convenient shorthand. Even though only

---

1. See the exchange between Kiser and Schneider 1994 and Gorski 1995.
2. On the idea of a distinct "state effect" or logic in the modern era, see Mitchell 1999; and Scott 1998.

individuals actually have preferences, make decisions, and take action, organizations can structure individual behavior, however perversely, in ways that make it meaningful to talk about organizations as if they were actors.[3] Yet although all organizations produce outcomes, how and whether they impose uniform standards of behavior on the individuals who inhabit them varies considerably. Understanding this source of variation is important, since without some microlevel theory of the organization, the processes through which ideas, values, or other factors get aggregated and reproduced as organizational preferences and actions will remain obscure. The frequency of references to esprit de corps, institutionalization, and corporate identity in theorizing about the state suggests that organizational-level factors are significant (Evans 1995, 46–49; Huntington 1968). Yet scholars of contemporary Southeast Asian political economy have scarcely begun to investigate the structures and processes that create organizational identities and behavior.[4]

If governing capacity is taken to mean the government's ability to implement its declared policy in a consistent and rule-abiding way, the problems encountered by the organizations responsible for policy implementation will vary according to political context and policy content. For example, the more a policy generates resistance, the harder it will be to implement (Grindle 1980). Institutional context will also matter: where police and judicial systems are authoritative and consistent, much of the burden of ensuring rule-abiding policy implementation is lifted from other state organizations. It follows that organizational-level strategies that work in one context may not be suitable in another. Nonetheless, certain core organizational attributes can be seen as the building blocks of governing capacity within state systems, even if some of these attributes are dispensable in certain policy areas or institutional contexts.

Many of the organizational attributes that this book identifies as providing for consistent, rule-abiding policy implementation approximate familiar Weberian notions of state rationalization.[5] In contrast, more personalized, informal organizations are shown to be maladapted to implementing declared government policy in a consistent way—although they may be highly effective on many other measures. The following account of how organizational structures, routines, and norms affect policy implementation builds on Weber but also draws on more recent organizational sociology.

Organizational Structures, Routines, and Norms
Organizational structures include recruitment processes, career paths, remuneration systems, and decision-making structures. They are key determinants of an

---

3. Morgan 1998 presents various conceptualizations of how organizations act.
4. The most comprehensive studies of selection and socialization in state organizations examine industrialized countries, potentially biasing our understanding of "modern" state organizations. See, e.g., Bourdieu 1989.
5. For Weber's analysis of rational-legal authority and bureaucracy, see Weber 1978, 217–26, 956–68. In a Southeast Asian context, see Hutchcroft 1998 on the importance of rational-legal state organizations.

organization's effectiveness and self-discipline. Without discipline, organizational action will reflect a haphazard combination of individual, idiosyncratic preferences, opportunistic behavior, and official policy. Obviously, it is not the only condition of effective regulation. Political resources also count, but the frequency with which politically dominant states fail to discipline private actors demonstrates that organizational discipline is necessary to translate political resources into consistent policy implementation.

A single ultimate source of authority within the organization and clear lines of accountability and hierarchy (internally and with respect to outside systems) are obvious sources of coherence and discipline. Reasonable stability in organizational design (as opposed to frequent restructuring of offices and functions) also appears to promote organizational effectiveness (Collins and Poras 1994). And adequate official remuneration is important.[6] The degree to which formal hierarchies and rewards actually constrain behavior, however, varies from organization to organization. Because individuals are at least potentially opportunistic (they may break rules if the balance of expected rewards and risks suggests that it is in their interest to do so), organizations need to generate meaningful incentives for individual compliance. To this end, organizations can adopt monitoring and sanctioning systems to make it likely that rule-breaking will be detected and punished (Solnick 1998). Ultimately, however, governing capacity does not rest solely on extensive auditing, detailed contracts, and sanctioning systems to cover every contingency; something else must come into play if these systems are to work.

The salience of internal sanctioning systems increases the more the organization—not potential future employers, outside political actors, or the private marketplace—constitutes the primary arena in which officials stand to reap rewards. This is why the rational-legal bureaucratic structures identified by Weber—exclusive, long-term employment, formal financial remuneration through salary, and the appointment of administrators on the basis of individual achievement rather than election or hereditary right—are significant. In addition, selective, performance-based recruitment systems entail high (often nontransferable) entry costs and are thus a plausible source of member loyalty to an organization, which in turn reduces the burden placed on formal monitoring and sanctioning systems.[7] More fluid systems, which offer options for early exit and lateral entry, entail a much looser connection between the individual and the organization. Such systems may make it possible to apply market principles to government organizations themselves and thereby, as envisaged by a popular (and influential) strand of public-administration theorizing, improve government efficiency.[8] This theorizing, however, by largely assuming that the rule of law is secure and corruption rare, begs much of the question about the sources of effective government.

---

6. Although the relationship is not entirely straightforward, higher public sector salaries are associated with lower rates of corruption. See Rijckeghem and Weder 1997.
7. See esp. Hirschman 1970.
8. See e.g., the review of "new public management" in Christiansen 1998, 273–78.

Organizational routines too influence discipline and effectiveness. Office procedure, reporting systems, and the established practices for interaction with outsiders are all organizational routines. Routines structure behavior by defining tasks, modes of analysis, and cognitive categories. They thus make up and reproduce an organizational culture that provides individuals with competencies for particular types of action and understandings of social reality or "the way things are done" (Swidler 1986; Powell and DiMaggio 1991). In this way, they can be seen as informal institutions with the potential to influence the content of individual notions of interest and the kinds of opportunism engaged in.[9] Routines that define tasks and modes of behavior have implications for governing effectiveness. What, for example, do reporting systems report? How easy is it to retrieve and use information? How much do ascriptive value orientations intrude on supposedly technical tasks? In addition, governing capacity is likely to be affected by whether practices tend to be formal or informal, structured along personalized networks or depersonalized functional offices, rule-based or at odds with the organization's structure and norms, results-oriented or attuned to meeting the demands of form over substance.

Routines, like structures for recruitment and career development, potentially establish loyalty—or at least underline the organization as an institutional field of action—through internal "housekeeping" or projects that establish the organization as a distinct entity. Such projects include the creation of traditions, encouragement of extracurricular activities, promotion of organizational badges (literal or symbolic, such as songs, awards, and newsletters), and the organization's record of itself in annual reports and official histories. These organizational projects and rituals are important insofar as display, ceremony, and myth all serve to establish claims to identity and significance (see, for example, Apter 1999).

Finally, organizational norms can be a source of discipline and effectiveness. Explicit standards for proper behavior, such as those reflected in the content of induction courses, promotion criteria, and disciplinary rules, may elicit compliance or motivate behavior directly. For example, norms that ascribe legitimacy and status to legal rules are a prerequisite for government that abides by its own laws (Barret-Kriegel 1989). I assume that governing capacity in the financial sector will be supported the more regulatory organizations understand their role as legitimately requiring them to act, at times, in ways that run counter to the private interests of those they regulate.

An organization's explicit values and norms can be significant even when (as is often the case) they are honored mainly in the breach. A large gap between principle and practice makes it hard to sustain systems that generate organizational discipline. It is hard to introduce incentive-based pay and disciplinary systems that minimize corruption, for example, when official rhetoric emphasizes personal

9. Institutions—whether broadly social or organizational—can play this role because individual notions of self-interest are necessarily learned, even if the complexity of the social environment means that institutions are not determinative. See Granovetter 1985.

moral rectitude and dedication as the basis for correct behavior. Ongoing lip service to principles that are obviously at odds with reality may in fact aggravate tendencies to disregard official goals. It is worth emphasizing, however, that an organization in which routines and norms are not in basic contradiction with each other is not the same as one in which formal rules are strictly adhered to. As recognized in organization studies and demonstrated by the effects of work-to-rule strikes, obsessive rule-following is almost always dysfunctional (Morgan 1998, 165). Just as the inefficiency of devising contracts to cover a wide range of eventualities creates incentives for hierarchical organizations to replace specific contracts with generalized authority structures (Williamson 1975), so a proliferation of organizational rules is generally an indicator that organizational discipline is weak.

Organizational Attributes as Mediating Structures
The structures, norms, and routines of a government organization not only shape the organization itself but also help determine the interface between the state and other actors, a vital area for understanding governing capacity. Porous, personalized organizations create scope for individual interventions by outsiders and tend to reward individualized accommodation with outsiders, which will potentially restructure organizational routines. The implications for governing capacity are fairly clear: individualized interventions generally target the policy implementation stage and, almost by definition, impede consistent, rule-abiding policy implementation (Grindle 1980, 15–19). Hence, in the case of financial policy, the structures, routines, and norms that govern relations between bankers and regulators merit direct attention. Looking at this aspect of the banker-regulator interface allows one to say something about the quality of the ties that connect the state with business actors, not just whether ties exist or which side appears to have the upper hand politically.

This perspective may be particularly relevant in the Southeast Asian context. Many authors have argued that the political vulnerability of ethnic minority Chinese, who remain Southeast Asia's main entrepreneurial group, helps explain their presence in speculative economic fields and their efforts to forge particularistic ties with politicians and officials (e.g., Yoshihara 1988, 89–94). It is arguable, however, that the political vulnerability of ethnic minority entrepreneurial actors and their consequent need to engage in patronage-based business activity derives from the way the state is constituted. The vulnerability of minorities such as the Chinese in Southeast Asia has its roots in government policy (see, e.g., Chirot and Reid 1997). Although this could be a matter of pure political expedience, potentially fostered by all states, those with personalized, informal, and loosely structured state organizations will be most able to complement exclusionary politics with particularistic engagement. Thus there is a high degree of congruity between Indonesian state organizations under Suharto and the blend of discrimination and personal privilege that marked the regime's relations with Chinese business. In contrast, the more rationalized Malaysian state, despite being overtly constructed along racial lines, produced more formalized, predictable discrimination against the Chinese, with very different consequences for governing capacity and financial sector outcomes.

STATE ORGANIZATIONS AND CENTRAL BANKS IN SOUTHEAST ASIA

Modern state organizations vary considerably in their structures, routines, and norms. Japan, Singapore, and Taiwan have fairly developed rational-legal bureaucracies, whereas state organizations in Thailand, Korea, and Malaysia show significant deviations from these standards; those of Indonesia and the Philippines are generally judged the least Weberian.[10] This categorization of regional states corresponds with various proxy measures of state capacity and rationalization: extractive ability, corruption, the efficiency of legal institutions, and the development of public sector organizations.[11]

Southeast Asian states are not all of the same type. Thai state organizations underwent a period of development and rationalization in the late nineteenth century as a result of reforms that gradually separated the bureaucracy from the ruler's personal household and organized it along functional lines (Siffin 1966; Brown 1992). The bureaucracy did not fully institutionalize standards of performance-based merit and formalized procedure, however. In the 1950s its routines accommodated personalized agreements, channels of influence, and informal linkages with political and business spheres (Riggs 1966). This style of governing persisted even as political change dramatically altered the balance of power among bureaucratic, political, and private actors from the 1970s onward.[12] One of its byproducts has been pervasive bureaucratic and political corruption (Pasuk and Sungsidh 1994).

According to most accounts, state organizations in the Philippines reflect a more extreme form of patronage-based organization. The introduction of electoralism in the American colonial period laid the basis for a relatively politicized bureaucracy, frequently in the hands of local political bosses (Anderson 1998, 192–226; Sidel 1999). Since then, struggles to gain the private booty accessible through public office have replicated patterns of nepotism, plunder, mediocrity, and ambiguity in the bureaucracy (Varela 1996; Hutchcroft 1998). Only very recently have some observers detected signs of change in these patterns (World Bank 2000).

Central banks in the region exhibit many of the same characteristics as the states of which they are a part. This is most obvious in the Philippines, Indonesia, and

10. A recent data set that ranks state organizations according to their degree of Weberianness rates Singapore as the most Weberian, with a score of 13.5, and the Philippines as the least, with a score of 6. Other Asian countries included in the survey were Taiwan (score of 13), Korea (12), Malaysia (10.5), and Thailand (8). See Evans and Rausch 1999.
11. See Appendix 2.
12. See "Murder and Progress in Modern Siam," reproduced in Anderson 1998, 174–91.

Singapore, where the central bank has been thoroughly absorbed into the wider state system. The result in Singapore is a financial sector regulator that shares with the rest of the state a personnel system based on high academic achievement, effective disciplinary mechanisms, and a pragmatic, results-oriented approach to regulation. In Indonesia the result is a central bank that since the late 1960s has combined a formal commitment to technocratic expertise with internal systems responsive to informal, sometimes even unspoken, patterns of influence. Like other state organizations in Indonesia, the structures, norms, and routines of the central bank reveal a consistently large gap between professed value orientations and actual routine behavior.

The Philippine central bank, while sharing some features with the Indonesian central bank, has been more structurally open to outside influence. This influence is visible in the pattern of senior appointments, which suggest a less career-based system, and in instances of direct overlap of identity between senior central bankers and private bankers. Also in line with other Philippine state organizations, but unlike those of Indonesia, central bank staff have been subject to private intimidation and lawsuits filed by bankers under central bank investigation (Hutchcroft 1998). Finally, while other central banks in the region have made use of outside consultants, the Philippine central bank has seen its internal structure most directly penetrated by foreign institutions (Broad 1988, 148–53).

The Thai central bank, the Bank of Thailand, displays a comparatively greater sense of organizational identity and elite status than other state organizations in Thailand. According to Ammar Siamwalla (1997a, 70), the "structure, organization and ethos of the Bank of Thailand was established during the 1950s and 1960s, by the then governor of the Bank, Dr. Puey Ungphakorn, a revered figure among the country's technocrats and academics. The institution that he led was imbued with a spirit of fierce integrity. In a country in which corruption is rife, the Bank of Thailand was considered to be the only institution where it was unthinkable that any corrupt practices could be found."

Several organizational attributes help explain this reputation. The role played by a member of the Thai royal household in the bank's establishment and its subsequent recruitment of officers from many of Thailand's elite families lent it an aura of aristocratic tradition.[13] The central bank's preference for conservative monetary policy derived in part from the adverse effects of earlier episodes of inflation on the real incomes of senior civil servants and policymakers, a class to which many bank officials belonged (Warr and Bhanupong 1996, 21–27). Most bank officials were career central bankers or, in the early period, recruits from the civil service (Bank of Thailand 1992, 381–82; Nukul Commission 1998, 173). The bank also prioritized human resource development under Puey's governorship, maintaining a large staff scholarship and training program from the 1960s (Ammar 1997a, 70; Bank of Thailand 1992, 384–87).

---

13. The bank's longest-serving governor, Puey Ungphakorn (1959–71), came from a Sino-Thai family of modest means, however. His position in the central bank was based on academic ability (he had earlier won a scholarship for doctoral study in England) and a reputation for personal integrity. See Ammar 1997b, 7.

Supporting this emphasis on staff development and continuity, the Bank of Thailand has also demonstrated a concern with organizational identity—reflected, for example, in the content and presentation of its commissioned history and in comments by former governors on mechanisms to "create a sense of belonging to the organisation" (Bank of Thailand 1992, 388). In this respect the Bank of Thailand is similar to the central bank of Malaysia, which also displays a high degree of organizational self-consciousness. The two central banks share other similarities, but Bank Negara Malaysia (especially in its early years) placed more emphasis on its regulatory mission, internal discipline, and the maintenance of formal, distant relations with the financial industry.

This difference may have something to do with why the prestige and reputa- tion of the Bank of Thailand fell abruptly with the Thai baht in 1997. By the 1990s if not before, the central bank was enmeshed in personal relationships linking finance ministers, some senior Bank of Thailand officials, and private bankers. The relationship between the financial industry and Thai regulatory authorities has been interpreted positively, as a consultative partnership (Unger 1998, 83–108), but details that emerged later show a pattern of interaction more accurately described as private and sometimes illegal collusion, with key actors occupying overlapping positions or maintaining personal ties across official and nonofficial spheres (Nukul Commission 1998; Haggard 2000, 52–54; *Business Times*, 17 January 2000; *Nation*, 4 July 2000). Further, although identified after the fact, signs of stress in the organization appear to have preceded these episodes. Problems of leadership and factionalism were cited as contributing to declining morale and standards in 1990s (Ammar 1997a, 70). A major inquiry after the events of 1997 also described a number of problems related to the organization of the bank rather than to the skills of its personnel: an increase in political interference, the low pri- ority accorded the personnel department, remuneration systems that did not ade- quately reflect capability and merit and therefore adversely affected staff loyalty, overcentralization of authority, and an internal culture that made advocating dis- senting opinions difficult (Nukul Commission 1998, 169–73).

Overall, the variation among states and central banks in Southeast Asia shows that countries in the region do not fit any one postcolonial or "developing state" model. Their different organizational characteristics can help explain their dif- ferent strategies and experiences with regard to governing the financial sector. Before I develop this argument, however, it is legitimate to ask where these organizational attributes came from and whether they have any independent significance.

STATES IN POLITICAL AND ECONOMIC CONTEXT

States are shaped by a variety of pressures and opportunities, ranging from inter- nal political struggles to external military threats and the economic resources provided by geographic location or world market trends. The attributes of particular state organizations, therefore, are a product of the specific contexts in which they evolved; however, organizational-level characteristics have enough independent significance to be considered as explanatory variables in their own right.

Incentives to create efficient, authoritative state organizations depend on the domestic political cleavages rulers confront, the degree of political uncertainty or insecurity they experience, and their need to mobilize military resources (Tilly 1985; Rich and Stubbs 1997; Stubbs 1999). The dispersal or concentration of polit-ical power plays a critical role in state formation and rationalization. Some dispersal of power, logically and historically, appears to be a condition for politi-cal leaders to have any incentive to develop depersonalized state structures (Silberman 1993). On the other hand, acute political instability or widely dispersed power centers can make it impossible to build or maintain such state structures (Migdal 1988; Geddes 1994).

Economic conditions also influence the way state organizations develop. Abun-dant natural resources reduce incentives for political leaders to create capable bureaucratic organizations to raise revenues. Easily collected revenues such as windfall gains from oil resources can therefore lead to the atrophy of revenue-collecting organizations—which constitute the base of most other administrative capacity (Chaudry 1989). Incentives to create such capacity, however, do not ensure that rulers have the means to do so. Hence, very low per capita incomes and severe resource constraints are likely to impede the development of rationalized state organizations.

Economic and political conditions thus create incentives for the construction of particular types of state organizations and set limits on the resources available for state-building projects. The attributes of state organizations, however, are not reducible in any straightforward way to their political or economic environment. There is a positive association between per capita national income and the devel-opment of rationalized state organizations, but variations in wealth do not com-pletely correspond with variations in state rationalization. In 1965, for example, per capita GDP in Korea was $104; in the Philippines, $189. Yet Korea had a much more rationalized set of state organizations than the Philippines. The comparison between Indonesia and Malaysia also suggests that economic factors are not deter-minative. Indonesia's state organizations in the 1990s did not resemble those of Malaysia in the 1960s, even though levels of economic development and natural resource endowments were similar. It is in fact possible that the causal relationship runs from rationalized states to rates of economic growth and hence, over time, wealth.[14]

Neither is political context determinative. High political instability and total political centralization are clearly not conducive to developing rationalized state

---

14. Evans and Rausch 1999 argues that there is an association between Weberian state structures and rates of economic growth.

organizations, but between these extremes it is difficult find any predictable relationship between political conditions and state rationalization.[15] Even where unconstrained political leadership appears as the primary reason for the failure to develop a rationalized bureaucracy—in the Philippines under Marcos, for example, or Indonesia under Suharto—it is also the case that the kind of bureaucracy these rulers confronted affected their choices. The state that Suharto inherited and ruled for over thirty years formed an organizational reality that both permitted and relied upon personalized interventions. In the long run, it was an unsustainable system: political expectations, generational pressures, and the sheer level of personal extraction ran counter to its logic of rotation and disbursement of benefits (Sidel 1998). In the interim, Suharto's power and interests left their imprint on the Indonesian state not according to a uniquely determined political logic but through processes that reflected the structures, routines, and norms of extant state organizations.

Given sufficient incentives and resources, political leaders may invest in refashioning state organizations, but the organizational context in which they do so influences their response to a given set of political or economic pressures. Different regulatory systems and state structures can thus emerge in countries with otherwise similar political economies. For this reason, the structures, routines, and norms of state organizations are worth examining in their own right as factors that influence governing capacity.

GOVERNING CAPACITY AND FINANCIAL SECTOR OUTCOMES

Governing capacity, or the ability of a government to implement its declared policy consistently and in a rule-abiding way, has implications for financial sector stability. The centrality of money and credit in an economy, the vulnerability of financial markets and institutions to disruption and loss of confidence, and the serious consequences of financial instability are all reasons why some sort of active government role in the financial sector is virtually unavoidable. How the government fulfills that role will thus have important consequences. It matters, for example, whether prudential banking regulations are enforced or bypassed, whether state-owned banks are corrupt, and whether financial subsidy schemes are administered according to plan or diverted to other uses. Two other implications of governing capacity in the financial sector are the increased latitude for policy choice that it creates and its role in determining how capital mobility is experienced.

15. The lack of consensus is suggested by ongoing debates over the implications of state strength, autonomy, and democracy. See Katzenstein 1978; Migdal 1988; Haggard 1990; Evans 1995. Although the usual dependent variables in analyses of state capacity are rapid economic growth and industrialization, consistent policy implementation is frequently an implicit element of capacity in such accounts.

Policy Options

The ability to implement policy consistently is likely to increase the government's policy choices.[16] For example, it should increase a government's latitude to appropriate financial assets directly, to become engaged in financial intermediation, to pursue strategic financial policies aimed at influencing the distribution of credit, and to regulate the activities of private financial institutions. Governing capacity is important for the viability of these basically interventionist policies because, like prudential regulation in the banking sector, they all entail an active government role in implementation and hence the scope for failure if that implementation lacks discipline and consistency.

All other things being equal, the more a policy vests in government agencies a significant discretion over the use of resources, the more fertile ground it creates for corruption, rent-seeking, and distortion of policy at the implementation stage (Rose-Ackerman 1999). Greater levels of organizational discipline are therefore required to implement policies that devolve significant responsibilities on government agencies. Most studies of interventionist financial policies suggest that in the absence of high levels of government autonomy, self-discipline, and coherence, financial-industrial policies tend to degenerate into costly exercises in channeling rents to favored interests (e.g., Haggard, Lee, and Maxfield 1993). In financial systems where competition is restrained, financial markets relatively undeveloped, and financial flows predominantly national rather than internationalized, the task of maintaining financial stability is less challenging if financial policy is relatively noninterventionist. In the absence of these conditions, it is not at all clear that nonmarket interventionist financial policies are more difficult to implement than market-based prudential policies.

Governing capacity determines not the political ability or propensity of a government to pursue particular policies but how costly they will be. Some policies are inherently costly and unviable, however consistently implemented—perhaps particularly if implemented consistently. Some policies are better suited to realizing particular goals than others. Market-oriented financial policy, for example, is more conducive to rapid financial development than a policy of financial repression, which maintains interest rates at below-market levels (Fry 1995). This book, however, is not about the marginal efficiency of different interest-rate policies or how to stimulate financial market development. To the extent that it is interested in aggregate economic outcomes, it is concerned with very large effects such as crises and chronic low growth, which have the potential to make policy politically unviable. With a few exceptions, policy itself is not independently determinative when it comes to such very large effects. Rather, a large element of the cost or benefit of many policies has more to do with the way they are administered than with the fine details of the policy itself. Further, in some cases, perverse policy choices can be traced to underlying implementation problems.

---

16. Katzenstein 1978 is among the earliest to relate state structure to national policy options.

This argument is supported by the absence of a clear association between broad financial policy orientations and outcomes across the Asian region. Taiwan, Japan, Korea, Singapore, Malaysia, Thailand, the Philippines, and Indonesia have pursued a wide variety of financial policies, from high levels of government intervention over the price and allocation of credit to relatively market-based systems with minimal constraints on competition.[17] Similar policy orientations have been associated with very different economic outcomes in different countries. For example, policies that involved moderately high levels of government appropriation of financial assets or intervention in the allocation of finance have been very costly in Indonesia and the Philippines but viable over long periods in Taiwan, Malaysia, and Singapore. If this difference in policy sustainability can be related to underlying levels of governing capacity, then capacity is something that increases the range of viable policy choices open to a government.

Open, Developed, and Competitive Financial Systems
Governing capacity also alters a country's experience of capital mobility and integration with global financial markets. States with higher levels of governing capacity are better able than those with lower levels to maintain national policy goals under conditions of capital mobility. Potential challenges for government policy stem from internationalized financial systems, and governing capacity is expected to reduce these challenges.

There is a high degree of reciprocity among levels of international openness, development, and competition in the financial system. Competition tends to increase with financial openness and to increase the rate of financial development, which in turn tends to make a financial system more open. Financial liberalization, therefore, which increases competition in the financial sector, generally precipitates an escalation in the growth rates and international flows of financial assets. The potential for instability in these circumstances is high: many of the most serious financial crises since 1980 followed episodes of financial liberalization and increased exposure to international capital markets (Diaz-Alejandro 1985; McKinnnon and Pill 1996). Many of the reasons relate to the increased need for governments to play stabilizing roles in financial markets as they become more open, developed, and competitive. When financial markets are open and developed, the likelihood and costs of financial instability increase because of contagion via cross-national linkages, the sheer size of financial flows compared to the national economy, the potential for domestic banking crises to generate currency crises, and the monetary policy dilemmas imposed by capital mobility.[18] Prudential regulation also becomes more technically complex and politically difficult, as regulators con-

17. This paragraph draws on accounts of financial policy in Lee 1990; Lamberte et al. 1992; Haggard, Lee, and Maxfield 1993; Patrick and Park 1994; Haggard and Lee 1995; Cole and Slade 1996; Tan 1996; Warr and Bhanupong 1996; and Hutchcroft 1998.
18. For recent discussions of these issues, see Reinhart and Reinhart 1998; Gruen and Gower 1999; and Noble and Ravenhill 2000.

front financial institutions with multinational operations and may rely on the cooperation of foreign authorities.

Although some risks and challenges are specific to the internationalization of financial markets, financial development and competition—as well as being preconditions of certain forms of internationalization—are likely to play significant roles themselves. As financial assets increase in size relative to the national economy, financial market failure becomes much more costly: the effects on the real economy are likely to be more profound and the political pressure for public bailouts harder to resist. In addition, greater numbers of financial market players, along with more diverse and complicated financial products, make the tasks involved in prudential regulation commensurably more complex. Financial development may be accompanied by the development of such market-based solutions to these problems as sophisticated risk analysis services and accurate market pricing of risks. There is no reason to believe, however, that these will develop automatically as the ratio of financial assets to GDP rises.

Levels of competition within the financial sector are also likely to make a difference. The more banks and financial service providers compete with each other, the more dynamic financial markets will be. This may have many advantages in delivering better-quality, lower-cost financial services. It also, however, increases the need for formal prudential regulation, as removing limits on price-based competition in the financial sector removes the scope for certain forms of private sector self-regulation and increases incentives for risk-taking.[19]

Examples from the Asian region suggest that the openness, development, and competitiveness of the financial system can have an independent effect on financial sector outcomes. As some financial systems evolved in these ways, they became more prone to crisis and experienced more costly crises. Thailand and Malaysia, for example, both show this pattern. Japan and Thailand until the 1990s confirm that limits on competition in the financial sector could be conducive to certain forms of private sector self-regulation which, if not optimal, were consistent with reasonably stable and effective financial systems. In both countries, regulatory limits on entry and price-based competition as well as informal collusive practices among bankers were significant features of their pre-reform financial systems. In addition, close links between banks and firms—relatively formalized in Japan's main bank system, informal in Thai conglomerates—may well have reduced problems of asymmetric information otherwise inherent in the creditor-borrower relationship (Aoki and Patrick 1994). These systems utterly failed to cope when regulatory limits on competition were eased and the economic environment changed, exposing the weakness of formal prudential regulation.

On the other hand, the independent effects of openness, development, and competition do not fully explain patterns of financial stability or instability. Many finan-

19. Hellman, Murdock, and Stiglitz 1997 explains why limits on competition in the financial sector can be advantageous.

cial systems in which regulation or collusion limit competition are both hugely inefficient and unstable, the Philippines being a case in point. Indonesia in the 1960s and the Philippines in the 1980s also illustrate the potential for crises to occur at low levels of financial development. The hazards associated with openness are clearly not insurmountable, as some countries maintain high levels of financial and monetary stability with comparatively open systems: Singapore and Malaysia have always operated in conditions of high capital mobility, yet Singapore has maintained an exceptionally good record of financial stability, and Malaysia has an imperfect but comparatively good record. The experiences of both can be related to underlying levels of governing capacity: high in Singapore, moderate in Malaysia.

For a variety of reasons, governing capacity influences the way a country manages the challenges of financial openness. One reason is that as financial markets become more developed, competitive, and internationalized, the information that market participants require in order to act prudently becomes more complex and diffuse. These conditions increase the need for governments to enforce disclosure rules and accounting standards and to provide information. The management of an internationalized economy calls for other specific government capabilities. For example, it requires the ability to monitor private international transactions, including capital transactions.[20] Reliable capital-account monitoring and the tracking of the foreign assets and liabilities of domestic firms, however, are administratively demanding. Intensive monitoring also opens the door to abuses of power by state officials and hence may be particularly resisted in countries that do not have records of consistently implementing declared policy.

Managing the challenges of internationalization requires an ability to retain the confidence of mobile investors without necessarily acceding to their immediate demands. The cases in this book suggest that governments are most able to realize policy objectives that go against the preferences of mobile investors if they can convince investors that specific adverse policy decisions do not entail significant generalized risks. This kind of credibility is plausibly related to governing capacity. For example, managing the political and economic challenges of an internationalized economy has on several occasions led the Malaysian government to take actions that were either detrimental to certain classes of foreign investors or perceived by them as such. Yet for the most part, Malaysia's comparatively disciplined implementation of these specific policies—reducing foreign ownership in the banking and natural resource sectors, for example, or imposing limited capital controls—and general record of reasonably consistent policy implementation meant that these initiatives were low-cost ones. Indonesia found attempts to implement similar policies much more costly.

Governing capacity may also ease the macroeconomic problem presented by the unsustainability of maintaining a fixed exchange rate and an independent

20. Accurate capital-account monitoring is now accepted as a necessary component of financial governance. On monitoring, transparency, and prudential regulation as part of the "new international financial architecture," see Kahler 2000.

monetary policy under conditions of capital mobility.[21] Governing capacity cannot directly affect this relationship (virtually a truism) but provides the government with policy options that make a trade-off between domestic price stability and exchange-rate stability less necessary. First, by making government appropriation of financial assets more viable, governing capacity can effectively lock up domestic liquidity without resort to monetary levers. Second, governing capacity makes temporary controls on short-term capital flows more feasible, effectively reducing capital mobility. Third, governing capacity makes possible a range of other temporary controls, from restrictions on real estate speculation to ad hoc regulations on the use of credit cards or margin lending, again reducing the need to use monetary policy to maintain domestic price stability.

Finally, governing capacity affects the way a country manages economic internationalization because of its implications for international cooperation. Prospects for cooperation, in turn, are important because unilateral efforts, however well implemented, are sometimes inadequate for dealing with international or transboundary problems.[22] Further, governments have the ability to do more than devise new regulatory mechanisms that suit an internationalized environment. Governments imposed cooperative limits on capital mobility in the early postwar years, and the subsequent removal of these controls did not occur without deliberate changes in government policy (Helleiner 1994). Although any reversion to a cooperative global regime involving capital controls is politically unlikely at present (Cohen 2000), many countries made substantial efforts to strengthen international standards for prudential regulation and crisis management in the 1990s (Kapstein 1994; Eichengreen 2000). But since cooperation on such regulatory matters requires participating governments to implement cooperative agreements, governments with limited ability to enforce their own prudential policies will have similar difficulties implementing international standards of financial governance.

New Organizational Forms for a New Era?

Many would argue that this discussion of governing capacity and capital mobility is fundamentally mistaken because globalization profoundly alters the terrain in which governments operate. It is possible, for example, to assert that globalization is conducive to increased private sector self-governance rather than to a greater role for governments. Recent episodes of financial market instability, however, and the actual trend of increasing government regulation make this idea hard to sustain empirically. It is slightly more plausible that governing the financial system in a world of global capital mobility requires states that are, above all, flexible, adaptable, and responsive to the demands of financial markets (Cerny 1996). If so, state organizations built on a demarcation between public and private interest and

---

21. This basic incompatibility is often termed the Mundell-Fleming thesis, after work by Robert Mundell and Robert Fleming in the 1960s.
22. This was widely recognized in studies of interdependence in the 1970s. See Cooper 1968 for an early account.

designed to promote organizational identity, regularity, and discipline might be maladapted to delivering appropriate financial policies. A more ominous interpretation is that if globalization empowers forces that are antagonistic to core principles and practices of Weberian states, then it may indirectly promote a new kind of patrimonial, patronage-based state (Theobald 1995). No assumptions need to be made about the functionality of this kind of state for governing the globalized financial system to support predictions that it will become increasingly common; globalization may simply mean a deficit in government capacity and legitimacy (Pauly 1995 and 1997; Strange 1996).

There is evidence that certain types of state development and government activism actually support internationalized economies (Katzenstein 1985; Rodrik 1998). Nonetheless, it remains a moot point whether internationalization and capital mobility will, over time, erode the kinds of state organizations that provide for this kind of government activism. The following chapters on Indonesia, Singapore, and Malaysia offer an implicit commentary on such debates because these countries have, for most of the time, had highly internationalized economies. Chapter 6 explicitly examines the interrelationship among capital mobility, strategies for governing the financial sector, and the nature of state organizations in Southeast Asia. First, however, it is necessary to investigate the genesis of particular state organizations and central banks in the region, to see how their organizational attributes have affected patterns of financial policy implementation at the domestic level.

3.

Indonesia: Ambiguity and Financial Instability

When President Suharto resigned in May 1998, after thirty-two years in power, his cultivated image as Indonesia's *bapak pembangunan*, or father of development, was looking particularly ragged. The flames from burning buildings in the capital city had barely been extinguished; riots and organized violence had killed over a thousand people in Jakarta itself; the national currency had plummeted, and the country was in the depths of an extraordinarily severe recession. *Krismon*, the monetary and financial crisis that struck Indonesia in 1997, had become *kristal*—total crisis. As in 1966, student protests added a reformist tone to the ouster of a long-serving leader in circumstances of economic collapse. The city landscape conveyed in television images of the 1998 protests, however, showed that plenty of development of a sort had taken place in the intervening years.

The main roads through central and southern Jakarta provide physical evidence of one of Suharto's developmental legacies: the multistory buildings that line the wide avenues are, overwhelmingly, banks or other financial institutions. Many are gleaming marble and glass towers, built in the decade before the crisis when billions of dollars of foreign capital poured into the country and the liberalized financial sector took advantage of new freedoms. By the end of 1998 virtually all Indonesian banks were insolvent, and most of the large private ones had been nationalized. Many of the companies listed on the Jakarta Stock Exchange were also insolvent. Their debts contributed to another Suharto-era legacy: foreign debt of over $150 billion, 130 percent of GDP.[1] The concrete and steel towers of the brand new stock exchange building (which also houses the local offices of the World Bank, Indonesia's main institutional aid donor) stood as a partially empty reminder of the days when optimism reigned.

To what extent is the history of Indonesia's financial sector related to that of its state organizations? Tracing the changes in the Indonesian state and the central bank since the early nineteenth century shows how the organizational attributes of both have affected the scope and implementation of financial policy. As the colonial state took on more of the features of a rationalized bureaucracy, financial and monetary policies became more ambitious and more effective. Not all organizations

---

1. This is the official estimate of private and government debt as of March 1999. See Bank Indonesia, *Laporan Tahunan 1998/99*, 57.

of the colonial state acquired these traits to the same degree, however; to the extent that war and revolution in the 1940s permitted continuity, it was largely the less rationalized organizations that survived. The central bank itself was a partial exception, but over the first decade of independence it took on more of the attributes of other state organizations. The disorganization of the state at this time meant that financial and monetary policies were not implemented consistently, and the government was increasingly forced into adopting unsustainable policies. The political centralization brought about by the new regime from 1966 allowed for much greater organizational coherence, but it was a coherence that only minimally resembled rationalized bureaucratic forms, even in supposedly technocratic organizations such as the central bank. Consequently, the state's organizational attributes allowed for a large gap between policy and practice in the financial sector. The result was a financial system that was frequently a burden on the economy and the public purse, regardless of financial policy orientation.

COLONIAL FOUNDATIONS

The Evolving Indies State

For nearly two centuries, Dutch authority in what became known as Netherlands India was vested in a transnational trading company, the VOC (Verenigde Oostindische Compagnie, or United East India Company), until its financial collapse at the end of the eighteenth century. The VOC had a patrimonial structure that required company servants to trade extensively on their own account. The salary drawn by employees "was of merely symbolic significance," and by the end of the eighteenth century, perquisites of office "were considered so normal that instead of receiving a nominal salary, an annual 'office charge' had to be paid to the Company," according to W. F. Wertheim (1964, 112–13). VOC directorships, like other state offices in the Netherlands at the time, tended to be hereditary. Although highly effective at first, this system was unable to secure the company's commercial interest when the growth of British trade in the Far East freed employees from dependence on official lines of oversight and reward (Adams 1996).

Administration was taken over by the Dutch government early in the nineteenth century (apart from the interregnum of 1811–16, when Stamford Raffles of the East India Company, acting on behalf of the British government, replaced the Napoleonic-era Governor-General Hermen Willem Daendels). The Dutch governed through a colonial bureaucracy that combined political, administrative, and commercial functions.[2] This structure of government changed over the first half of the nineteenth century (in part because of the attempt by Daendels to imitate the Napoleonic reforms that had been introduced in Europe) but retained many of its early features (Wertheim 1964, 115–16). Government finances relied on state

2. Furnivall 1939 remains the most comprehensive examination of the colonial system.

trading and tax farming, and under the regime of state-run forced production
known as the Cultivation System (approximately the middle decades of the
century), officials received a percentage of the agricultural produce in their areas
of responsibility (Furnivall 1939, 116; Rush 1990; Diehl 1993). Some governors-
general engaged in business on their own account or had business backgrounds.
The regular rotation of incumbents, however, signals that the office was
depersonalized.

The system of government involved considerable blurring of public and private
functions. The revenue farms, for example, delegated more than the sale of monopoly distribution rights: the enforcement of these monopolies was largely carried
out by private parapolice employed by the farmers themselves. Their authority to
operate was never spelled out in law but, as James Rush puts it, was "considered
by the Chinese [farm operators] to be a firm, though unwritten, part of the farm
contract." Routine breaches of the law were accepted and attracted punitive action
only when "blatant clandestine activities exacerbated other excesses."[3]

Part of the reason for this informality in policy implementation lay in what John
Furnivall described as a system of government that rested on authority, not law,
under which officials aimed to achieve particular goals rather than to follow the
dictates of procedural rules.[4] The impulse to rule through law was not absent, particularly after the constitutional reform of 1854, but was confined to Europeans
and those who acquired European status through commercial activity. In matters
relating to the indigenous population, the exercise of "gentle pressure" and
personal authority beyond the law remained common practice. Flexible policy enforcement was also "encouraged by an environment among the residency elite in
which the exchange of favors was raised to the level of adat (accepted and honored
custom)," writes Rush. Gifts, retail credit, and low-interest loans subsidized the
standard of living enjoyed by European officials, with transfers mediated by "social
customs that permitted well-heeled Chinese supplicants to curry favor with the
Colonial Service" (Rush 1990, 124, 128–33).

Direct bribery, in contrast, was not acceptable even before the administrative
reforms of the end of the nineteenth century (Furnivall 1939, 160; Rush 1990,
133). Over time, however, standards of propriety required a clearer distinction
between public and private realms, and the notion that public and private interests
could conflict—which had received lip service from the early 1800s—took on more
concrete expression. By the 1920s, officials who accepted commissions and gifts
from the private sector or moved on to lucrative positions in private companies
after retirement attracted serious complaints (Wertheim 1964, 118–23). This shift
in public morality coincided with changed perceptions of the proper organizational
form for the modern era. In a novel written in 1921 by Semaoen, the Communist
Party (PKI) is shown to have the correct, modern form of organization. Hence,

3. This paragraph is based on Rush 1990, esp. 59–62, 75–81, 117, 135.
4. See Lev 1985 on colonial law; and Furnivall 1939, 124, 158, 187–90, 260.

"PKI leaders did not rely on their personal individual connections through traditional patron-clientelism, but rather created the public image that the PKI was an impersonal, rationally-functioning machine," writes Yamamoto Nobuto (1997, 73).[5]

The greater formality of government-business interaction may in part have been a function of the increasing influence of private business, which could now successfully press its case in The Hague or Batavia and had less need of informal accommodation in the field (Wertheim 1964, 122). It also related to other changes in the colonial state as newly acquired tasks led to a massive extension of state activity. This late-colonial state was, to use Harry Benda's term, a *Beamtenstaat*: an apolitical polity concerned with sound administration per se (Benda 1966). Overall, it was an organized and functional apparatus, if labored and unresponsive in many ways. Many observers considered Netherlands India to be a comparatively well-run colony, with a high level of infrastructure and administrative capacity.[6]

This describes the Dutch side of the state. A policy of indirect rule meant that the other side of the colonial state was rather different. Indirect rule entailed turning the local aristocracy, the *pryayi*, into an official class of bureaucrats, the *pangreh praja*, which would simultaneously serve as agent of the Dutch administration and rule in a supposedly traditional manner over the local inhabitants (Sutherland 1979). This system built on localized centers of power with fluctuating boundaries rather than on a unified Java-wide (let alone Indies-wide) polity (Moertono 1981). Javanese ideas of power envisaged a personalized center of authority inseparable from ethical and spiritual stature (Anderson 1990, 17–77).

Under the Dutch, administrative boundaries were remade and hardened; traditional control over the population increased greatly; and local rulers were slowly transformed into functionaries (Onghokham 1978). But as Sutherland has argued (1979, 160), many of the practices and principles of these official strata continued to be informed by older Javanese systems that stressed the importance of ceremonial display, personal loyalty, the cultivation of patronage networks, and ethical attributes. Nonsalary income was significant—though not for the most part based on private landholding (Onghokham 1978, 135)—and essential, given that official salaries were inadequate for meeting the cultural role expected of native rulers. This role was subsidized partly by extractions from the local population but also by Chinese opium farmers through gifts, bounties, and loans (Rush 1990, 118–22).

In the early twentieth century, the *pangreh praja* took on more of the attributes of a Weberian bureaucracy. From household apprenticeship of relations or friends, recruitment and training systems were taken over by government schools. Other reforms to native government introduced modern organizational forms and functions (Benda 1966, 595–600). In addition, local officials migrated to the Dutch side

5. Other movements at the time rejected this model in favor of familial organization. See Shiraishi 1997, 81–85.
6. E.g., Furnivall 1939, 298; Wertheim 1964. See also the contemporary impressions of a visiting British official in Bell 1928.

of the expanding state—in the government-run Opium Regie, for example, and in the Credit Service—where officials adapted to an administrative system in which promotions and duties were more specified, formalized, and merit-based—although nonsalary incomes were not eliminated (Rush 1990, 223–26, 234).

After 1931, however, reform gave way to "retraditionalization" (Onghokham 1978, 157) and a return to indirect rule with the ethnic group as the main administrative unit. Among the "most obvious victims in this reordering of colonial governance were the Western-trained Indonesian civil servants outside the ranks of the hereditary hierarchy in Java" who were to be replaced by traditional *adat* leaders (Benda 1966, 601–2). In parallel, efforts to resurrect and codify supposedly traditional legal institutions consolidated the colonial order's legal pluralism, on one side of which, according to Daniel Lev (1985, 63–66, 69), there existed "legal equality, personal rights, challengeable authority, knowable written law. . . . On the other was the privileged authority of officialdom, where discretion counted for more than law and influence peddlers more than lawyers." It would be the Indonesian side that won out in the institutions that survived the transition to independence.

The Java Bank and the Financial System

Indonesia's central bank, Bank Indonesia, had its origins in the Java Bank (Javasche Bank), which received its charter in 1827 and began operations in 1828. Its establishment marked a further step toward the formalization of colonial government in the area of money and finance; a tremendous increase in monetary regulations had already occurred in the late eighteenth century (Klein 1991, 421–32). The Java Bank was a commercial bank and the only financial institution in the colony with the right to issue notes. Its currency, however, did not become (compulsory) legal tender until 1914 and never fully displaced the variety of other monies that circulated in Netherlands India.

The original intention of the bank's main promoter in the Indies, Commissioner General Du Bus (himself a Belgian capitalist), was that it should be a private institution, and most sources describe it as such, although some acknowledge that most of its capital was subscribed by officials in Batavia because private capital in the Netherlands was unenthusiastic (Laanen 1980, 18).[7] In fact, the government took about 50 percent of the shares, and a trading company, the Nederlandsche Handelsmaatschappij (NHM), took 15 percent (De Bree 1928, 1:213–14; Rahardjo 1995, 29). By the turn of the twentieth century the Indies government was receiving 65 to 70 percent of the bank's annual dividend, although this percentage dropped to around 50 percent in the 1940s.[8] The bank was in this sense always a

---

7. Those who refer to the Java Bank as private include Wardhana 1971, 343; Laanen 1980, 17, 33, 36; Laanen 1990, 250; Klein 1991, 436; Eng 1996, xviii; and Prince 1996, 58. Sutter 1959, 87, is more cautious, calling the bank "a private corporation, operated under government control." Furnivall 1939, 102–3, describes the bank as substantially government owned.
8. De Bree 1928, vol. 2, reproduces a summary of the annual accounts of the Java Bank for the years 1900 to 1927.

public institution, even though its shares were actively traded and it was meant to be profit oriented.

On the other hand, the level and type of public control over the bank was not constant. Its second largest shareholder, the NHM, had an ambiguous relationship to public authority and illustrates the uncertainty of this category. The NHM was co-owned by the Dutch king and private investors. As well as enjoying monopoly privileges in the Indies, its finances and operations were closely entwined with both the Indies government and the Dutch Colonial Ministry in what Willem Mansvelt (cited in Furnivall 1939, 149) called a "labyrinth of borrowing and lending." The Java Bank's other original shareholders were a mix of colonial officials and private English and Dutch traders in Batavia (De Bree 1928, 1:213–14). Its original management (president, secretary, and directors) were all shareholders, although one of them may also have been representing the NHM, of which he was president. The government was represented from 1830 by a government commissioner, generally the director-general of finance (De Bree 1928, 2: app. 26).

Senior personnel tended to have a long association with the bank. Some directors served for fairly short periods, but the president generally held his position for at least five years, frequently more (there were only three presidents between 1828 and 1863, and six of the bank's fourteen presidents between 1828 and 1941 served for ten years or more) (Rahardjo 1995, 63–66). Although generally an internal appointment, the president did not always have a prior connection with the bank. The seventh, N. P. van den Berg (1873–89), had worked for the NHM and then a commercial bank in Batavia. His experience with the Java Bank qualified him to move on to become president of the Dutch central bank and to be offered the position of governor-general of Netherlands India.[9]

Van den Berg's appointment illustrates a shift in the bank's orientation toward technical skill: he had demonstrated his ability to perform in business and was highly regarded for his publications on money and finance before joining the Java Bank. In contrast, the bank's first president, C. de Haan, was appointed largely because other candidates for the position were either unwilling or too valuable to be transferred from elsewhere in government.[10] De Haan, who had been a justice official, had no background in banking or finance and little understanding of the Java Bank's functions. The other directors in early years were no better equipped to run a bank of issue, admitting in their first report to shareholders that "they had not succeeded in obtaining the necessary information for the investigation of the principles on which similar establishments were conducted elsewhere" (Berg 1996, 62).

As well as increasing its personnel skills, the bank became a more complex organization over time. Initially, its organizational structure consisted simply of the directors, a bookkeeper and a head of administration.[11] Their record keeping

9. On Berg, see Eng 1996, ix–xi, xxiii–xxvi.
10. Details about de Haan are from Rahardjo 1995, 34–35.
11. The following paragraphs on the structure and hierarchy of the Java Bank are based on Rahardjo 1995, 30–45, unless otherwise indicated.

appears to have been sporadic.[12] By 1895, the bank consisted of four functional offices, all operational as well as branch offices. By this time, if not earlier, the bank's balance sheet was published weekly in the official gazette (Berg 1996, 67). By 1939 a separate audit department and three nonoperational units had been added. The latter included an economics and statistics section, which (along with the other nonoperational sections) was considered by a new Indonesian employee in 1950 to have a particularly "serious and sacred" atmosphere (Abdullah 1995, 12). By the end of the colonial period the Java Bank had a slightly more elaborate organizational structure (Rahardjo 1995, 51). Lengthy annual reports were pro-duced and published on time (except for the years of Japanese occupation); the rotation of managing directors proceeded smoothly according to set procedures; and the rewards of employment at the bank were considerable: in addition to gen-erous fixed salaries, the bank paid out a percentage of its profit in annual bonuses to the professional staff and maintained a pension and provident fund.[13]

In parallel with this shift to a more differentiated and publicly oriented organ-ization, the government's control over the bank was progressively formalized. In addition to placing a government commissioner with the bank from 1830, the bank's president and secretary were, until 1870, appointed by the governor-general, with the King's approval; other directors were chosen by the shareholders. After 1870, senior managers were appointed by the president and two directors who had to be permanent and salaried. These functionaries, in turn, were appointed for fixed terms by the governor-general from a list of nominees prepared by the direc-tors and a newly established board of commissioners.[14] In 1895, government over-sight was further enhanced by the establishment of the Government Commissariat, which included the Resident of Batavia and a Finance Department official. Gov-ernment control was codified in the Java Bank Act of 1922.

As a profit-oriented institution, the bank performed indifferently for much of the time until the twentieth century. In its first decade profits were meager, and the bank was virtually insolvent by 1839; then its assets stagnated, falling to pre-1838 levels by 1890.[15] One reason was that regulatory limits on its credit issue between 1854 and 1875 reduced its commercial scope (Laanen 1980, 34). The bank also lost ground to the commercial banks established in the Indies from 1857 onward. It took a conservative approach to banking, discounting government bills and offering finance at relatively low interest rates only to large European exporters and Chinese commodity traders. As its public role and competence increased from the late nineteenth century, the scale and profitability of its operations also grew

---

12. In a reconstruction of the bank's accounts, much of the data from 1841 until about 1853 had to be estimated (Laanen 1980, 84–85).

13. These expenditures are recorded in the bank's annual reports.

14. This board comprised members of the Dutch commercial community, professionals, the president of the NHM, and others appointed by the government (Rahardjo 1995, 41). According to De Bree, from 1887 to 1888 they included one E. Douwes Dekker, who may have been the author of *Max Havelaar* (a well-known anticolonial novel published in 1860) or one of his descendants.

15. All figures on assets are from the consolidated accounts of the Java Bank in Laanen 1980, 84–91.

considerably. The bank's annual dividend averaged 17 percent between 1915 and 1940.[16]

The Java Bank's public role centered on currency management. At its founding it was given responsibility for managing the currency system in return for note-issuing privileges. But blurred lines of authority, lax colonial accounting systems, fiscal problems, and few regulatory limits on the issue of notes undermined any attempt it made to ensure currency stability. It was at this time no more a rationalized organization than the rest of the colonial state. A later bank president blamed the government for "willfully perverting the currency of the colony" by introducing large amounts of copper money which the bank, "notwithstanding the reiterated protests of its Directors, was forced to issue" but maintained that the fault was due to the mismanagement of the directors (Berg 1996, 62). Conditions began to change in 1848, when the bank was required to abide by limits on note-issuing set by the governor-general. These limits were revised in 1859, and the bank abided by them despite the constriction on commercial activity they entailed. Only in 1875 did the Dutch government agree to a directors' proposal to replace quantitative limits with a set proportion (40 percent) of reserves (Berg 1996, 64–67).

The bank's 1846 currency purge to deal with the oversupply of copper currency (created by government policy) and the smuggling of copper coins was an early attempt at currency rationalization. Like later purges, it was not entirely effective: old coinage continued to circulate; many foreign monies were extensively used (particularly in Sumatra and Borneo); and smuggling remained a problem (Klein 1991, 437–44; Prince 1996). There was also an inflow of counterfeit coins and private tokens from China and Singapore (Pridmore 1968, 79–91; Berg 1996, 87). In the nineteenth century the circulation of foreign (noncounterfeit) currencies was mostly tolerated, and foreign money was accepted by government offices, but later the attempt to regulate the currency in circulation became more serious. Twelve separate currency purges were completed between 1900 and 1930, and large amounts of irregular currency were withdrawn. Even so, "right up to the end of the colonial regime in 1942 some areas had continued quite unpurged," as Peter Klein (1991, 440, 445–46) points out.

Although standardizing the currency in circulation did not become a particular concern until the twentieth century, monetary policy from 1854 focused on maintaining parity between the Netherlands currency and that of the Indies through regular shipments of specie (Prince 1996, 59). This meant following the Netherlands onto the gold standard in 1877, which was maintained (except for a hiatus in 1914–25) until the Netherlands devalued its currency in 1936. The Java Bank under the presidency of van den Berg was a strong supporter of the gold standard. Interestingly, van den Berg was one of those who appeared to view the bank as a private institution in that he likened it to the Netherlands central bank,

---

16. Calculated according to the book value of the capital. See the summary in *Report of the President of the Java Bank (1947–1949)*, app. F.

which he approvingly described as having "always kept free from any State intervention, or any meddling with State finances."[17] On the other hand, he justified the Java Bank's support of the gold standard on the grounds that "it is one of the first duties of every Government [to] take any reasonable precaution . . . to prevent that [monetary] standard from fluctuating" (Berg 1996, 65, 76). The bank fulfilled this task competently for most of the time until 1940, although its preoccupation with external value probably contributed to its failure to supply adequate small-denomination coinage for use in domestic transactions (Klein 1991, 449; Prince 1996, 59–67).

Another element of the bank's public role was to provide credit to the government. It unwillingly eased the government's financial problems through currency issue in the 1830s, but the adverse effects of this experiment prompted a restrictive regulatory framework for the next three decades. At this stage, however, the fiscal position of the colonial government was strong. When deficits became more common after 1875, the gap was initially made up by loans from the Netherlands Department of Finance (Booth 1990, 211–17). In the twentieth century the bank's advances to government became substantial, even as it criticized the Netherlands Bank for its lending to the Indies government (Laanen 1980, 89–91; Prince 1996, 65).

For much of the colonial era, neither the government nor the Java Bank had much of a financial policy. A private financial sector did not exist until government economic policy entered a more liberal phase in the second half of the nineteenth century; before that the government and the Java Bank had provided credit to whatever private enterprise there was (the NHM stayed out of banking until the 1880s). Commercial banks began to operate from 1857, prompted by a shortage of credit in the Indies (Allen and Donnithorne 1957, 186–92; Laanen 1990). Mostly they were Dutch banks, although two British-owned banks already operating in Asia also opened offices.

The Dutch banks soon found that they had overestimated the demand for banking services and began investing in agriculture. Competitive pressures meant that they "advanced money freely without adequate security, and multiplied their risks by discounting their own bills." When business in the Indies was hard hit by the decline in sugar prices in 1883–84, most of the Dutch banks ran into severe trouble. They were saved "with the help of the Java Bank, the N.H.M. and some financiers in the Netherlands," according to Furnivall (1939, 197–98). As a result of the restructuring that followed, commercial banks that focused on short- and medium-term financing emerged as institutions separate from the specialized agricultural banks engaged in long-term investment (although one major commercial bank did retain ties to a newly formed agricultural bank, and the NHM engaged in both businesses). The banks' earlier practice of discounting their own bills on the Amsterdam market was also brought to an end.

17. In this estimation of the Netherlands Bank he was mistaken. See Furnivall 1939, 83; Conant 1927, 289–90.

The Java Bank provided support for business in times of distress, such as the downturn in the 1880s, but doing so did not prevent it from pursuing policies that were perceived to be unfavorable for private business and banks. An early attempt by a private bank to challenge the Java Bank's note-issuing monopoly was scotched in 1863 (Allen and Donnithorne 1957, 187). The bank was not afraid to take unpopular action in other areas. For example, as president, van den Berg was strongly in favor of following the Netherlands onto the gold standard, even though the move was not supported by Dutch business in the Indies and the local press was almost unanimously against it. On the other hand, he opposed the establishment of a mint in Java, despite its being "warmly advocated by the commercial community" (Berg 1996, 75, 64). This orientation may have changed for a time early in the twentieth century, when the bank "made itself the monetary mouthpiece of private enterprise" and urged a looser monetary policy (Klein 1991, 446). Except when relations with the Netherlands Bank were strained between 1919 and 1924, however, the bank emphasized currency stability. In the face of local calls to devalue the currency during the depression, it raised the bank rate rather than see the external value of the currency decline (Prince 1996, 63–67). The Java Bank also continued its commercial banking activity, greatly annoying its competitors (Wardhana 1971, 342).

Over time, commercial banks became much larger actors in the Indies, experiencing strong growth in the early twentieth century until the downturn of the 1930s. Foreign banks, both European and Japanese, increased their presence under a relatively open-door policy; local Chinese banks were established and, after 1929, two small banks owned by indigenous Indonesians began operating (Furnivall 1939, 335–36; Allen and Donnithorne 1957, 193–94; Sutter 1959, 89–90; Twang 1998, 41). In this period, the government's financial policy became more active. Some private actors, including the Indies Bankers' Council, made proposals for prudential constraints and greater legal regulation (Vleming 1992, 152–54, 159–62, 145). An extensive official survey of Chinese business carried out by the taxation service in the 1920s criticized the "over-extension and unscrupulous use of credit facilities, particularly on the part of European banks, brokers' offices and trading houses," for financing speculative activity in commodity futures markets (cited in Vleming 1992, 151, 158).

The Java Bank was not involved in the limited attempts to introduce a degree of regulation in these areas. Most of the large banks were tied to the Netherlands or other metropolitan centers, as were most large firms, and because these private-sector players tended to remit surplus funds for investment, a money market barely developed in the Indies. Banks in the Indies also preferred to rely on the Dutch market in times of distress rather than on the Java Bank as a lender of last resort (Wardhana 1971, 340). It is significant that private actors did not see the Java Bank as an easy source of funds—in contrast to the government-owned Philippine National Bank, which was continually raided from its establishment in 1916 onward (Hutchcroft 1998, 67–69).

The Java Bank acquired further central banking responsibilities in the twentieth century by providing clearinghouse facilities for interbank payments, as well as recording its own physical management of currency in circulation in much greater detail than before (Laanen 1980, 64; Vleming 1992, 139; Prince 1996, 61). At the close of the colonial era it also began to monitor the activity of commercial banks, reporting on their assets and liabilities from 1948 on. One of its first tasks after reopening in Jakarta in 1946 (having been closed during the Japanese occupation) was to oversee the liquidation of the Japanese banks (Rahardjo 1995, 47–50). Until this time, although the Java Bank's reports survey the domestic and international economy (and government finances) in detail, they virtually ignore the banking industry.

The Java Bank was involved in a limited way in the government's financial policy initiatives in the area of small-scale finance for the indigenous population, village banks, and postal savings, all of which developed in the twentieth century (Furnivall 1939, 357–61; Laanen 1990, 258–64). A civil servant who promoted the idea of such institutions in the 1890s suggested that the rationale was to reduce the "pernicious influence" of Chinese and other private moneylenders operating in rural areas.[18] His account is instructive for the way if conceptualized public authority and government activity. He noted that the government had in 1892 provided interest-free advances to indigenous coffee growers and was therefore moving in the direction of becoming a credit provider. He went on to acknowledge that some might object to the scheme on the grounds that it constituted state interference but argued that since the natives were bound by public duties, it was right and reasonable for the state to protect them—in this case by providing credit at reasonable rates through a state enterprise which "should be replaced by private initiative later, but under state supervision." The idea, he said, was something he often discussed with the then president of the Java Bank, who thought the bank "would be happy to exercise its control over such an establishment and prepare the way as far as administration and guidelines were concerned." Although this scheme was not adopted, a range of government savings and credit institutions were established and became moderately successful. Starting in the 1930s, their activities began to be recorded in the annual reports of the Java Bank.

STATE AND FINANCE, 1945–1965

Japanese occupation between 1942 and 1945, followed by four years of revolutionary struggle, destroyed much of the colonial infrastructure of government. War and revolution severely damaged its physical and economic basis and also did much to finish the process of undermining previous systems of political authority, which had begun with the spread of ferment in Indonesian society in the 1910s

18. See Fokkens 1992, esp. 50–56, on which this paragraph is based.

(T. Shiraishi 1990). Soon after independence was declared, wrote Benedict Anderson (1972, 107), "it became increasingly clear that virtually all of the institutions and organizations of the occupation era depended for their integrity and vitality on the backbone provided by Japanese military power." The difficulties were not only due to the disruption of occupation and revolution but also related to the Japanese promotion of nonbureaucratic groups, including the man who became Indonesia's first president, Sukarno. Sukarno's theatrical style of popular politics combined with the spread of military and revolutionary values among the youth to produce a society that was highly politicized (Anderson 1966, 1972). The extent of social mobilization and the intensity of nationalist feelings pushed the Indonesian leadership to an early declaration of independence, before the country had a chance to recover administratively, politically, or economically from World War II. The ensuing four-year militarized conflict against the Dutch meant that when sovereignty was ceded in 1949, the country was in almost complete disarray. The contrast could hardly have been greater with the slow and orderly transition to independence in Malaya and Singapore, where the new structures emerged according to plans laid out by the old.

The New Indonesian State

After the transfer of sovereignty the number of government employees grew as a result of the politics of patronage in a series of short-lived alliance governments. The weakness of the state in military, economic, and administrative terms included extensive penetration of state organizations by societal groups whose loyalties were generally given to other institutions or causes (Anderson 1990, 102–3). The suspension of parliamentary government in 1957 focused political competition between the army and its political enemy, the PKI (Partai Komunis Indonesia). These two organizations were the most disciplined, coherent bodies in Indonesia, more able than any other to provide for the institutionalized expression of interest.[19] A series of massacres in the closing months of 1965 and early 1966, however, physically destroyed the PKI.[20] And the army, though undergoing considerable rationalization over the 1950s, became extensively involved in commercial (and often corrupt) activities from the 1960s on (Crouch 1988, 24–42, 273–303). President Sukarno, with no organizational base, relied on his popularity and ability to ignite mass emotion to maintain his position as the center of authority. By the end of the decade, the use of appointments and favors to placate rival groups, saw the administration decay rapidly, with hundred-member cabinets and blatant manipulation of state trading and financial organizations. Political competition, subversion by the United States, separatist rebellions, and

19. On the transformation of the armed forces from a geographically splintered set of loosely organized, revolutionary, and idealistic corps (Anderson 1972, esp. 20–33 and chap. 11) to a unified, structured organization, see McVey 1971, 1972.

20. These massacres resulted in upward of 500,000 deaths. Pipit 1985 provides a firsthand account of the period.

military confrontations fed upon one another and weakened an already fragile economy.

These conditions in turn fed the growth of patrimonialism and the use of state resources for personal and political ends. Corruption was common and hugely exacerbated by the inflation of the 1960s, which devastated official salaries (Mackie 1967; Smith 1971). State organizations at this time lent themselves to the development of collaborative, informal relationships between largely ethnic Chinese entrepreneurs and government power-holders. These ties had become established during the revolution, when the Dutch blockade and the desperate need of the nationalists for finance and war matériel forced them to rely on the commercial networks and skills of ethnic Chinese Indonesians.[21]

There was also a direct overlap between those in official positions and those involved in business from the early years of revolution and independence. Mohammad Hatta, the republic's vice president and major economic policymaker, came from an extended business family; his relatives and close associates included most of the prominent indigenous Indonesian, or *pribumi*, businessmen of the 1950s (Twang 1998, 137–39). There was at this time a close association among political party leaders, the heads of government agencies, and business actors (Robison 1986, 46–62). In some cases, this was a necessity. Sumitro Djojohadikusumo, for example, recalls being sent to represent the Republican government at the United Nations in 1947 and supporting himself through a smuggling operation he organized, since no money was sent him from Indonesia (Sumitro 1986, 34).[22]

The new government's policy was fundamentally oriented to promoting private interests; not exclusively those of power-holders but also those of a fledgling, largely imagined, *pribumi* capitalist class. The increasingly "statist" economic structures and policies after 1957, when the Dutch businesses that dominated the modern sector were nationalized, did involve discrimination in favor of state-owned corporations (Anspach 1969, 193). One needs to bear in mind, however, the nature of the Indonesian state at this stage. Many of the nationalized corporations were seized in uncoordinated actions by their Indonesian workers and were only subsequently taken over by power-holders, often in the military. In other cases, the military acted without political sanction (Thomas and Glassburner 1965, 168–73). More generally, the disorganization and indiscipline of most state organizations, including the state corporations, meant that they were vehicles for private interests more often than institutionalized public organizations (see, e.g., Robison 1986, 47). The fractured structure of authority over the state development bank at this period illustrates that state organizations were far from being under monolithic state control, even in formal terms; control and oversight of the bank were divided among its managing directors, its supervisory council, a special executive command staff, the Bapindo committee for re-tooling the state apparatus, and an employees' council.[23]

---

21. Twang 1998 describes the formation of these relationships.
22. See also Soedarpo 1994, 43–48, which recounts his early, intertwined, official and business career.
23. See Bapindo, *Laporan Tahunan 1962 Bank Pembangunan Indonesia*, 1965, 115–17. The bank was bankrupt by 1966 (Emery 1970, 188–91).

Indeed, the meaning of Indonesia's independence and the state that emerged from it was that public institutions existed to serve societal interests (Anderson 1990, 99–109). This did not mean that the distinction between public and private which had developed over the colonial period was submerged, or that corruption or abuse of office were alien concepts. Although corruption was common and attempts to end it halfhearted, corruption scandals were scandals, some of which prompted parliamentary inquiries and resignations (Sutter 1959, 1081–87). The abuse of public office represented a discrepancy between norm and reality (Wertheim 1964, 129), a gap that contributed to the low esteem in which government came to be held.

State institutions represented a vaguely defined general interest rather than a distinct government interest. No group other than the army and the PKI showed much commitment to building or sustaining rationalized organizations. The major study of the parliamentary period (Feith 1962) could be taken to imply that there was such a group—leaders committed to a rational, problem-solving approach to government, whom Herbert Feith terms administrators—and that it was politically defeated. Viewed from the perspective of administrative organizations, however, this characterization has been disputed (Willner 1970, 265), and, in Feith's own account, "administrators" were distinguished mainly by the priority they accorded to economic development and by being attuned to Western ideas of economic development. Sumitro, a Western-trained economist, makes it clear that this orientation did not entail any liking for administration. As he describes his role in issuing Republican currency in 1946, "It was an awful job, really an organising job" (1986, 33).

Bank Indonesia and the Financial Sector

After the transfer of sovereignty in 1949 the Java Bank's status as the bank of issue was not assured, as many Indonesians wished to make state-owned Bank Negara Indonesia (BNI), established in 1946, the new country's central bank.[24] The Dutch, however, motivated by concerns about the repayment of Indonesian debt to the Netherlands and fears about the impact of monetary instability on Dutch business, successfully insisted that the Java Bank retain its position. Some on the Indonesian side, such as Vice President Hatta, also believed that retaining it lent the new government credibility (Rahardjo 1995, 53–54). The Java Bank remained in Dutch hands until 1951 and was legally constituted as the central bank, Bank Indonesia, in 1953.

In 1951, Indonesia's leading financial authority, Sjafruddin Prawiranegara, replaced the Dutch president, who resigned when the government announced plans for the bank's nationalization (Sutter 1959, 960). Sjafruddin remained at the helm of the bank until 1958. His appointment was a concession both to meritocracy and to the Dutch, whose confidence he enjoyed. He was not tainted by corruption

24. BNI was originally intended as the central bank and was officially opened in the building that had housed the Java Bank in Yogyakarta (Rahardjo 1995, 1–3, 50–54). The notes it issued, known as ORI (Oeang Republik Indonesia), financed much of the Indonesian revolution (Oey 1991, 68–87).

(Kahin 1989) and had been known as a fiscal conservative and for his opposition to patronage demands when he had been finance minister (Feith 1962, 169). Sjafruddin was initially unwilling to take up the position, recalling later, "I wanted to retire from public life. . . . I felt that I had to earn enough money for the education of my children and I could only do that in a private capacity. At that time—maybe because of my Dutch education—I would not have thought of abusing my power as a public servant to make money! Then we thought of the public service as an honorary job." He accepted the post on condition that he and other Indonesian staff enjoy the same salary scale and privileges as the Dutch staff (Sjafruddin 1987, 103).

Initially, the Java Bank maintained a fair degree of continuity in structure and personnel. A monetary council, consisting of the head of the bank and the ministers of finance and economy, set monetary policy. Otherwise the organizational structure of the bank after it was renamed and brought under the new Central Bank Act in 1953 was not much different from what it had been in 1948 (Rahardjo 1995, 50, 61, 93). Until this time, the format of the annual report also remained unchanged, only extending its scope to report also on local banking activity. From 1951, Indonesians were increasingly recruited to board positions and as employees; until then, there had been only two Indonesians in professional staff positions and one Indonesian member of the board of directors.[25] The recruitment process of was seen by an Indonesian clerk at the bank in a less than favorable light: "I saw that there was a principle that they [new professional staff] had to speak Dutch well. I also saw that many of them came from *pamong praja* families, for example children of *bupati*.[26] There were also some that came from the army" (Abdullah 1995, 16). The great majority of educated Indonesians at that time, however, would have been the Dutch-speaking children of civil servants (Sjafruddin himself had been a colonial Finance Department official), so their appointment was consistent with a concern for educational qualifications. The bank also adopted a program of on-the-job training and rotation for new recruits (Rahardjo 1995, 100). The fact that many Dutch personnel were retained until 1953 also indicates a concern with continuity, skills, and effectiveness.[27]

The competency of these Dutch employees has been questioned. Ali Wardhana, for example, writes that the Java Bank failed to develop "a truly central bank-minded staff" (1971, 342), and Sumitro says of the Dutch advisers and officials in the central bank and Ministry of Finance that "I didn't have much respect for any

25. There were also Eurasians and Chinese Indonesians who held such positions but they were not perceived, in a contemporary account, to be "Indonesian." See Abdullah 1995, 12.
26. The *pamong praja* was the renamed *pangreh praja*, the colonial native civil service. A *bupati* was the head of an administrative unit, both an aristocratic ruler and a senior official.
27. According to personnel lists in the bank's annual reports, in 1952 almost all head office staff were Dutch; of twenty-nine senior officers, only three were Chinese (in the accounting and foreign exchange departments) and one Indonesian (although some of those counted as Dutch are likely to have been Eurasian). In 1953 Indonesians were still a small minority (12.5 percent) of the staff officers in the head office (Rahardjo 1995, 94).

of them—they had no clue about economics—but they were very good at administrative procedure" (Sumitro 1986, 35). These assessments probably say more about those making them, both macroeconomists involved in Indonesian economic policy under Suharto, than about the quality of the Dutch personnel Sjafruddin chose to retain; they had maintained stable monetary conditions before the war and were acknowledged to have skills in administration and commercial banking (*Far Eastern Economic Review*, 6 April 1961), which was a significant activity for the bank.

Sjafruddin had a fairly strict attitude toward the nascent Indonesian banking industry. In one account, he "treated the Indonesian banks much as the Dutch had done. On technical grounds, he may have been right, but that was not the point" (Sumitro 1986, 36). The Dutch had been unenthusiastic about the rapid establishment of new banks and urged caution in lending and liquidity (De Javasche Bank, *Laporan Tahun-Buku* 1949–50, 43–47). One Indonesian who established a bank (Bank Niaga) in the 1950s recalls that "the main difficulty was obtaining a banking license from Bank Indonesia," but he goes on to say that "fortunately, Sumitro [an old friend] was then Minister of Finance, which made it a bit easier" (Soedarpo 1994, 49). Apparently many others had connections that were equally effective: eighteen private Indonesian banks had been established by 1952 and forty-two by the end of 1956, by which time they accounted for 11 percent of domestic credit outstanding. Minimum capital requirements were introduced in 1955, in reaction to unscrupulous activity by many bankers whose operations, Bank Indonesia noted, were often capitalized on state handouts. Bank Indonesia attempted some supervision but acknowledged that regulations were hard to enforce, given the lack of skilled personnel (Anspach 1969, 142–43).

Bank Indonesia was initially able to maintain at least some organizational continuity and discipline, corresponding with at least some operational success: until about 1958 the overall condition of the financial system and wider economy was precarious but had not reached crisis point.[28] Like other state organizations, however, the central bank was eventually overwhelmed by the politics of the time, a process that is reflected in all facets of its organization. The discontinuity in personnel at the senior level became marked after 1957. Sjafruddin left as governor in 1958 to take up a position in the rebel government in Sumatra. By 1960, none of the managing directors of 1952 were still serving, and of the fifty-six senior officers in the head office only seven are listed as having been with the bank in 1952. Several reorganizations took place, often without any apparent rationale, producing a confused organizational structure that lacked a clear hierarchy, even on paper (Rahardjo 1995, 109–26), and culminating in a major upheaval of the entire state-owned banking sector in 1965 which made Bank Indonesia a unit within a massive conglomerate structure. How much the bank was functioning at all between 1960 and 1965 is doubtful; it stopped publishing its reports even before hyperinflation

28. See Higgins 1957 for an account of stabilization policy.

set in. One reason was a government policy of releasing minimal financial data that foreign interests might exploit, but "a shortage of funds and other problems" also delayed the production of reports (Emery 1970, 172–73). Data from this time are not considered reliable (Arndt 1984, 143).

Extremely low salaries in the 1960s were not conducive to retaining skilled staff, and patronage determined many senior appointments. A managing director of the bank in the late 1960s says his salary was not enough to feed his family (interview, former Bank Indonesia officer, Jakarta, April 1997).[29] By 1966 the number of directors had grown from the three or four of the 1950s to fifteen (Rahardjo 1995, 127), which, given that salaries had been eroded by inflation, suggests there were opportunities for outside gains. Further, some of the new board members appointed from 1951 were politicians or businessmen. The governor from 1963 to 1966, for example, had left the PKI in 1953 to join another political party and owned business interests (Sutter 1959, 961, 1086). He was arrested for corruption soon after the change of regime in 1966.

Bank Indonesia was subject to prevailing ideas about the nature of public institutions. In the debate that preceded its nationalization in 1951, advocates of nationalization emphasized that as a private institution the Java Bank could not work in the public interest; to guarantee the public interest, the bank had to be owned by the state.[30] The meaning of public interest at this time is illuminated in the discussions over the form the central bank would take. Many parliamentarians opposed a corporate form because they associated it with profit-seeking, which they considered inappropriate for a state institution; the government, preferring a corporate form in the interests of continuity and reputation, insisted that there need not be a correlation between profit-seeking and corporate status. Establishing the bank's institutional interests, or indeed its potential role as a source of profit for the government, was therefore very much against the climate of the time. Bank Indonesia was intended to serve societal, not state, interests. In this it was similar to the many government credit institutions established in the 1950s, as well as schemes such as the Benteng program to provide *pribumi* businessmen with preferential access to foreign exchange and import licenses (Anspach 1969, 139–42, 168–78; Robison 1986, 44–45). These expectations permeated the central bank. A former employee recalls his surprise at the directors' negative reaction to his union activity and to his criticism of a bonus paid to senior officials, many of whom were Dutch: since the directors were part of the Indonesian nation (*bangsa Indonesia*), he could not understand why they favored Dutch officers and objected to his strug-

29. I informed all persons I interviewed that I was researching central banks and banking in Southeast Asia and that I would be using in published work the data I collected. I obtained no written consent to quote them, but I have not identified by name or company affiliation either those who preferred that I not do so or any others who, I thought, might conceivably be damaged by such identification. I did not record my interviews but made only a few notes, usually writing up the conversation immediately afterward and later transferring some of my longhand copy to computer files.

30. This account is drawn from Sutter 1959, 961–72.

gle for justice for the *bangsa Indonesia*: "What else could be the meaning of the independence we had struggled for?" (Abdullah 1995, 20).[31]

As political conditions and the tenuous organizational coherence of Bank Indonesia broke down after 1957, the financial system and the economy rapidly deteriorated. The unchecked flow of credit through Bank Indonesia and other state-owned financial institutions led to hyperinflation in the 1960s. Statutory limits on central bank advances to government were repeatedly overstepped. Legal economic activity stalled, production by many nationalized corporations collapsed, and illegal trade became widespread. By the time President Sukarno lost control of the government to the military in 1966, the financial system was in utter disarray, and foreign reserves were exhausted. The government was facing a severe fiscal crisis (Mackie 1967; Arndt 1984).

STATE AND FINANCE, 1966–1998

The New Order State

The New Order, as the regime headed by Suharto after 1966 was known, brought profound changes to the nature of state organizations. The military and civilian bureaucracy increased in size far beyond levels seen in the Sukarno period; the reach of state organizations expanded as never before into the countryside; and the state apparatus developed a degree of cohesion and order (Emmerson 1978; Evers 1987, 672). Political centralization, the development of corporatist quasi-state organizations, and the forcible depoliticization of mass organizations underlay these changes. The regime also used the organizational strength of the armed forces to maintain control over the civilian bureaucracy (MacDougall 1982). The government's emphasis on administration and depoliticization meant that it bore some resemblance to the *Beamtenstaat* of the colonial era, focused on "the strengthening of the state qua state" (Anderson 1990, 111).

This does not mean that state organizations had structures, routines, and norms conducive to high levels of organizational discipline. Even if the state could be described as a "bureaucratic polity," it was one in which informality and personalized accommodation with outsiders were routinized.[32] An official's real status depended on securing wealth, clients, and favor rather than formal title (McVey 1982, 88). Official ideology promoted the idea of the family principle in the state, and norms of familial responsibility by senior officials for the welfare of their subordinates were still operative in the 1990s.[33] When senior figures in the bureaucracy moved to new positions, it was normal for their assistants to move with them.

---

31. "Lantas apa artinya kemerdekaan yang telah berhasil kita perjuangkan?"
32. Cf. Thailand, the original "bureaucratic polity" analyzed in Riggs 1966.
33. This is captured by the notion of *bapakism* (see Feith 1962, 127; and Anderson 1972, 236). Shiraishi 1997 analyzes its historical genesis and development in the New Order.

Over time, the New Order state became even less oriented to the organizational interests of its agencies and more attuned to the private interests of power-holders. By the 1980s, it increasingly served the regime—the president, his family, personal associates, and favored administrators—more than any organizational component of itself (Robison 1994, 52). Suharto's personal centralization of power helped the demands and interests created by deregulation from 1983 triumph over bureaucratic interest. The bureaucracy was incapable of amending these new priorities, even when they were detrimental to an organization's interests.[34] The constituency for change was created by the transformatory force of capitalism in Indonesia, as individuals associated with the state acquired wealth in ways that went beyond taking bribes to encompass commercial activity (Robison 1986). This process eventually created groups for whom state organizations served purely instrumental purposes and for whom the state-oriented organizational goals of the early New Order took on subsidiary and conditional roles.

The legalist emphasis of the New Order was only superficially at odds with its underlying informal and personalized routines. The absence of the rule of law marked a basic continuity with earlier legal institutions as, right from independence, the *pamong praja* officials who found their way into the judiciary, prosecution, and police were inclined to procedures that Lev calls "fundamentally patrimonial, discretionary, and authoritarian" (1985, 72). Adoption of the "rule of law" as a mobilizing slogan in the early years of the New Order coexisted with a generalized reliance on informal, personal mediation rather than legal procedures and institutions (Lev 1972; Lindsey 2000). An apparent formality in government organizations was similarly deceptive. Formal rules and structures were constantly referred to and created in substantial volume. Again, this New Order practice marked some continuity with the past: in the 1960s a foreign scholar working inside the bureaucracy identified the "respect, almost bordering on veneration, for the appearance of legality and correctness of form" (Willner 1970, 266, 286). Such a proliferation and veneration of written rules made rule-abiding policy implementation inconsistent with functional performance.

The New Order state also failed to remunerate its employees through salary alone. Indonesia's former foreign minister, Adam Malik, justified the payment of commissions and other gifts to officials on the grounds that it was customary and that official salaries were insufficient. Corruption, he said, "occurs only if people misuse their power" (*Singapore Trade and Industry*, September 1973, 39). Private business activity and outside employment were expressly prohibited for state officials in 1974. Yet inadequate salaries at the lower levels of government employment made such activities a necessity. Even in the middle ranks of the civil service, supporting a middle-class lifestyle required outside work or business. Family businesses commonly operated in areas related to the responsibilities of an official.

In 1996 a law—substantively no different from one already on the books—again prohibited such activity, but again, no attempts were made to enforce it. An early

---

34. The replacement of the customs service by a foreign firm for the decade to 1997 is an example.

official inquiry into corruption never had its findings acted on, and few offenders were prosecuted, even during a series of campaigns against corruption in the 1970s. Inadequate funding meant that government agencies as well as employees often had to develop their own quasi-legal funding sources. By the 1990s the systematization of extralegal fund-raising was reflected in the routinized size of kickbacks and percentages on government contracts or aid funds (Winters 1996, 136; interview, foreign aid agency, Jakarta, March 1997). State organizations had come to depend on practices acknowledged as corrupt, so that the eradication of corruption, as Willard Hanna put it "might mean the critical dislocation of the whole shaky national structure. . . . the emerging attitude seems to be that one must first refashion the system and meanwhile tolerate enough korupsi to keep it functioning. . . . [According to the head of the state oil company, Pertamina], 'If you can arouse and vitalize Pertamina by means of corruption, then let us all be corrupt'" (qtd. in Quah 1982, 176).

Within this state system, Indonesia's high-profile technocrats played supportive, often vital, roles. These people, all trained as economists, were adopted by the military early in the New Order and placed in key positions in economic ministries and agencies, or as special advisers to Suharto (Crouch 1988, 165–66, 183; Bresnan 1993, 62). The changing fortunes of this group are often presented (e.g., by Winters 1996) as a struggle between "technocrats" and "nationalists" within the state: at times of economic crisis Suharto favored the technocrats and their policies; when the government was flush with funds, the nationalists won out.

It is misleading, however, to interpret the technocratic element as constituting a core of bureaucratic rationality within the state. In the first place, most of the technocrats did not belong, in origin or orientation, to any state organization. All the economic advisers who first earned the label were recruited from outside the bureaucracy, and their elevation occurred at a time when the bureaucracy was demoralized and ripe for attack (Bresnan 1993, 60). They were academic economists whose identities remained tied to their profession rather than to any state organization. In recollections of their careers the technocrats are overwhelmingly concerned with Western economists, debates over economic theory, and their individual professional relationships. None describe the state organizations in which they worked, often in leadership positions, in detail or with any sign of affection (see Sumitro 1986; Sadli 1993, 37–38; Prawiro 1998). Their academic sponsor in the early New Order, Sumitro Djojohadikusumo, was neither a bureaucrat by training nor an administrator by inclination but an academic and a politician with business connections.[35]

The New Order technocrats enjoyed their influence not as a result of their official positions but because their professional expertise and credibility gave them the

---

35. Sumitro took a position in the secessionist government in 1957 and became trade minister in 1968. His son Hashim was one of the better-known *pribumi* tycoons of the late New Order. Hashim's interests in the 1990s included shares in three ailing banks. Hashim's brother-in-law was governor of the central bank at the time and his brother was married to one of Suharto's daughters (*Australian Financial Review*, 7 November 1997).

ability to get the foreign finance tap turned on in times of crisis (Anderson 1990, 112; Bresnan 1993, 63–72; Winters 1996, 52–82). Even in noncrisis periods they remained oriented toward outside institutions as their primary source of validation, often holding positions in universities concurrently with their government appointments, working as outside consultants, and becoming deeply involved with the many teams of foreign consultants and aid officials in Jakarta.

The technocrats themselves adopted principles of *bapakism* and traditional Javanese political culture. One recalled an instance of how he learned to adjust to this indirect way of operating. At a meeting to consider the introduction of a new rice strain, when Suharto called for comments, "most people behaved in the typical Javanese way and politely stayed quiet. I, however, had not yet been fully 'brainwashed,' and stated bluntly that the whole idea was nonsense and amounted to cheating the people. Widjojo [the acknowledged leader of the technocrat group] later advised me never to speak up like that again!" (Salim 1997, 56). As a means of understanding their working environment with Suharto, one economist suggested reading Benedict Anderson's essay on power and rulership, implying that Indonesia's technocrats were part of the ruler's household, "granted their positions and the perquisites that go with them as personal favours" (Bresnan 1993, 74).[36]

The technocrats never institutionalized their expertise in any agency. As one of them noted, "Our only weak spot was that we were not good managers. Widjojo did not place much emphasis on management when he was head of Bappenas [the development planning agency]. He was able to produce five-year development plans (Repelita) and the Development Budget was on time for many years, but Bappenas was not highly regarded as an organisation at that time" (Sadli 1993, 49). The apparent inability to retire people such as Widjojo and Ali Wardhana underlines the personal rather than organizational nature of technocratic involvement in the Indonesian state. The more colorful Marzuki Usman, also a foreign-trained economist, said that he could not have revived the capital market to spectacular growth in the late 1980s had he relied only on formal government organizations and official procedure (interview, Jakarta, May 1997).

The agencies that these economists led relied heavily on outside expertise from the World Bank and the Harvard Institute for International Development (HIID), as well as other foreign consultants. Initially, both the World Bank and HIID teams were located inside the economic agencies (the latter retained offices in the Ministry of Finance building as late as 1997) and played a major role in drawing up reforms, proposing and evaluating projects, drafting legislation, and helping write the five-year economic plans.[37] In addition to their official roles, World Bank consultants were called on unofficially. One foreign consultant admitted that he had far more access to the minister of finance than even senior officials of the ministry.

36. See "The Idea of Power in Javanese Culture" in Anderson 1990, 17–77.
37. On the use of consultants and the influence of outsiders, see Higgins 1957, 40–45; Mason 1986; MacIntyre 1995; and Winters 1996, 68, 148, 168.

He would make an effort to work with those officials, but "if the Minister asks for something to be produced tomorrow, the only way to get it done is to sit down and write it myself. Otherwise it would take weeks" (interview, Jakarta, March 1997).

Even allowing for exaggeration, it is an extraordinary degree of dysfunctionality that can spread an evening's work over two or more weeks—especially as the economic agencies were not bereft of trained staff: as early as 1980, sixty-five of the ninety-nine middle- and senior-ranking officers of the Ministry of Finance had postgraduate degrees; many had more than one (*Financial Directory of Indonesia* 1980, 6–15). Indeed, training efforts figured prominently from the 1970s onward (Mason 1986, 46–48; Lippincott 1997). By the 1980s the economic agencies had a sizable pool of officers with good formal qualifications and experience. That outsiders should still be playing such substantial roles in the 1990s implies organizational weakness rather than personnel deficiencies.

Obscure standards, personalization, and permeability characterized virtually all state organizations of the New Order period, despite episodes of reform, training efforts, and economic change. Societal groups rarely used formal channels to influence the government with any success, although some did organize to make the attempt (MacIntyre 1991). Even when external demands led to a change in policy, its implementation was frequently distorted by individualized interventions and organizational disarray; this was the case with financial policy despite deregulatory reform and the involvement of a supposedly technocratic economic agency: the central bank.

Bank Indonesia: Internal Organization

Like other state organizations, Bank Indonesia became more stable under the New Order. In contrast to the frequent restructuring under the previous regime, which saw the number of departments in the head office increase from twelve to twenty-one, organizational structure changed little after 1966. According to its new governor, the bank was "deeply divided between those who had achieved their position through the patronage of Jusuf Muda Dalam, and all other employees . . . [yet] in the end, very few people were forced to leave the Bank. Such upheavals are incompatible with the community and consensus orientation of the Indonesian culture" (Prawiro 1998, 55). Staff at the most senior levels were all replaced by 1968, but staff continuity thereafter was high. Until the regime was in crisis in 1997–98, governors all served out their five-year terms of office and moved on, normally to other bureaucratic or cabinet positions. Managing directors also served out their appointments but were more likely to move on to positions with private banks after financial liberalization in the 1980s.[38]

The central bank did not, however, completely monopolize employee rewards. First, the governor was not always internally recruited, and some managing directors came from outside agencies, reducing internal reward opportunities for those

38. See Appendix 3 for Bank Indonesia's governors and senior staff continuity.

who started their careers with the bank, despite long staff tenure. Second, while still serving with the central bank, some senior officers sat on the boards of private or other banks in which Bank Indonesia held equity, and some continued the association after retirement from the central bank. Third, although the bank did operate an employee welfare and pension fund, inadequate retirement benefits are suggested by the accounts of retired officials and employees who served as part-time examiners for a small-scale credit scheme, with the bank explaining this with reference to the "human aspect of the story of uplifting the spirits of these retired people" (SEACEN n.d.). The official rewards of bank employment were not large: salaries were higher than in the rest of the civil service, especially after increases in the 1980s, but continued to lag behind the private sector, making employment at the central bank relatively unattractive for new graduates (*Jakarta Post*, 28 August 1996).

To some extent, Bank Indonesia's internal practices supported a formal commitment to technical merit. From the early 1970s the sponsored education of bank staff increased, and by the mid-1970s Bank Indonesia was employing a reasonable number of economics graduates. Officers also took part in many short-term training courses abroad.[39] In addition, Bank Indonesia made use of external consultants; as with the New Order's use of consultants in the wider state system, however, this can be read as evidence of the permeability of state organizations as much as a commitment to technical expertise. Still, according to several former and serving employees, the bank gave more priority to meritocratic considerations and less to an individual's connections than did other state organizations, including the Ministry of Finance. Although some graduate recruits in the early years of the New Order were asked to join the bank because they were known to the governor or senior staff, others reported rising to senior positions despite having no influential family connections or patrons. Formal qualifications were considered important and were pursued as a route to further promotion.[40]

The kind of expertise valued by the central bank was not always suited to its role as a bank regulator. According to a former official, it placed more emphasis on recruiting and training macroeconomists than on developing the auditing and accounting skills necessary for prudential supervision. According to the same source, there was also sometimes a gap between position and responsibility as, for example, when the officially designated legal officer was excluded from drafting new banking regulations (interview, former Bank Indonesia official, Jakarta, April 1997). After banking liberalization in the 1980s there was a common perception that the central bank lacked professional expertise and that it had inappropriate auditing procedures (*Far Eastern Economic Review*, 20 December 1990). It was also criticized for a lack of clarity in its regulations and directives and for issuing reg-

39. There are many course reports by participants in the Bank Indonesia library but no aggregate figures.
40. These observations were made by current and former bank staff interviewed in Jakarta in 1997. See also Abdullah 1995 for the memoirs of a former Bank Indonesia officer.

ulations that could not be implemented without bias (*Far Eastern Economic Review*, 12 October 1989; *Jakarta Post*, 1 February 1995). Bank Indonesia's own account of its supervisory role does not mention any problem other than the lack of qualified personnel at state banks, signaling either an unwillingness to address problems frankly or an inclination to downplay the seriousness of its supervisory role.[41]

Bank Indonesia's internal disciplinary systems were obscure and frequently ignored. As well as civil service–wide rules, it had its own employee code, issued in the form of a small handbook (Bank Indonesia 1994). Some if its directives are extremely vague, such as the instruction not to do anything that would bring the bank into disrepute; others are clear prohibitions, such as a ban on outside employment without permission. Some procedural rules for dealing with offenses are complex to the point of being comic, such as the formula for determining how an employee who stole 15 million rupiah would be dealt with (Bank Indonesia 1994, app. 21/10). Perhaps more relevant than its content is the fact that no employee interviewed recalled such a codification of internal rules. All were vague as to what conflict of interest or other disciplinary rules existed.

Prescribed sanctions were rarely enforced. During a trial of officers accused of fraud (a rare event, despite the many abuses in the banking schemes and activities that Bank Indonesia supervised), one of them maintained that other staff had been known to commit similar offenses but had only been transferred to provincial branches as punishment (*Jakarta Post*, 25 April 1997). In 1997 several officers were suspended because of their alleged collusion with problem banks: they were suspected receiving bribes of up to 60 billion rupiah or $24.8 million (*Jakarta Post*, 16 April 1997). After they were arrested, the defendants acknowledged receiving money from a banker, Hindoro Halim, on a regular basis over four years.[42]

Their accounts are noteworthy in several respects. First, not only did they emphasize that more senior officers were involved, but their decision not to cite the bank for violations of banking regulations was made on the basis of an anticipated negative reaction by the head of the bank supervision department, Hendrobudiyanto (a former Golkar representative and state bank officer). A colleague had warned one of the defendants, "What, you are going to blacklist Hindoro? Look out, he's a close friend of Pak Hendro [Hendrobudiyanto]." Second, Hendrobudiyanto's claim to know the bank owner well was apparently enough to ensure that a meeting of the central bank's senior management, including the governor, had approved advancing funds to the bank. Reportedly, the governor, acceding to the proposal, laughed and said, "Six billion at six percent—no need to be a banker, give a lunatic help like that and he'll make a profit. Just deposit it [and make a profit] without lifting a finger." Third, Bank Indonesia's internal audit unit only began to take action against one of the lower-level staffers only when he announced that he wished to resign. He and some other junior officers

---

41. See Bank Indonesia's presentation on supervision to a meeting of Southeast Asian Central Banks (SEACEN n.d.).
42. The details and quotations that follow are from *Forum Keadilan*, 8 September 1997, 12–22.

were "administratively sanctioned"—in his case, by being sent to the human resources department and having his pay cut by 50 percent. Note that this punishment was meted out to people who were suspected of having received hundreds of thousands of dollars in bribe money. Fourth, the internal audit unit took no action over accusations made against Hendrobudiyanto because their mandate did not cover Bank Indonesia's senior management. Finally, the defendants appeared to distinguish between ways of receiving payment by outsiders: some payments were bribes, but others were just *uang hadiah biasa*—the "usual (monetary) gift or reward" (*Forum Keadilan*, 8 September 1997, 16). In November 1997 four Bank Indonesia directors were sacked, some allegedly in connection with this case, and three of them (including Hendrobudiyanto) were later arrested.

This account of the central bank's internal organization points to many features that are a long way from Weberian rational-legal ideals. The inavailability of further information may reflect the bank's very limited efforts at institution-building. Former and current Bank Indonesia officers interviewed in 1997 could think of little that the bank had done to develop either internal traditions or staff loyalty. The one symbol of organizational membership spontaneously identified by all officers who had joined the bank in the 1950s and 1960s was the wearing of neckties, a mark of the social position they acquired as central bank officers. The absence of internal organizational mythmaking corresponds with a marked lack of public organizational display. Bank Indonesia's annual reports and published documents are striking in that they record virtually nothing about the bank as an organization or about the people in it. The annual report did not even publish total staff numbers until the 1990s, and the practice of listing midlevel officers by department was discontinued after the 1950s. A commemorative volume issued by the bank in 1983 appears to have disappeared.

Bank Indonesia's Public Role and Relations with Government

Despite standing at the center of the state-dominated banking system until the 1980s and retaining responsibility for bank supervision thereafter, Bank Indonesia failed to regulate the banking sector according to declared policy. It fulfilled its monetary policy tasks with much more success. Although the divisions occupied with banking accounted for most staff members, the allocation of training effort, promotion, and prestige in the bank tended to favor macroeconomists. After the change of regime, economics graduates replaced law graduates as governors, and outsiders promoted to senior positions were all economists. Bank Indonesia was not formally empowered to pursue monetary policy goals independently, but the commitment to a balanced budget brought in by the new regime institutionalized a block on central bank provision of credit to government. With this potential source of pressure removed, the bank was reasonably successful in maintaining monetary stability (Cole and Slade 1996, 18, 39). Part of the reason for the emphasis on its macroeconomic role was undoubtedly Indonesia's experience of hyperinflation in the 1960s. This focus was also in line with the bank's organizational resources, which lent themselves to the administratively undemanding task of monetary policy rather than the active implementation required for bank regulation and supervision. As one official put it, "Monetary policy can be executed by less than 10 persons. Governance requires hundreds" (qtd. in Root 1996, 98).

Responsibility for financial policy was more disbursed. Key decisions were taken outside the bank (Grenville 1994, 94; Cole and Slade 1996, 40, 101, 110; Prawiro 1998, 251), and other government agencies were involved in regulating the financial sector. As an instrument of government financial policy, Bank Indonesia was used as an "agent of development" to finance officially prioritized sectors and organizations. Small-scale credit operations and rural finance were supported to some degree, but the greater part of the central bank's direct credits went to high-profile (and notoriously corrupt) government agencies, to bail out the state oil company after 1975, and to distribute subsidized credit to favored individuals (MacIntyre 1993, 148–52). This role was reduced after 1983, as the proportion of total banking-system credit accounted for by the central bank's direct credits or rediscounts dropped to 7 percent (Hamilton-Hart 2000a, 122).[43] The largest cases of central bank direct financing during the 1990s supported what were essentially President Suharto's family interests: his son's clove monopoly and "national car" project (Schwarz 1994, 153–57; Bisnis Indonesia, 28 April 1997).

A similar pattern can be seen in the central bank's role in the state-owned banking system. State-owned banks dominated the credit system until the end of the 1980s and remained significant even after reform. Before reform, they were heavily dependent on the central bank for discounting and direct credits. Given this position, Bank Indonesia was structurally involved in the use of state bank loans, which were a "central plank in the patronage networks that sustain political power and cement networks of support," according to Richard Robison (1994, 68–69). There was also room for opportunistic behavior at lower levels in this system. As reported by David Jenkins, "Standard practice is that a borrower pays a certain percentage of the total credit granted as a kind of commission to the bank official receiving the loan" (Far Eastern Economic Review, 27 March 1981). From 1993 onward, levels of bad debt at the state banks had become a matter of public discussion, and Bank Indonesia announced that it would prioritize forcing payment by those who intentionally refused to pay (Indonesian Observer, 9 June 1994). Its complete failure to do so can be judged from the condition of the state banks: despite being recapitalized in 1992, they required substantial off-budget funds in 1996 (McLeod 1997, 14), and less than two years later their levels of bad debt were even worse than those of private banks.

Most often, Bank Indonesia appears to have stood as a ready source of finance as and when required. It was not removed, however, from the personalized practices characteristic of the state banks. This interaction can be illustrated by the case of the state development bank, Bank Pembangunan Indonesia, more often

43. The most comprehensive account of Indonesia's financial liberalization is Cole and Slade 1996.

known as Bapindo, whose supervisory council included the minister of finance and the governor of Bank Indonesia (or their representatives). Bapindo remained dependent on Bank Indonesia, the government, and foreign finance agencies for most of its funds (World Bank 1983, 28), and its loans were mainly directed to the private sector (Bapindo 1980, 138). Its recurring problems are particularly well known because of its sustained and intimate relationship with the World Bank. World Bank involvement included allocating significant resources to training Bapindo staff, improving its procedures, maintaining a nearly continuous advisory presence, and reviewing major lending decisions.[44] In other respects, however, there is no reason to believe that Bapindo was very different from other state banks.

In 1994 a scandal involving Bapindo erupted when it emerged that the bank had lost $449 million in loans to a little-known Sino-Indonesian businessman called Eddy Tansil. During the trials of Tansil and the Bapindo directors, a number of revelations about the bank's operations were made.[45] Its loans to Tansil had begun in 1989 and increased to $430 million over the next years, even though none of his companies had a track record or access to expertise in the area of his proposed ventures (*Tempo*, 19 February 1994). Indeed, Bapindo officers knew that Tansil was a bad credit risk and had turned down his unsupported loan request in 1987 (Majidi 1994, 169). Tansil later said he had paid a Bapindo director 500 million rupiah as thanks for credit disbursed. Apparently this was a significant enough sum—or person—for him to remember the details, but his payoffs to the bank were more widespread: he said he had paid several other individuals at Bapindo whose names he did not remember (Majidi 1994, 225–26).

These payoffs may have smoothed the process but were not the only mechanism Tansil used. His business and loan requests also involved three influential people. The first was Coordinating Minister for Political and Security Affairs Sudomo, who introduced Tansil to the Bapindo directors and wrote in support of his loan applications several times from June 1989 onward. His letters show that no attempt was made to keep knowledge of the credits, or his role, restricted: he addressed some letters to the directors collectively; he wrote them on official letterhead; and some are signed off by Sudomo in his official capacity, complete with official crest above his signature (*Forum Keadilan*, 31 March 1994). He also wrote to other state banks that were involved in the syndication of the early loans. The accused Bapindo directors said the letters carried a lot of weight and were interpreted as directives (*Indonesian Observer*, 1 June 1994, 24 August 1994). As one of them put it, "Sudomo is our leader, a leader of the nation. Because of that we respected [*hormati*] his references' (Majidi 1994, 265–66). It was common practice for influential people to send the state banks unsolicited references. Letters from the influential asking for consideration even have a specific term, *surat katebelece*,

---

44. On training and staff rationalization, see Bapindo 1985, 188; and Bapindo 1990, 112–14. On the World Bank's involvement, see World Bank 1983 and 1991.
45. In late 1996 Tansil escaped from jail. For background details on the Bapindo directors, see *Forum Keadilan*, 31 March 1994, 11–15.

which the press applied to Sudomo's letters, of which a former banker said that "state bank bosses often can't tell what's a reference and what's an instruction" (*Asian Wall Street Journal*, 3 March 1994).

A second person allegedly drawn into the loan decisions was J. B. Sumarlin, considered one of Indonesia's technocrats, who was at the time minister of finance; by 1994 he was head of the state audit board and also acting as a World Bank adviser (Majidi 1994, 184–86). One of the Bapindo directors maintained that it was Sumarlin who pressured them to reverse their decision, recorded on 2 June 1992, to discontinue financing Tansil unless certain conditions were met. Another director said that they "tak berdaya karena instruksi Pak Marlin"—that is, they were effectively powerless in the face of instructions from Sumarlin (Majidi 1994, 197–265). Sumarlin denied that he ever issued such instructions, and although unnamed sources supported the Bapindo directors' version of events (Majidi 1994, 238–39), his role remains unconfirmed. He (like Sudomo) was never cross-examined in court, and a key alleged intermediary, Oskar Surjaatmadja, died before the trials.[46] One long-time observer of Indonesian banking (and later deputy governor of Bank Indonesia), Anwar Nasution, came out bluntly with the view that Sumarlin could be dubbed "crook of the year" (qtd. in Majidi 1994, 116).

Finally, Tansil had some association with Suharto's youngest son, Hutomo Mandala Putra, more often known as Tommy. At one stage Tommy had a 60 percent interest in a Tansil company that received credit from Bapindo. During 1991 he sold the greater part of his shares in this company and ended his ownership interest entirely in August 1993 (*Tempo*, 19 February 1994). His role in securing the loans to Tansil has not been made public, and early on, the Indonesian press stopped mentioning him in connection with the affair (*Asian Wall Street Journal*, 9 May 1994); however, a large part of the Bapindo loan was drawn in cash, and Tommy sold his shares back to Tansil soon afterward (Cole and Slade 1996, 138).

What was Bank Indonesia's role in the case? Its governor maintained afterward that he knew "absolutely nothing" of either Tansil or the bank's loans to him, even though he had concurrently been a member of Bapindo's supervisory council (Majidi 1994, 166). Tansil's loan requests, however, had been discussed by all Bapindo directors, who kept records of their decisions, and one of them was a former Bank Indonesia officer. The initial loans had also been syndicated with other state banks, and as Sudomo's letters show, there was no attempt made to restrict knowledge of the credits, even though they ought to have run into the controls set by the Monetary Authority and External Debt Coordinating Team (Majidi 1994,

---

46. Oskar Surjaatmadja was yet another person linking different government and private organizations. He was a Finance Ministry official who had been on Bapindo's supervisory council throughout the 1980s, as proxy for three successive finance ministers (Bapindo, *Operations of Bapindo*, various issues). By 1991 he was also acting government commissioner on Bank Indonesia's board of governors (Bank Indonesia, *Report for the Financial Year 1990–91*). In 1993 he was appointed to the board of Astra International, after the Soeryadjaya family lost control of Indonesia's second largest conglomerate to a group of businessmen close to Suharto (*Asian Wall Street Journal*, 15 March 1993).

303–4). Moreover, Bapindo's credits to Tansil's companies are included in a list of debtors behind in payments to the state banks as of the end of 1992.[47]

Given these circumstances, not to mention its official supervisory responsibilities, the central bank must have known of the loans and the problems involved. Two days after the first allegations about Bapindo were made public, the Bank Indonesia governor and the minister of finance discussed the state banks with a World Bank team. Later, the governor called a five-hour meeting between Bank Indonesia officials and external economists. When the publicity storm about the case was at its height, the World Bank president held a long meeting with the Bank Indonesia governor and others, including the ever present advisers and crisis managers Ali Wardhana and Widjojo Nitisastro (Majidi 1994, 34, 43, 114–15). Bank Indonesia itself apparently never pursued any action against Bapindo for breaches of the banking law. Insofar as the available information allows one to judge, the case confirms the central bank's role of passive accommodation to the regular processes of personal extraction of state bank resources, followed by conciliation with Indonesia's major aid donor.

Bank Indonesia and the Private Financial Sector

Until liberalization in the 1980s, the relationship between the private sector and state financial institutions, including the central bank, was largely a matter of channeling loans to private actors. The number of private banks that survived the consolidation of the sector in the late 1960s accounted for a very small percentage of banking assets. As a result, although few private banks ran into financial difficulty in the 1970s, these episodes did not seriously threaten the financial system as a whole. In some cases, partnerships with other private sector actors provided rescue funds. Sino-Indonesian businessman Sjamsul Nursalim (Liem Tek Siang), for example, acquired half of Bank Daging Nasional Indonesia in 1980 after it had defaulted on its obligations and its major owner, Sultan Hamengku Buwono IX, was unable to raise finance elsewhere (Robison 1986, 341).

Bank Indonesia and other government agencies did sometimes provide struggling financial institutions with equity infusions in addition to central bank credit. This meant that despite officially losing its commercial banking role in 1968, the central bank acquired interests in commercial operations (Nasution 1983, 63). The bank also retained a commercial venture, known as Indover, through its branch in the Netherlands, which later became linked to one of Indonesia's largest conglomerates, the Astra group and its banking arm (*Far Eastern Economic Review*, 26 April 1990). Indover and a related company remained as subsidiaries of the central bank and handled some of Indonesia's official foreign exchange reserves in the 1990s. Alleged mismanagement by Indover between 1993 and 1998 reportedly cost Bank Indonesia $1 billion (*Business Times*, 30 August 2000). This was not an iso-

---

47. Most commentators consider the list substantially correct. See Robison 1994, 65–66; and Schwarz 1994, 75.

lated case. Several institutions in which Bank Indonesia held an interest performed badly, despite having central bank officials on their boards—in contrast with the improvement of problem banks under the management of Malaysia's central bank. Violations of related-party lending limits and other abuses occurred in banks that were under the close surveillance of Bank Indonesia. Bank Harapan Santosa, for example, owned by Hendra Rahardja (Tan Tjoe Hien, brother of Eddy Tansil of the Bapindo scandal), reacted to Bank Indonesia's concerns about its condition by channeling loans to affiliates through related finance companies and by making back-to-back loans through other commercial banks. Eventually Bank Indonesia appointed one of its staff to the Bank Harapan Santosa, but this move, too, proved ineffective in halting irregular practices (*Infobank*, September 1998).

Another problem bank lost $600 million in guarantees and loans to a related party, even as it continued to receive injections of central bank equity and had a central bank officer on its board. This was Bank Pasifik, which first received an undisclosed amount of equity from Bank Indonesia in 1982, with further amounts injected as it experienced increasing problems (*Asian Wall Street Journal*, 18 April 1996; *Jakarta Post*, 8 March 1997). Not only was Bank Indonesia a party to these activities, but its rescue of the bank also illustrates the New Order's habit of tolerating massive failure and fraud. In this case, Ibnu Sutowo and his family, the private owners and managers of Bank Pasifik, were able to claim ongoing state support despite having led the state oil company into a $10 billion debt crisis in 1975. Personal ties, not past performance, determined access to privilege.[48]

Financial liberalization did not alter this pattern of forbearance. Liberalization started in 1983 and reached its height at the end of the decade, when restrictions on entry, expansion, and pricing were largely eliminated. Although credit subsidies were slashed, well-placed private actors were more than able to compensate for the partial loss of direct credit from the state banks through participation in the liberalized financial sector. Substantial gains were made through Jakarta's newly deregulated stock exchange; in addition, the rapid expansion of the banking sector proved lucrative. By the end of 1996 the number of local private banks had risen to 164, and thirty joint venture foreign banks had been established. The assets of local private banks increased by 244 percent between 1991 and the end of 1996 (Bank Indonesia, *Indonesian Financial Statistics*). The distribution of bank assets among individual banks suggests that deregulation reinforced more general patterns of commercial success under the New Order.

For the most part, the banks that emerged with the largest asset bases after financial reform (cf. Table 3.2 with Table 3.1) were owned by individuals who enjoyed a significant level of private access to Suharto or other public figures; had previously benefited from state concessions such as monopoly rights, loans from

48. While heading the state oil company between 1967 and 1975, Ibnu Sutowo developed "the largest private indigenous business group in Indonesia" (Robison 1986, 350). In 1958, Sutowo had been dismissed from his post by General Nasution, allegedly for corruption. Another of those transferred for irregularities at the time was then Colonel—later President—Suharto (Crouch 1988, 40).

Table 3.1. Largest Private Banks in Indonesia, 1982

	Assets (Rp billion)	Market Share (%)	Major Owner(s)	Corporate Group (rank, c. 1986)
BCA	247	18	Liem, Suharto family	Salim (1)
Panin	203	15	M. Ali Gunawan	Panin (17)
Duta[a]	140	10	P. T. Berdikari	
BUN	123	9	Ong Ka Huat	Arya Upaya (12)
Niaga	105	8	Soedarpo S. Julius Tahija Bank Indonesia	Soedarpo (28)
Bali	101	7	Djaja Ramli Sukanto Tanudjaja	Bali (11)
Buana	96	7	Tan Siong Kie	Rodamas (8)
All private banks	1,356			

Sources: Bank Bumi Daya, *Financial Institutions in Indonesia*, 1983; Robison 1986; Yoshihara 1988; Sato 1994, 119; Suryadinata 1995; Cole and Slade 1996, 108.
[a]Bank Duta was formerly known as Bank Dharma Ekonomi; it was jointly owned by P. T. Berdikari, a state-owned enterprise, and a Sino-Indonesian entrepreneur.

Table 3.2. Largest Private Banks in Indonesia, 1996

	Assets (Rp trillion)	Market Share (%)	Major Owner(s)	Corporate Group (rank)
BCA	26.6 ('95)	18 ('95)	Liem, Suharto family	Salim (1)
Danamon	22.0	11	Usman Admadjaya	misc.
BII	17.7	9	Widjaya family	Sinar Mas (4)
BDNI	16.6	8	Sjamsul Nursalim Hamengku Buwono	Gajah Tunggal (19) misc.
Lippo[a]	10.2	5	Riady family	Lippo (3)
Bali	8.0	4	Djaja Ramli	
Niaga	7.9	4	Julius Tahija Soedarpo S.	Tahija (23) Soedarpo (23)
BUN	6.3 ('97)	3 ('97)	Ong Ka Huat Bob Hasan	Ongko (12) Bob Hasan (6)
All private banks	200.87			

Sources: Annual reports of the banks; Bank Indonesia, *Indonesian Financial Statistics*; *Jakarta Post*, 22 April 1997; *DC/ICN*, 28 September 1998; Hill 1996, 111; Backman 1999.
[a]Lippo bank was formerly Bank Perniagan Indonesia. The Riady family acquired it from Hasyim Ning in 1982. It merged with Bank Umum Asia in July 1990.

state banks, and import licenses; or had business partnerships with members of the presidential family or its associates. With the partial exception of Bank Danamon and Bank Bali, these banks were also related through common ownership ties to large nonbanking conglomerates, which expanded rapidly from the 1980s on.

Personal ties to power-holders are most obvious in the case of Bank Central Asia (BCA), the largest private bank before and after reform. BCA was owned by long-time Suharto crony Liem Sioe Liong (Sudono Salim) and his family, along with two of Suharto's children. Liem's business relationship with Suharto dated back to the 1950s, when Suharto was still serving as an army officer and Liem ran a small business supplying the military. After Suharto came to power, Liem family companies, loosely grouped together in Indonesia's largest conglomerate, the Salim group, experienced phenomenal growth. The special privileges and favorable deals enjoyed by Salim companies, often at public expense, have been extensively catalogued.[49] BCA's association with Suharto was so close that it became a particular target during the unrest in the last weeks of the New Order (hundreds of its branches and ATMs were attacked), and as Suharto lost his grip on power, the bank suffered massive deposit withdrawals.

Bank Danamon, the second-largest bank in the 1990s, also had close a relationship with power-holders or brokers. Its major owner, Usman Admadjaya, had earlier been a supplier to a state company and a contractor for infrastructure projects (Suryadinata 1995, 2). In the 1990s, Bank Danamon had business ties and joint ventures (including a small bank) with companies controlled by Liem Sioe Liong and far exceeded the ceilings on credit expansion declared by the central bank in the mid-1990s without any penalty. With loans growth of 41 percent in 1995 and 56 percent in 1996, it was the fastest-growing major bank at the time (*Business Times*, 23–34 August 1997). In 1991, Minister of Finance Sumarlin was accused of using money from the government pension fund to help Bank Danamon (Schwarz 1994, 77). Another source holds that Admadjaya's access to Sumarlin was facilitated by religious ties—they attended the same church—and that this link gave Bank Danamon access to the government credit it needed to remain solvent (Backman 1999, 218). A rumor that one of Suharto's daughters held a secret share in the bank reflected the general perception that Danamon's spectacular growth could be due only to preferential treatment. When Danamon was nationalized in the wake of Indonesia's financial crisis, its level of related-party lending was, at 44 percent, lower than that of many other nationalized banks, but it was found to have advanced particularly large credits to companies owned by Suharto's family and his regular golfing partner (*Profil Indonesia*, No. 4, 1998–99; *Infobank*, January 1999).

Lippo Bank was majority-owned by the Riady family, long known as business associates of Liem Sioe Liong (Mochtar Riady managed Liem's bank until 1990).

49. See Robison 1986, 296–315; and Backman 1999, 113–17.

The rise of their bank paralleled that of the Lippo group of companies: from being the twenty-fourth largest Indonesian conglomerate in 1986, it became sixth largest in 1988 and third largest in 1993 (Mackie 1990, 109; Sato 1994, 119; Hill 1996, 111). The family is known for its tendency to seek out influential partners in Indonesia and overseas, its profit-taking through manipulating listed companies, and its alleged involvement in a campaign finance scandal surrounding U.S. President Bill Clinton (Backman 1999, 339–46). Two other large banks, Bank Internasional Indonesia (BII) and Bank Daging Nasional Indonesia (BDNI), were also related to large, rapidly expanding conglomerates. BII's major owners were members of the Widjaya family, beneficiaries of important land-use concessions for oil palm plantations and logging under Suharto. Their diversified business group, Sinar Mas, was one of Indonesia's largest. BDNI was jointly owned by Sultan Hamengku Buwono IX and Sjamsul Nursalim. The sultan was a former cabinet minister and vice president of Indonesia in the 1970s; Sjamsul Nursalim was among the New Order's most successful tycoons.

Bank Niaga's political connections were less spectacular, but as it was the only *pribumi*-owned bank among Indonesia's ten largest private banks, its success was something of a political necessity for a regime that periodically came under fire for allowing Chinese-owned businesses to dominate the corporate sector.[50] Bank Indonesia had an early equity interest in the bank (Robison 1986, 247), and a former central bank official served on its board in the 1990s.

Another bank that demonstrated the tendency of commercial success to correspond with personal connections was Bank Umum Nasional (BUN). Established as a political party bank in 1952, it benefited early on from having the minister of economic affairs and minister of finance serve concurrently as its directors (Robison 1986, 49–50). By the 1980s, majority ownership of the bank lay with Ong Ka Huat (Ongko Kaharuddin), whose business group by 1998 had bad debts of over 1.3 trillion rupiah, owed to state banks—much less than the first tier of Suharto family and cronies but among the twenty largest state-bank debts (*Kompas*, 25 June 1999). BUN's position was also bolstered, if temporarily, by the interest in the bank held by a close confidant of Suharto, Mohamed "Bob" Hasan (The Kian Seng), in the 1990s. Hasan was associated with at least two other banks as well, but his business empire was heavily centered on logging and related industries. Like Liem Sioe Liong, he had a long personal association with Suharto and business ventures with his children. His private influence over the Department of Forestry and other state organizations was a major factor behind Indonesia's utterly ineffective implementation of forest management policies (Dauvergne 1997, 70–93).

What of the three banks that had dropped out of the list by 1996? Bank Duta's relative decline is perhaps surprising, as it was owned by three quasi-private foun-

---

50. On the economic role and political marginalization of ethnic Chinese Indonesians, see Robison 1986, 271–322; and Mackie 1991.

dations (*yayasan*) controlled by Suharto. Bob Hasan joined the board in 1995. Bank Duta had in fact grown very rapidly until it lost some $400 million through illegal foreign exchange trading in 1990. The affair was an early indicator of Bank Indonesia's ineffective regulation, despite its being the channel through which Bank Duta received $16.5 million in credit from the World Bank in 1989 and 2 billion yen from the Export Import Bank of Japan in 1989 and 1990 (Bank Duta, *Annual Report* 1995). After it was bailed out by businessmen close to Suharto, including Liem Sioe Liong's Salim group (*Asian Wall Street Journal*, 19 May 1995), Bank Duta continued to be a major recipient of Bank Indonesia liquidity credits and appeared to be making a recovery in the mid-1990s: its assets grew by 35 percent in 1995 and 55 percent in the first three months of 1996 (Bank Duta, *Annual Report* 1995; Jakarta Stock Exchange, *JSX Statistics*, 1996).

The second bank to lose relative position by 1996 was Panin Bank, which had one of the highest levels of public ownership among Indonesia's listed banks (most of the others listed a minority of their shares). Control of the bank remained with its largest shareholder, Mu'min Ali Gunawan (Lie Mo Ming), who was related by marriage to the Riady family and had gone into joint ventures with both Ibnu Sutowo and the Suharto family (Robison 1986, 347, 353). Gunawan's relationship with Riady was not close, however (Riady earlier left his position at Panin because of disagreements with him), and after the early 1980s his relatively few business ventures with politically connected figures were eclipsed by those of the major tycoons of the late 1980s and early 1990s. Panin was described as "the most conservatively run bank in Indonesia" (Credit Lyonnais Securities 1996, 23), and by 1996 its market share had slipped to 2.7 percent of private bank assets (*Jakarta Post*, 22 April 1997).

The third private bank to lose its position was Bank Buana, part of Roda Mas, one of the larger private business groups early in the 1980s (Robison 1986, 390; Yoshihara 1988, 233) but one that grew less rapidly than the other Indonesian conglomerates thereafter (Hill 1996, 111). Its major owner, Tan Siong Kie, goes virtually unmentioned in studies of politically connected business in the Suharto era. Yet Buana and Panin were the two largest banks to survive Indonesia's financial crisis without requiring recapitalization funds from the government.

Bank owners with privileged personal positions ensured that their banks functioned to maximize the owner's interests rather than the bank's corporate interests. The most obvious mechanism was to lend the bank's deposits to companies owned by the bank's controlling shareholders. According to Bank Indonesia figures before the crisis, many private banks exceeded regulatory limits on related-party lending. Yet apart from issuing warnings, the central bank never took any action against the seventy banks that it acknowledged, in early 1996, to have breached lending limits. The issue was regularly aired in the press, which also published estimates of intragroup lending by individual banks and groups of banks (*DC/ICN*, 23 September 1996, 6 November 1995). Like estimates of nonperforming loans at the time, however, these figures were later found to understate the actual amount of related-party lending indulged in by most banks—a gap that could have been anticipated, given the common perception that false accounting, as well as incestuous lending, was very common at the private banks (*Jakarta Post*, 10 January 1996; *Indonesian Observer*, 1 July 1995). It was eventually revealed that related-party loans accounted for 91 percent of BDNI's total credits, 44 percent of Bank Danamon's, and 78 percent of BUN's (*Profil Indonesia*, No. 4, 1998–99, 64). Most of these loans turned out to be nonperforming.

Although the problem was underestimated, many banks were known to be in poor condition before 1997 (Nasution 1992). Even basically insolvent banks continued to enjoy central-bank support—or at least avoided being closed down by the central bank—despite ongoing breaches in banking regulations. Until 1997 the only loss in the banking sector to cause significant change in the ownership of economic assets was the 1992 collapse of Bank Summa, a midsized bank owned by the Soeryadjaya family, who also owned Astra, Indonesia's second largest conglomerate. When the Soeryadjayas were forced to sell Astra because of Summa's losses, it was taken over by a group of Suharto cronies: Usman Admadjaya of Bank Danamon, Liem Sioe Liong of BCA, and Bob Hasan of BUN all emerged with shareholdings of between 9 and 10 percent (*DC/ICN*, 12 October 1998). Astra's former owners, despite an earlier association with Suharto's wife, were regarded as the least "political" of Indonesia's major business owners by the late 1980s (Mackie 1990, 119).

The fastest-growing banks could count on an inflow of deposits to fund their loan portfolios, but many weak banks also used direct support from Bank Indonesia. As one banker later stated, Bank Indonesia funds were intended to provide his bank with an income stream over the coming years, as central bank funds lent at 6 percent were invested in Bank Indonesia bonds yielding 13 to 14 percent (*Tempo*, 6 June 1999). Such use of central bank liquidity and tolerance was, however, dwarfed by Bank Indonesia's final effort in the closing months of the Suharto regime, when it gave out 164.5 trillion rupiah in emergency support to private banks.[51] After Bank Indonesia increased interest rates because of pressure on the currency in August 1997, the number of banks experiencing problems and drawing upon central bank funds increased. This flow of funds, however, remained a trickle until the IMF-mandated closure of sixteen small banks in November sparked a run on several private banks. Thereafter, the central bank's advances swelled to astronomic proportions, as Indonesia's currency plunged to hitherto inconceivable depths in January 1998, and the largest private banks experienced deposit runs in May 1998 (Colin Johnson 1998).

Rumors soon surfaced that Bank Indonesia's emergency liquidity support (known as BLBI, *bantuan likuiditas* Bank Indonesia) was being abused by bank owners to fund offshore debt payments, speculate against the rupiah, or simply

---

51. The exact amount is unclear. The Rp 164.5 figure is based on the Supreme Audit Board's report, which was leaked early in 2000.

invest overseas (Cole and Slade 1998, 64; *Jakarta Post*, 29 July 1999). Some banks received an amount of BLBI that exceeded their total assets (*DC/ICN*, 28 September 1998; *Jakarta Post*, 9 February 2000). Later external audits of Bank Indonesia supported allegations of widespread misuse use of BLBI (*Financial Times*, 3 January 2000; *Business Times*, 11 January 2000; *Jakarta Post*, 11 February 2000). A parliamentary investigation found evidence to implicate former ministers, finance officials, and central bank officers (*Jakarta Post*, 8 March 2000).

Like the many pre-crisis instances of Bank Indonesia's failure to implement policy consistently, the abuse of BLBI during the crisis can be traced to several mechanisms. One was that established patterns of personal exchange involving smaller amounts facilitated larger transfers. A newspaper account of how Usman Admadjaya secured trillions of rupiah in Bank Indonesia financing for Bank Danamon alleged that he used an intermediary to distribute 30 billion rupiah among central-bank officers. Danamon would ultimately receive 26 trillion from Bank Indonesia. Another source cited in the same article alleged that bankers such as Sjamsul Nursalim of BDNI (which received Rp 28.5 trillion from the central bank) and Usman Admadjaya were acting in concert with senior officeholders and that they actually received only 30 or 40 percent of the liquidity credits (*Infobank*, January 1999).

A second mechanism was direct pressure from political actors, Suharto most of all. Syaril Sabirin, central bank governor starting in early 1998, said that during the crisis Bank Indonesia had been ordered to override normal procedures for advancing liquidity support (*Financial Times*, 3 January 2000). His predecessor, Soedradjad Djiwandono, explained another failure to follow normal procedure by the central bank (in this case, its guarantee of nearly $1 billion in loans from a state bank to a private businessman) by saying that he had been powerless to go against Suharto's wishes (*Australian Financial Review*, 9 December 1999). Perhaps more important, personalized and instrumental use of the state apparatus had become routinized enough in the New Order to make direct intervention unnecessary in most cases: agencies such as Bank Indonesia would know in advance what was expected of them. When a Suharto family member whose bank was closed under IMF pressure in November 1997 protested the action, he argued that his bank had been closed because, unlike other private banks, it had not provided "gifts" to Bank Indonesia officials. It probably had no need to (Backman 1999, 91).

Personal intervention by Suharto often seems to have been tacit, inferred by other actors in state organizations rather than formally expressed. Thus, for example, a former senior judge recounting a "clear example of interference from my own experience" could report only that he *heard* that Suharto was very angry about a ruling he had made in favor of a labor activist; he could not prove Suharto's interference. But, he said, "the Supreme Court clearly broke the law in reviewing this case, which strongly suggests that there was an invisible hand at play" (Soetjipto 2000, 271). When it is commonly assumed that if there are signs of rules being overturned, then powerful figures are involved, the space for private manip-

ulation of official policy actually increases: the not-so-powerful as well as the powerful can profit in such a climate.

To these factors of opportunistic collusion, direct pressure from influential outsiders, and habitual anticipation of their demands can be added Bank Indonesia's
own internal disorganization: irregular record-keeping and lack of internal controls. Audits of its books as of May 1999 carried a disclaimer to the effect that
serious weaknesses in the bank's internal control mechanisms and accounting
standards impeded a fully authenticated report (*Jakarta Post*, 6 January 2000).
Muddled bookkeeping, lost certificates for gold reserves deposited offshore, and
missing documentation were all problems; evidence relating to the banks closed in
November 1997 was lost in a fire in Bank Indonesia's new building in December
1997. This kind of disarray not only impedes policy implementation directly but
also provides a prime environment for manipulation of an organization by insiders and outsiders.

As in earlier years, the central bank's organizational traits compounded the deficiencies in government capacity registered by the Indonesian state more generally.
The results for Indonesia's financial system and ordinary Indonesians have consistently been costly: the failure to implement policy according to its stated design
produced first a state-dominated financial system subject to systematic abuse, then
an unstable private-sector-led system. The consequences of the latter's collapse
may prove even more costly than the perennial drain associated with the state
banks. The government bailout and recapitalization of the banking system after
1997 amounted to an estimated 50 percent of GDP, and interest payments on government debt have been estimated at 32 percent of total government spending
(Fane 2000, 24).

In this and other episodes of financial instability, mistaken policy choices were
never the whole story. Indonesia's economic collapse in the mid-1960s has frequently been attributed to Sukarno's irrational or reckless policy choices, but this
assessment does not explain why he made them. Political pressures rendered disciplined government fiscal policy difficult, but it was the breakdown of the political process after 1957 that really brought on the economic disintegration of the
late Sukarno period. Among many factors behind this breakdown was the government's organizational inability to administer the policies that the political situation
demanded.[52] The policies themselves, such as restricting the role of foreign business and promoting local banks and businesses, were similar to those pursued—
with much more success—in Malaysia. In an increasingly precarious political
position and with no organizational resources to speak of, Sukarno employed the
one resource at his disposal: the demand for revolution and the economic policy
of a revolution. The Indonesian (like the American) revolution was financed by
printing money (Oey 1991, 70–86). That Sukarno, the superlative revolutionary,

---

52. On the political pressures generated by the structure of Indonesia's economy, see Glassburner
1971.

should seek to re-create and reinvigorate the revolution at a time when his position was deteriorating was a logical response to his circumstances.

Similarly, Indonesia's costly experiment with financial liberalization in the 1980s and 1990s was only superficially a case of mistaken policy. Indonesia deregulated its financial system too fast, had inherently flawed prudential regulations, failed to monitor the buildup of private sector foreign debt, and missequenced its liberalization policies. Policy during the crisis also exacerbated its depth and duration (McLeod 1998). Yet when these policy choices were made, Indonesia had very few alternatives. Its open capital account since 1970, for example, was widely considered a necessity to reassure foreign investors and induce flight capital to return (Fane 1994; Cole and Slade 1996, 42–45). Similarly, banking deregulation in the 1980s had to be relatively swift because more controlled reforms would almost certainly have foundered. With balance-of-payments crises in 1983 and 1986, an economic slowdown, and pressure from foreign aid agencies, it was almost impossible to maintain demonstrably flawed, restrictive financial policies (MacIntyre 1993; Pangestu 1996, 141–44; Winters 1996).

Many of these constraints reflect the structure and capacities of Indonesia's state organizations. Because of its turbulent transition to independence, the country's political leaders were unable to draw on the resources of a functioning bureaucracy to deliver the kind of economic and financial policies demanded by a highly mobilized population. Even though organizations such as the central bank had by the late colonial period developed structures conducive to coherent, disciplined policy implementation, few survived intact the disruption associated with occupation and revolutionary struggle. In the case of the central bank, early postindependence efforts to maintain organizational continuity and discipline were overcome by political pressures, the disarray of the rest of the state system, and prevailing ideas about the nature of state organizations. From 1966, the centralization of power and enforced mass depoliticization restored a degree of organizational coherence and continuity to the central bank. Like other state organizations in the New Order, however, Bank Indonesia did not develop into a rule-based, meritocratic organization but combined a formal commitment to technocratic expertise with internal systems that were responsive to informal, sometimes even unspoken, patterns of influence. Its disciplinary code for employees was vague and loosely enforced, its organizational routines often at odds with declared norms. The bank's leadership, reflecting the values and orientations of Indonesia's economic technocrats, emphasized macroeconomic policy over financial regulation or internal administration. These organizational attributes of the central bank, together with those of the wider state system, help explain the high costs associated with Indonesia's financial system. Other states, however, have successfully pursued policies that failed dismally in Indonesia.

4.

Singapore: Organized Authority and Financial Order

The regulatory zeal of the Singapore government has become an acceptable joke in the city-state, a way of selling T-shirts to foreign tourists. Souvenirs proclaiming Singapore to be "a fine city" neatly package two of its most famous characteristics: the commercialism of a state founded on international trade, and the strong arm of the regime that has governed Singapore since 1959.

Ritual invocations of Singapore's orderliness, however, do not reveal its foundations. The impressive record of financial stability that Singapore enjoys today is neither the legacy of long-standing colonial institutions nor the byproduct of a modern bureaucratic state insulated from the private sector. Rather, the rationalization of the colonial state was slow, and the expansion of its regulatory authority came comparatively late. In the financial sector its responsibilities remained limited in aspiration and practice. The public sector organizations of independent Singapore developed some core attributes of rational-legal Weberian state organizations, but the state's governing capacity also rests on informal institutions that link public and private spheres. As the interests, career paths, and identities of public and private actors, particularly in the financial sector, became ever more closely intertwined, these informal institutions became increasingly important. Both formal and informal state institutions underlie the government's active financial policy and the financial sector's ability to weather financial storms experienced in neighboring countries.

STATE AND FINANCE IN THE COLONIAL PERIOD

Until it became a separate crown colony in 1946, Singapore was part of an administrative unit known as the Straits Settlements, which included Penang and Malacca, now in modern Malaysia. The crown itself did not govern until 1858, when the East India Company was dissolved, and did not break from the company practice of governing the Straits Settlements as an appendage to India until 1867. Company rule was thus maintained until a much later date than in the case of Netherlands India. The government of the Straits Settlements laid the basis for Britain's later expansion in Asia but was, in many respects, an irregular government. Although the language of treaty-making and agreements between Britain and local rulers in Southeast Asia appears in histories of the British advance into the region, until the mid-nineteenth century "Britain" was, in this context, an agglomeration of private traders, freebooters, and company representatives, backed up by personal connections to administrative and political actors in London.

Colonial Administration

Penang, the first of the Straits Settlements, was established as a trading post in 1786 by Francis Light, a country trader acting under loose instructions from the East India Company.[1] By his own account, soon after landing he "hoisted the Flag, taking possession of the Island in the name of His Britannic Majesty and for the use of the Honourable East India Company" (qtd. in Tregonning 1965, 44). The blurred nature of his endeavor was reflected in an enduring mixture of legal formalism and personal discretion in government. No code of laws reached Penang for more than twenty years; Light and his successors acted more or less independently in running it. Eventually, after the company petitioned the king for a charter of justice for the settlement, a Court of Record was established in 1807. A court had already been set up a year before, and its first magistrate had already been dismissed for corruption. The new court saw an astonishing number of cases. In 1811, "a typical enough year," it issued 8,800 summonses, 7,700 of them in the Tamil language—a reflection of the strategies acquired by Penang's immigrants from the company's South Indian jurisdiction. The total population of Penang was only 25,000 at the time.

The government financed itself through revenue-farming because the company never attempted to acquire the administrative staff necessary to tax the rapidly expanding trade of the island. The administration generally ran at a substantial loss, whereas private trade by company representatives was profitable. Out of concern over persistent revenue shortfalls, the resident in 1816 pushed the company into becoming an active trader on Penang, "the only time in its Southeast Asian existence when the Company emulated its seventeenth-century commercial role" (Tregonning 1965, 67). The modest administrative staff of around twenty people was also cut with a view to reining in expenditure. When Singapore became the capital of the unified Straits Settlements in 1832, just nine officers were responsible for administering all three territories.

Singapore had been established as a company post in 1819, with an even smaller administrative basis, on the personal initiative of Stamford Raffles, who acted in advance of company approval. Raffles himself spent very little time on the island and had little to do with its administrative or physical development. He was involved in trade on his own account, and one of his few administrative acts was to appoint as harbormaster "the incompetent but favoured husband of his sister"—on whom he also bestowed a monopoly for provisioning ships (Tregonning 1965, 153, 159).

1. This account of the first decades of company rule on Penang is based on Tregonning 1965, 41–73.

For the whole period of company rule there was hardly a civil service, certainly not one resembling Weber's bureaucratic machine. Recruitment was not on meritocratic grounds but by patronage of the directors of the company.[2] The covenant of service forbade private trading, but inadequate salaries (especially in relation to the high cost of obtaining positions) made it a necessity. In 1859, a year after the transfer to the India Office, a total of twenty officers were administering the Straits Settlements. Except for the top two or three posts, salaries were so low that as a review in 1859 recorded, "No officer of the Indian Civil Service will willingly go to the Straits for permanency, except in the position of governor. To be transferred there at the beginning of his career . . . would involve so large a sacrifice of prospects on the part of a young Indian Civil Servant, that he cannot reasonably be expected to make it" (Lord Canning, qtd. in Singh Bal 1960, 55–56).

After the shift to crown rule, the state apparatus acquired an increasingly administrative orientation. Greater numbers of professional civil servants filled senior posts, and officers who had been appointed through examination gradually displaced those who had moved into government positions through personal nomination (Heussler 1981, 28–33, 263–64). Before the move to crown rule, some recruitment decisions had appeared to found minor dynasties in government offices as sons, nephews, or other relatives followed family members into the civil service (Makepeace, Brooke, and Braddle 1921, 434–40). But although debt and private income did sometimes supplement official salaries, the relative unpopularity of government service and the constraints imposed by limited incomes on incumbents' style of life suggest that these other sources of support were not large. Soon after the transfer to crown rule, for example, a contemporary noted that "whatever it may be under the new regime, the official world here certainly has not hitherto taken a prominent lead in social affairs, due to the expensive nature of hospitality" (Makepeace, Brooke, and Braddle 1921, 507).

The government remained dependent on a restricted range of revenue sources for most of the colonial era. From the 1820s, opium farms never provided less than 30 percent of government revenue, sometimes more than 50 percent (the opium farms were shared with the Malay rulers who governed nearby Johor semiautonomously for the next century), nor did the importance of opium revenue diminish over time. Between 1904 and 1908 it actually yielded a higher proportion of total revenue, 55 percent on average, than during the decades of company rule (Trocki 1990, 96–97, 188).

The farm system went hand in hand with the abdication of most governing authority as regards the majority of the population, the mostly immigrant Chinese community. The system of policing the farms and, indeed, policing in general was based on collaboration between the government and the leadership of Chinese economic groups, or *kongsi*, which controlled the farms and constituted the main source of authority for Chinese laborers.[3] The farm system's de facto delegation

---

2. This paragraph is based on information in Singh Bal 1960.
3. On the practical authority of the *kongsi* and their relationship with the colonial government through the institution of the opium farms, see Trocki 1990.

of authority to private actors became less tolerable over time. In 1888 the governor stated, "In a Colony properly administered, it is not possible to have an imperium in imperio. The Government must have the paramount power, and it is not so in the eyes of many thousands of Chinese in the Straits Settlements" (qtd. in Lee 1991, 137).

There remained some reluctance to make actual changes in the system of revenue-raising and rule; given the lack of administrative resources, it was cheaper and less bothersome to leave things as they were. Consequently, the opium farms were not closed until 1910, in line with the trend of bureaucratic rationalization sweeping the region at the time. The change in Singapore came later, however, than the replacement of opium farms in the Dutch and French colonies of Southeast Asia. The farm system was abolished in Singapore mainly as a result of internal changes in the previously self-policing Chinese communities: the economic change that broke down the structures of capital and labor control within Chinese groups eroded the ability of the revenue farmers to maintain the farms as profitable ventures (Trocki 1990, 213–19, 234).

Official involvement in the provision of infrastructure also increased at this time, moving into areas previously in private hands, such as the local docking company (expropriated on fairly generous terms in the early 1900s) and other port services (Makepeace, Brooke, and Braddle 1921, 11–20). The government organizations assuming these new responsibilities were now markedly different from those of the company era. Official salaries slowly improved as a result of persistent complaints by officials, an increasing desire to uphold the status and capacities of the colonial service in London, and support from the local business community. Commercial actors supported calls for an inquiry into the civil service after officers made complaints about pay and morale in 1909.[4] The Colonial Office was concerned that business was draining off the best university men, and it recognized that conditions in the Malayan Civil Service (MCS) were less favorable than those in the Indian Civil Service. Salary increases in the 1920s, however, made the MCS one of the best-paid services in the empire. When the conditions of service in Malaya were criticized in London as overly lavish, the Straits Settlements government argued that the point of comparison should not be the other colonies but the local context, where, it maintained, professional men lived far better than government servants yet were the people with whom the MCS officers were expected to live on close terms.

The rules under which MCS men would maintain their status in colonial society gradually became more restrictive. In the late nineteenth century there was some debate over land speculation and commercial activity by civil servants. At the time, landholding was accepted simply because of its prevalence (especially on the Malay Peninsula), with the proviso that commercial interests not interfere with official duties. Rules were tightened early in 1900. In 1913 the Colonial Office forbade

---

4. Unless otherwise stated, the following paragraphs on the civil service are based on Heussler 1981, 135–36, 261–70, 38, 128.

retired governors of all colonies from taking directorships in companies that had interests in the colonies in which they had served. In addition, all officers who took up company directorships after retirement would lose their official pensions. Some did so anyway, but according to one source the numbers who moved into private positions were never large, and the MCS was "remarkable for its imperviousness to corruption" (Heussler 1981, 278).

Thereafter, the service increasingly established a distinct, bureaucratic identity. In 1921 the initials MCS began to appear in official documents. One governor "made a point of placing MCS after his name, ahead of his public honors, to emphasize the importance he attached to esprit de corps," recounts Robert Heussler (1981, 262). From the end of the nineteenth century, with almost all its officials formally recruited by examination and as the site of the colonial secretariat, Singapore gained a reputation as a center of form-filling and bureaucracy. Individual officers might rotate through the secretariat and more independent, multitasked jobs in the field, but the secretariat aura was established. Late in the colonial period a contemporary scholar, Rupert Emerson, would note that Singapore, in contrast to the Malay states, "pales into a drab uniformity to the established Imperial pattern" (1964, 269).

Although the development of bureaucratic agencies and capacities was slow, the in-principle commitment to legal procedure and the right of private actors to influence decisions that affected them had long been features of government. From near the beginning of the company's administration, judges—called court recorders—were members of a separate judicial service and enjoyed much better salaries than civil servants, even the governor (Heussler 1981, 25). Private lawyers could enter the judicial service, and some continued in private practice concurrently (Makepeace, Brooke, and Braddle 1921, 424–25). The frequent appointment of local lawyers to judicial posts was a concern of the Colonial Office from the 1880s (Heussler 1981, 35).

The importance of legal training and the separation of some legal functions in a distinct service coincided with a relatively independent, organized, and influential European private sector. The chambers of commerce established throughout Asia dealt with many wholly commercial issues of common interest, but they also served to articulate the views of the commercial community in areas under East India Company rule, making it their practice to lobby both the company and political actors in Britain. A common feature of these chambers, described by Ian Nish (1962, 82) was that their rules "made it imperative on parties who were elected to serve on the committee, to do so or be subject to a penalty; thus those who wanted to pursue private profit rather than the welfare of the group were penalised by a fine." Both before and after the establishment of the Singapore Chamber of Commerce in 1837, merchants sometimes combined in defense of their interests, and eventually in 1886 the government decided to treat the Chamber of Commerce as a representative body, with the right to nominate a member to the Legislative Council. Many unofficial members of the council took an active concern in governing issues, and some were frequent critics of government (Makepeace, Brooke, and Braddle 1921, 39–42, 448). Commercial interests were most involved on financial issues but also exercised informal influence on government through representation on many advisory boards and investigative commissions (Emerson 1964, 298–99). This kind of incorporation of and consultation with private interests was a routine part of the governing process by the early twentieth century.

These two potential sources of constraint on administrative actors—the elevation of legal processes and the influence of an assertive private sector—eventually contributed to the regularization of government by marking off the official sphere as one governed by consistent rules and formal representations. The administrative resources that would allow such regularization to become a reality, however, were slow in coming. Further, the early recognition of private sector claims may have curbed inconsistent government, but it was sometimes a direct obstacle to the development of public institutions. Both implications can be seen in the evolution of colonial banking and monetary arrangements.

Banks and Money in the Colonial Era

The history of currency in the British territories of Southeast Asia has been described by William Spalding as "a tale of confusion and chaos arising out of adherence to the silver standard" (1924, 162). Until the long-term decline in the price of silver against gold after 1870, however, the impression of monetary disorder was due to the multiplicity of coinages rather than the fact that they were silver based. The dominant coins in use in the Malay Archipelago at the time of the East India Company's establishment of the Straits Settlements were different varieties of "Spanish" dollars, originating mostly from the Americas. Dutch silver and copper coins, minted both in Europe and in Netherlands India, were also becoming widespread.

The company did not take effective steps to supply a regular local currency until 1848, although it had periodically shipped its subsidiary coins to the area. Early in the nineteenth century the administration in Penang proposed issuing a monopoly coinage for the island, from which it anticipated considerable profit. The government in India did not approve, but contemporary reports refer to a locally manufactured tin coin, inscribed on one side with a Chinese character and on the other with initials that may have been those of Penang's governor at the time (Pridmore 1968, 16–21). If so, it would have been in line with the ad hoc and personal nature of the early company rule.

The government in India made successive but unsuccessful attempts to introduce Indian rupees to the Straits Settlements. The newly established chamber of commerce there declared its opposition to the rupee as early as 1837 (Pridmore 1968, 33), and in 1856 it led the opposition to a later attempt to introduce the rupee as legal tender (Nish 1962, 82). Although the actual standard of value was the dollar (Pridmore 1968, 39), it had no legal status. Officially, the unit of account used by the government after 1826 was the rupee but it was never in general use.

Official policy simply added to the bookkeeping tasks of government officers, who were obliged to receive and make payments in a range of coinages and record the transactions in rupees, at somewhat arbitrary rates of exchange. Only when the Colonial Office took responsibility for the territory in 1867 was the inconvenient practice laid to rest and a range of locally circulating silver dollars accepted as legal tender.

The government did not even attempt to outlaw the use of the many foreign coins that passed through the trading post, one of the mediating points in a regional circuit of trade, capital, and labor flows that extended from India to China (Hamashita 1991). The major coins continued to be silver dollars from South America, the Dutch silver guilders that seeped in from Netherlands India, and, later in the nineteenth century, Japanese silver yen and the United States trade dollar. Dutch doits from Netherlands India were widely used, as were "tokens" issued by local merchants. These more or less blatant copies of official coins were intended for local use, trade, and circulation in Netherlands India, where they were accurately enough perceived as counterfeit currency. Despite official agreement to suppress the trade in these coins in the 1840s, old issues continued to circulate in Dutch areas into the twentieth century (Pridmore 1968, 79–91).

After many delays and frequent complaints (by both commercial actors and administrators) about periodic shortages of coins and confusion over their value, the company in 1847 sent out copper coins struck for use in the Straits Settlements. Before then, "the value of copper currencies had been upset by a number of factors, among them depreciation, fluctuations in value, imitation of Dutch doits by the merchants, and finally the import in excessive quantity of the merchants' tokens. For this reason the introduction of a government guaranteed issue with a definite fixed value related to the dollar was welcomed by all classes, and within a very short period the new coins took the place of the foreign coins," wrote Fred Pridmore. Circulation of the merchants' tokens was prohibited in Singapore in 1848. The government eventually became concerned enough about the inflow of coins from neighboring territories to secure an agreement with the (British) Raja of Sarawak to prohibit the export of copper coins in 1891, but large numbers of these coins continued to be imported into the Straits Settlements (Pridmore 1968, 35–46, 76).

The government still did not issue its own major coins. In 1863 the Chamber of Commerce had proposed that a British dollar should be introduced, an idea supported by the governor (Pridmore 1968, 39). The first British dollars were minted in Hong Kong in 1866 and circulated in the Straits Settlements, but the mint was soon closed (and shipped to Japan) because of financial difficulties. The Singapore Chamber of Commerce, in concert with the Hong Kong chamber, repeated its wish for a British dollar in 1874, but although the government was sympathetic, it did not believe it would be able to issue a currency as cheaply as the Mexican dollar. In 1886 the Chamber of Commerce advocated the demonetization of some foreign currencies and again proposed the issue of a British dollar. The government did not act until partial currency reform in 1890 led to the issue of a British dollar for circulation in the East in 1895 (Makepeace, Brooke, and Braddle 1921, 46–47). In 1903 a standard coin specific to Malaya was issued, after which the Mexican, Hong Kong, and British trade dollars were demonetized.

The gradual move toward standardization and public responsibility for the supply of money was linked to the evolution of colonial banking. The first bank to operate in Singapore was a branch of the Union Bank of Calcutta, which opened in 1840, although a few firms had carried on banking business in 1830s (Makepeace, Brooke, and Braddle 1921, 175). The British-owned Oriental Bank opened a branch in 1846, prior to its incorporation by royal charter in 1856. By the 1880s other banks had offices in Singapore, including the NHM, the Dutch firm that dominated the commerce of Netherlands India until the second half of the nineteenth century.[5] The banking market was led by three note-issuing banks, all formed to carry out business in the wider Asian area and majority British-owned (although one, the Hongkong Bank, was incorporated in Hong Kong with a cosmopolitan ownership and board of directors). They were all incorporated by individual charters—special ordinances granted first by the company in the name of the crown and later by the British Treasury.

The idea of a government-issued paper currency did not take hold until comparatively late. It first arose in the Straits Settlements in the late 1870s, during the course of negotiations with the Hongkong Bank over its application to establish a note-issuing branch there.[6] The governor supported the circulation of Hongkong Bank notes in part because of that bank's unlimited liability for its notes. While there was no serious intent to carry out the idea of a government issue, the episode marked the "faint beginnings of a movement, pressed particularly by the Straits Settlements authorities, for a government as opposed to a private sector issue," writes Frank King (1987, 371).

This movement did not come to fruition until much later. One event that turned the government in this direction was the failure of a note-issuing bank, the Oriental, in 1884—a major event in Singapore (Makepeace, Brooke, and Braddle 1921, 503), even though the other note-issuing banks there stood behind the Oriental's notes and managed the crisis without government support. In Ceylon, however, the governor announced a public guarantee of the Oriental Bank's notes. The Treasury was very much concerned about the implicit precedent set by this use of public resources to guarantee private notes. Its solution was to advocate a state note issue in the colonies.

The government in Singapore, despite the shortage of small-denomination notes, was unprepared to issue paper money. The chartered banks opposed the idea, seeing it as a threat to their own note business and calling it a "slur on their private notes" (Lee 1990, 11). Later, a businessman would write that it was "a remarkable instance of the tenacity of our laissez-faire policy that even with regard

5. The NHM is the ancestor of today's ABN-Amro, which remains active in Southeast Asia.
6. The following paragraphs on paper money are based on King 1987, esp. 368–76, 348–50, unless otherwise identified.

to currency—a matter which, it is generally conceded, should be subject to Government control and regulation—the bulk of opinion during the first eighty years of the Settlement's existence was antagonistic to any Government interference" (qtd. in Makepeace, Brooke, and Braddle 1921, 49–50). The currency bill of 1896 was opposed by the unofficial members of the Legislative Council and by the Chamber of Commerce because they feared that a government issue would displace the private notes of the European banks.

The government did not issue its own notes until 1899—or the much-needed small-denomination notes of one dollar until 1905 (Spalding 1924, 169)—and did not claim a monopoly on issue until 1908, when the right of the Hongkong Bank and the Mercantile Bank to issue notes was suspended (the Chartered Bank's note-issuing privileges had ended in 1904). The private notes of these banks continued to circulate in small quantities until World War II (Lee 1990, 11). These gradual steps toward a government monopoly on note issue were spread over thirty years and came comparatively late. In contrast, in India the chartered presidency banks had their note-issuing role taken over by the government as early as 1862 (Collins 1993, 97, 121–22), and in Netherlands India the government-linked Java Bank had held a monopoly on note issue since 1828.

The change in policy concerning paper money was very much connected to concurrent shifts in bank regulation and the way public authorities interacted with private banks. The primary regulatory authority encountered by British banks in the East was the Treasury in London. The colonial banking policy that the Treasury inherited from the company era was considerably more restrictive than that in England itself at the time, where banks could simply incorporate as joint-stock companies.[7] Banking policy was also plural: banks operating in British territories and elsewhere were established under a variety of legal regimes. It was the note-issuing chartered banks that came under the regulatory purview of Treasury. A charter was required if a bank wished to issue notes that would be accepted by colonial treasuries or to bid for government deposits. Some charters prohibited nonbanking business, specified what kind of collateral the bank could accept, set the term of loans and required liquidity ratios, determined the amount of note issue in accordance with paid-up capital, provided for the inspection of the bank's accounts, stipulated limits on borrowing by directors, and held the shareholders liable for note issue.[8]

Neither the home nor the colonial governments were at all equipped to carry out the kind of supervision implied in the bank charters. From 1880 the Treasury increasingly withdrew from any pretense at supervision and argued for the abolition of the chartered banking system in order to avoid potential claims on the public purse by noteholders or depositors, should a bank get into difficulty (King 1987, 389). The more deregulatory banking policy was not a concession to the

---

7. See King 1987, 105–30 on the evolution of Treasury's role and colonial banking policy.
8. The Hongkong Bank's charter is reproduced in King 1987, 625–33.

banks; rather, it was an attempt to draw a firmer line between the government and the private business of the banks. The concurrent implicit recognition that this would not always be politically feasible was a major reason for the Treasury's increasing support of government-issued paper currency.

Attitudes in Hong Kong and Singapore moved more slowly. In theory at least, the governments in these colonies deferred to home authorities on banking issues. Yet they were active interlocutors of the banks, frequently representing their concerns and occasionally granting the banks' requests in advance of home approval. Bankers quite often held positions in the Legislative Councils of Hong Kong and Singapore (King 1987, 122, 157, 374). Government officers were not able to hold positions on the boards of private banks, but bankers served on several public committees and boards.[9] Home authorities were not entirely happy with these relationships. A Colonial Office official argued in the 1880s for continued Treasury involvement in colonial banking since, "we could not trust the Colonial Governments. The Bank Managers are generally members of the Legislative Council, and of great influence" (qtd. in King 1987, 390).

The Treasury had an even more formal and differentiated view of its own position and that of the banks. For example, when the Hongkong Bank's plan to rescue the Hong Kong mint from financial difficulties in 1868 included a proposal that it be granted exclusive rights to issue coins, the Treasury responded that it "would consider to be objectionable any arrangement which would place the coinage, in any of Her Majesty's possessions, under the control of private individuals or commercial firms" (qtd. in King 1987, 159). As we have seen, the coinage in Her Majesty's possessions was at the time substantially private or foreign and continued to be so for the next thirty years—not, however, by government grant of monopoly rights to private actors.

One reason for the Treasury's comparatively formal relations with the banks and its growing desire to distance them from the public sphere was the shift in notions of propriety developing in England. In the case of the Hongkong Bank, the relationship between the bank and the Treasury was not always harmonious, what Frank King calls but "a relationship of mutual assistance tempered by mutual distance" did develop (1987, 333–35). Underlying it were the organizational routines of government. In the words of John Stuart Mill, "The whole of the Government of [the Empire] is carried on in writing. All the orders given, and all the acts of the executive officers, are reported in writing, and the whole of the original correspondence is sent to the Home Government; so that there is no single act done in [the Empire], the whole of the reasons for which are not placed on record" (qtd. in King 1987, 334).

The paper flow generated by the process of fixing the local currency against gold is consonant with Mill's description. It also illustrates the practice of prefix-

9. The chartered banks had mixed views about accepting government-related roles. See, e.g., MacKenzie 1954, 181.

ing major policy changes in Singapore with extensive consultations and inquiries involving private actors. The first move toward adopting a government-issued, gold-backed currency began in 1893, when a committee of officials and private actors was formed to look at the question of gold standard convertibility. The three Chinese members and a European banker were against the introduction of a gold standard. The importance of commercial links with China presumably accounted for the attitude of the Chinese representatives. Bankers in Singapore had all along been opposed to a fixed rate, as were planters and miners, who stood to benefit from a falling currency (Makepeace, Brooke, and Braddle 1921, 48). In addition, foreign exchange business reportedly "became very profitable to the banks as silver declined in value, but a source of embarrassment and loss to traders," according to Charles Conant (1927, 593).

In 1897 the Singapore Chamber of Commerce established its own committee on currency and recommended fixing the currency against gold. Again, nothing was done until government consultation with business led to the appointment of a commission in 1903, which recommended the introduction of a Straits dollar and the demonetization of other dollars. The gold value of the new coin was not fixed until 1906, following the recommendations of yet another currency committee (Spalding 1924, 165–68). Those who were earlier opposed to gold had modified their views as a result of the extreme instability in the price of silver in the preceding years and the attendant "violent speculation" (Makepeace, Brooke, and Braddle 1921, 51).

To administer the new currency, the Currency Board was established by local ordinance in 1897. Like many other arms of government at the time, the Currency Board was formally supervised by a mix of official and unofficial representatives. Its chair was the financial secretary in Singapore, and other members eventually included the financial secretary for Malaya (after 1938) and a government representative from the Borneo territories (after 1950). Other representatives were often people eminent in the financial and banking world. Some were professionals: for example, in the early 1950s, Sydney Caine, the vice chancellor of the University of Malaya. He had previously had a Colonial Office career (1926–48) and had served on currency boards in other colonies; later, he was a coauthor of the report that prefigured the establishment of the Malaysian central bank (Singh 1984, 21). Board members were regularly replaced, but both ex officio and private members were generally comparative insiders.

The Currency Board met in Singapore, usually twice a year, but had very limited discretion. The minimum amount of cover for its currency issue was set by legislation at a very conservative 100 percent. From 1920, the actual backing of the currency was much higher: over 180 percent of currency liabilities between 1932 and 1936 (Lee 1990, 279). Most investments were in British government securities; according to Caine the only decision that members had to make was over the maturity of these securities, and even on that issue the crown agents in London were "inclined to take their own decisions in consultation with the Colonial Office and the Treasury without regard to the instruction of the Board" (Currency Board minutes, qtd. in Singh 1984, 21–22). This left the board to focus on other concerns, such as currency design and internal administration. Its reports give detailed attention to matters such as salary scales for clerical employees and accommodation arrangements for cashiers.

The actual management of currency affairs was carried out by the Currency Department of the Straits Settlements bureaucracy. Given the basically passive nature of a currency board system, not much discretion or active administration was required. Corrupt or inept management of the reserves or handling of cash could have undermined the system, but abuse of the reserves does not seem to have occurred, considering the rapid growth in the board's earnings, which were at high levels from the 1920s. The ratio of total expenditure to income (varying between 5 and 10 percent) tended to decline after 1924 (Lee 1990, 281). The bureaucracy was by this time well suited to the routine tasks of local currency administration, and major abuses of the currency fund were prevented by two related characteristics of the late colonial-era government: its habit of working by its own written records and procedural rules, and the continued decision-making power exercised outright or held in reserve by authorities in England.

Although the government withdrew from its earlier implied regulatory role with respect to the chartered banks, it did develop two savings institutions: the Central Provident Fund (a centralized pension fund established in 1955), and a savings bank attached to the post office. The Provident Fund really became significant only in postindependence Singapore, but the post office savings system was well established in the colonial period. The post office itself was an early creation of the company and maintained something of a commercial orientation. For example, in the 1870s it became involved in the business of conveying remittances to China, with the aim of breaking the hold on the remittance trade by Chinese brokers. This initially led to violent protests by Chinese workers against what was perceived as an attempt to farm a new postal monopoly. Ideas for a government savings bank had been floated as early as the 1830s but were not taken up until 1872, when the governor established a committee to look at the issue. A savings bank was opened in 1877, the post office report for the year explaining that its function was to encourage small savers and to make loans at lower rates than those available elsewhere. The government in England objected to this loan-making function and introduced regulations for the "safer investment of the bank's funds," which ended up largely in government securities (Makepeace, Brooke, and Braddle 1921, 135–48). The practice of channeling this growing pool of savings to the government continued for more than a century.

The growth in the financial industry over the colonial period did not occur without episodes of instability: periodic crises related to sharp changes in commodity prices, currency fluctuations, and unsound lending by the banks themselves. The structure and practices of the banking industry reduced financial instability, however, and lent themselves to private solutions in cases of stress. First, the dominance of the banking market by the two largest chartered banks limited competition. Unlike the profusion of banking companies in India, for example, where competition and innovation led to several cycles of rapid expansion followed by failures, the banking market in Singapore was concentrated. Among the variety of banks established, most maintained long-term ties with clients and tended to operate in separate market niches (Lee 1974, 66–78, 83–87). The Hongkong Bank was the most powerful of the chartered banks, and the others generally cooperated with it (Conant 1927, 591).

Second, the banks were generally conservative, operating with large liquidity ratios and often relying more on shareholders' funds than on deposits from the public.[10] They rarely engaged in long-term lending, tending to focus on relatively low-risk financing of trade operations. In addition, the larger and longer-lived banks developed internal audit and inspection systems to curb the potential for local managers to misappropriate funds or engage in risky projects.

Limits on competition would have helped the banks follow these conservative practices, but they were probably also inspired by a third factor: the nature of the legal system. The chartered banks had legal personalities with the right to sue and be sued, and their shareholders could be called upon to cover bank liabilities. The early emphasis on legal institutions in the Straits Settlements and the pro-creditor legal biases imported from British law gave them both the ability to limit banking losses through loan recovery and the incentive to follow prudent banking practices.

Finally, largely in consequence of these three factors, the banks proved them-selves willing and able to assume management of cases of instability. As noted, the other chartered banks met the obligations of the failed Oriental Bank in 1884, avoiding the kind of banking panic that might have led to government interven-tion. In a later case, three locally established Chinese banks combined in order to deal with serious losses they had incurred as a result of the depression and Britain's devaluation of sterling in 1931 (Wilson 1972).

Overall, by the end of the colonial period the government's ability to carry out an expanded but still relatively limited range of tasks in the financial sector rested on three underlying factors. First, there was a slow but steady development of rationalized bureaucratic organizations concentrated in Singapore. Second, the early in-principle commitment to legal rules and institutions led toward adminis-tration that was both rule based and predicated on the common law notion that legal rules should be consistent with common practice. Third, the involvement of the Colonial Office and the Treasury in London imposed a background constraint on irregular practices. The Singapore government did pursue modest initiatives to expand its role, but a budgetary constraint backed up by London and the local

10. Liquidity ratios and shareholder funds for the Chinese banks were particularly high. See Wilson 1972; and UOB 1985.

influence of private business ensured that the organizational capacities of the government were never tested against more demanding tasks.

CHANGE AND CONTINUITY IN THE POSTINDEPENDENCE STATE

The effectiveness of Singapore's government and bureaucracy are rarely questioned. Policy has been rigorously enforced, public-sector organizations efficient, and corruption rare (Quah 1996; Root 1996, 42–51). How this record was achieved ought to raise questions, since Singapore lacks many of the attributes commonly considered important for ensuring effective government. Transparency, especially concerning the government's economic activity, is low, and the government maintains a high degree of control over the flow of information (Seow 1998; Rodan 2000). Further, although legal institutions are efficient, several observers argue that the rule of law as an external check on government does not exist (Jayasuriya 1996; Seow 1997). To the extent that democratic checks and balances promote disciplined policy implementation, this restraint too is weak: the government continues to be able to co-opt, contain, or suppress most challenges (Rodan 1993b). In addition the government has taken an active role in promoting economic development since the 1960s, acquiring extensive commercial assets and using fiscal policy to influence investment patterns (Lim 1983; Asher 1999). How, in these circumstances, has disciplined policy implementation been maintained?

Governing capacity in Singapore rests on two bases. One is broadly consistent with the expectations about governing capacity outlined in Chapter 2: Singapore's core public sector organizations have structures, routines, and norms that approximate those of rational-legal Weberian bureaucracy, including overall administrative continuity, generous official rewards, hierarchical control mechanisms, and an embedded ethos of pragmatism and instrumental rationality. Because Singapore's state is neither bureaucratic nor insulated from private actors, however, its governing capacity also rests on a set of informal institutions that structure the behavior of elite actors who occupy positions in both public and private spheres.

The Core Public Sector

When Singapore acquired internal self-government in 1959, its economy and administration had more than fully recovered from the disruption that had accompanied the Japanese occupation and the postwar British Military Administration. A decade of stable, civilian colonial rule after the war meant that the new Singapore government had a functioning administrative apparatus at its disposal and was not facing a situation of economic collapse and high inflation. The government did face several political challenges in its early years—a suspicious business sector, active left-wing organizations with communist sympathies, outbreaks of interethnic violence, and conflict with Kuala Lumpur—but these were constructed as security threats that required the government to bolster its political and organizational strength.[11]

Organizational continuity was important in providing the government with the means to consolidate its position. A fairly high level of continuity in government organizations was a feature of the transition to self-government in 1959 and full independence in 1965. Ministries of national development and culture were created, but otherwise the departmental structure of the bureaucracy changed very little. The colonial-era organization of civil service employees into four divisions was maintained, as were salary scales, the format of the government directory, and the titles of official positions; the rotation of elite civil servants through different government agencies likewise continued after 1959 and still does. During Singapore's short-lived incorporation within Malaysia, between 1963 and 1965, merger never became an organizational reality in government on either side of the Straits.[12] Although its expulsion from Malaysia in 1965 reflected the priorities of the government in Kuala Lumpur, Singapore's emergence as a separate state was in fact in line with its distinct identity as an administrative center in the colonial period, an identity that had been enhanced by its being governed as a separate colony after the Second World War, with its own administration and, in the 1950s, its own political process (*Singapore Year Book* 1964, 25–55).

The personnel of the colonial civil service was not transmitted intact to the post-1959 government, but there was some continuity, despite the nonbureaucratic roots of the new political leadership and its strong criticism of the bureaucracy before assuming power. Some old-regime civil servants did leave the bureaucracy around 1959, and new recruitment in the 1960s meant that most senior bureaucrats in 1972 had joined the service after 1961 (Seah 1975; Chan 1976, 23). Partly this was due to the phaseout of British expatriates, but there was also turnover of local staff—for example, about a third of those in the Ministry of Finance over four years, significant but not revolutionary. Further, the most senior personnel in the Ministry of Finance in 1961 had generally been old-regime civil servants.[13] This degree of continuity protects functional effectiveness and helps ensure that the established routines of an organization are perpetuated.

Reward and sanctioning systems in core public sector organizations were strengthened over time. The principle of "fair comparison" with the private sector, affirmed in the 1960s as necessary to attract the best talent, led to significant salary increases in the early 1970s, early 1980s, and late 1980s. Ministers and senior civil servants were among the best paid in the world. Lee Kuan Yew stated in 1979 that

11. On the conditions under which governments respond to external or internal security threats by enhancing state capacities, see Rich and Stubbs 1997; and Stubbs 1999.
12. In Singapore, government departments and agencies also continued to produce their own annual reports.
13. Of the nine most senior Ministry of Finance officers in 1961, six were local Singaporeans listed in the *Government Directory* for 1957 or 1958; two others were expatriate officers.

it was desirable to retain at least a third of the nation's "best brains" in the public sector (Seah 1987, 109), and other senior ministers put forward similar views (Seah 1975, 19–20). Despite retention problems, the state sector had many of the nation's best performers in the 1980s (Lee and Low 1990, 160–61, 197). In the 1990s, state scholarships for tertiary education still attracted many of Singapore's best students. Both the material rewards of service and frequent public statements regarding the caliber of public sector personnel affirm the selectivity of its recruitment standards.

The positive rewards of government service are probably a factor behind the low incidence of corruption in Singapore, but there are also strong negative sanctions. In the early 1960s the powers of the anticorruption agency were increased and later changes gave it virtually unfettered powers of investigation and arrest (Quah 1978). Prosecuted cases have resulted in significant sentences for those convicted. Singapore's only cabinet minister to be accused of corruption committed suicide.[14] Changes to the corruption law in 1988 further strengthened its punitive scope—to the extent that the bill was criticized for appearing to introduce a presumption of guilt if an accused person dies or absconds during an investigation into corruption.[15]

Hierarchical control mechanisms in the public sector promote discipline and coordination in policy implementation. Most of the statutory authorities come under the purview of a ministry, and some of the companies in which the government holds an interest (known as government-linked companies, or GLCs) are subject to oversight by the auditor general and the Public Accounts Committee of Parliament. More significant control and coordination is achieved through a system of multitasking of key individuals and interlocking directorships in the state sector. This system of control through trusted senior personnel has operated since the early 1970s, and in the 1990s it covered all significant statutory authorities, GLCs, and policymaking ministries (Tan 1974; Vennewald 1994).

Policy flexibility and a very circumscribed role for ideology have also supported the government's capacity to implement policy consistently. A study of the organizational culture of the Economic Development Board, the main development agency, characterized its overriding ethic as one of "strategic pragmatism"—the ability to adapt behavior in light of new information and changing circumstances (Schein 1996). The government has used ideology as a tool and promotes an official ideology (Chua 1995, 9–39, 57–78), but its instrumental use does not interfere much with core practices of government. In economic policy the government has been catholic, pursuing both state ownership and private enterprise. Initiatives that proved overambitious, such as the "second industrial revolution," were abandoned or modified (Rodan 1989). The problem-driven approach to policy is coincidental

14. See Chan, Chai, and R. Iau 1987 on the affair, which did attract accusations of tardiness on the part of the authorities.
15. The Law Society of Singapore's concerns about the bill are contained in *Report of the Select Committee on the Corruption (Confiscation of Benefits) Bill* (Bill No. 7/88, presented to Parliament 16 August 1988).

with, if not related to, there having been few economists in senior positions. Government scholarships, the preeminent route to advancement, have favored degrees in engineering and hard science.[16] Engineers rather than economists have also made up the largest group of graduate staff in the Economic Development Board (Low et al. 1993, 96).

The issue of efficient government service is one of the few on which public complaints are encouraged, in contrast to the government's refusal to tolerate opposition on political issues (Chan 1975). The government's regular public surveys on the quality of public sector services show a reasonably high level of satisfaction with government services (*Straits Times*, 23 September 2000). And since the practice of subjecting organizations to this kind of external assessment acts as a source of discipline, the notion of performance-based promotion as value and practice has permeated the service. Through devices such as Work Improvement Teams and programs to upgrade the civil service (from the adoption of information technology to reducing service times for specific tasks) the public sector has remained subject to internal demands on its performance (Quah 1996). Academic merit is one of the principal performance-based measures in the public sector, a key criterion in the allocation of state scholarships, recruitment, and subsequent promotion.

In sum, the practices and embedded principles of the formal public sector show that it has developed many characteristics of rationalized government, including a commitment to appointment and promotion on the basis of performance. The acceptance of instrumental rationality also makes the government relatively pragmatic and promotes rule-abiding policy implementation, allowing unrealistic policy goals to be abandoned, and strategic flexibility is consistent with expressed principles. If Singapore were truly a bureaucratic state with a high degree of autonomy from the private sector, then an analysis of its governing capacity might stop here.[17] The image of an autonomous bureaucratic field, however, fails to describe the relationship among political authority, public institutions, and private actors in Singapore.

Political Authority, Public Institutions, and Private Actors

Political power is tightly concentrated in Singapore, but state organizations are not autonomous in the sense of occupying a sphere separate from that of private business. Individual bureaucrats occupy important roles, but they are integrated into a wider system of government which does not support bureaucratic centers of power. The flow of successful (presumably ambitious) officials to political positions suggests that real power is wielded by political actors in the cabinet. In addition, the civil service has not developed a sense of loyalty or emotive affinity among its members. Most accounts, like that of Seah Chee Meow, indicate that a "bureau-

16. In 1981, of 378 undergraduate and postgraduate awards only 52 were in the category of Humanities, Social Science, and Law (Tan 1983–84, 35).
17. Singapore's image as an administrative state in which the bureaucracy is the locus of politics owes much to the work of Chan Heng Chee. See Chan 1975 and 1976.

cratic ethos (such as pride in serving the bureaucracy) is not effectively instilled among the bureaucrats who tend to be susceptible to purely monetary considerations" (Seah 1975, 21).[18]

Rather than being bureaucratic, Singapore's governing elite occupies a mixed sphere that encompasses bureaucratic, political, and business actors. Relations between nominally private and public actors have increased over time, but senior politicians have never been completely isolated from business.[19] The line between business and government has been more systematically blurred as private sector individuals moved into state bodies and public sector personnel acquired private sector interests and positions.

Although no senior politicians in the 1960s had business backgrounds, the government made early efforts to cultivate the Chinese Chamber of Commerce, Singapore's leading business organization (Wee 1972, 27–80). The government also created links with private sector individuals by appointing them to directorships and managerial positions in state corporations, statutory authorities, and, less often, the People's Action Party (PAP). Statutory boards and GLCs generally have private sector individuals on their boards, and almost all members of what would now be called a Singapore establishment have served as directors on public sector boards. In the case of GLCs, not only do private sector actors serve as directors, but ownership tends to be shared with the private sector. Finally, state sector personnel have taken up positions in the private sector. Added to the more or less constant outflow of junior and midlevel officers from the bureaucracy has been a movement of senior state sector individuals into business as advisers, directors, and entrepreneurs since the late 1980s. Cross-cutting career paths that link public and private actors are especially evident in the financial sector.

Because public and private actors are intermixed at the apex of the Singapore power structure, the maintenance of clean and efficient government depends on governing institutions that encompass this mixed sphere. These institutions are largely informal systems that externalize many of the routines and norms of the formal government sector, such as the commitment to meritocracy, flexibility, performance-based indicators of achievement, and an entrenched acceptance of the government's right to govern. They are reflected and sustained by the selective incorporation and socialization of individuals into the governing elite. Rather like an exclusive private club, current members self-consciously admit new members according to set criteria that tend to reflect those by which they themselves gained entrance (Hirschman 1970). In Singapore, these criteria include academic performance, technical merit, and loyalty to the government.

In concrete terms, the process of selective incorporation and socialization has been carried out largely through the same channels as those that produce the amal-

---

18. This view corresponds with later studies; see Quah 1996, 80–81.
19. Examples of individual relationships connecting political and business spheres are given in Hamilton-Hart 2000b, which contains some other material used in this account of Singapore's governing structures. It is available from the website of *The Pacific Review* (www.tandf.co.uk).

gamation of public and private interests and actors: the statutory authorities, the GLCs, and the ruling political party. For statutory authorities, the practice of appointing nongovernment individuals to their boards grew out of colonial arrangements that provided for direct business representation in the Legislative Council and on statutory boards. The notion of representing outside interests faded quickly after 1959 (Pillai 1983). What these appointments provided was a way of socializing prominent members of the business community and, by example, the wider business sector. The process has also allowed the government to assess which individuals are trustworthy and thus to be cultivated.

The process of induction into senior governing positions is selective and progressive, based on verifiable measures of good performance. Public statements by leading figures such as Goh Keng Swee, Philip Yeo, and Lee Kuan Yew have repeatedly affirmed the importance of putting educated, skilled, and capable individuals into positions of responsibility. Besides safeguarding competence in government, structuring the integration of public and private sectors along performance-based norms protects the system of government itself. Private sector actors who assume public advisory or executive positions are not included because of their role in the economy, and even less because of any idea of interest representation; rather, individuals from the civil service, business, or the ruling party are chosen on the basis of prior success—success in external examinations, in outstanding university performance, or in business. According to one man who had himself experienced the process, putting oneself forward would invite suspicion (interview, Ho Kwon Ping, August 1997), but those who are successful may be *asked* to join the PAP and enter Parliament or act in a public position (*Singapore Business*, November 1990). They may then be brought further into the inner ring of those who govern Singapore by being given opportunities to demonstrate merit in public or quasi-public appointments. There are no apparent cases in which people who have been known to err seriously in one position are later given another position of responsibility— a record that stands in contrast to that of many neighboring states.

A final feature of the Singapore system is an institutionalized pattern of government-business interaction which avoids the aggressive testing of the limits of state policy (accepted in, for example, the United States). Private suits against government regulatory agencies are not part of the Singapore way of doing business. In regulatory matters the non-state sector has known that it must abide by the spirit and intention of policy goals rather than the letter of the law. The historical explanation has been the political and economic weakness of the local private sector (Rodan 1989). But now that local business is economically and politically much stronger, it is the particular way private interests are incorporated, along with the characteristics of the system into which they are drawn, that explains the durability of these norms of interaction. How durable they are, though, remains to be seen: there are signs that these informal disciplinary systems are precarious (Hamilton-Hart 2000b).

THE FINANCIAL SYSTEM: INSTITUTIONS AND INTERESTS

The financial system of Singapore at the coming of self-government in 1959 had completely recovered from World War II, inflation, and postwar controls. The banking market remained dominated by the same large banks, and most sectors of the economy had reverted to prewar ownership patterns: British interests tended to predominate, but local businesses were also significant, particularly in commerce, trade, and finance (Puthucheary 1960). The political climate in 1959 did prompt some foreign investors to move their operations to Malaya, which was perceived as being under more moderate, less interventionist government.[20] Overall, however, business confidence was not seriously dented, and Singapore's financial sector was stable. Under the familiar currency board system the exchange rate was steady and inflation low.

These background conditions of continuity and stability were as important to the subsequent development of financial sector institutions as they were to the development of state organizations. The gradual dismantling of the common colonial-era financial system that Singapore and Malaysia inherited was politically topical, and by the time the main financial sector regulator began operating, disturbances in the world economy were making themselves felt. Singapore, however, met these challenges on the basis of prior organizational consolidation and financial stability. The contrast with Indonesia, which faced the problem of setting up postindependence financial institutions at a time when the financial system was in a state of complete breakdown, is obvious. Not until 1967, when Malaysia began issuing its own currency, did Singapore need to alter the arrangements that governed its financial system (Lee 1974, 222–42).

The Monetary Authority of Singapore: Organizational Development
Singapore's de facto central bank, the Monetary Authority of Singapore, began operating in 1971. The MAS took over responsibility for banking supervision, foreign exchange monitoring, and the overseas investment of government funds from other departments, including the banking commissioner's office, which had been established as a consequence of the currency split in 1967 (Lee 1974, 235). The officers of the predecessor departments and agencies were all absorbed into the MAS, providing it with experienced personnel from the start. Some people with particular skills relevant to the financial sector were also recruited from outside the government (interviews, former MAS officials, Singapore, August 1997).

With the exception of an episode of major organizational disruption in 1981 (discussed below), the MAS has grown steadily. It tends to draw its senior managers from the public sector.[21] In line with a government system that typically

20. See the commentary in *Far Eastern Economic Review*, 1 January, 5 February, 9 April, and 20 August 1959.
21. See Appendix 4 for staffing levels and continuity at senior levels.

rotates elite civil servants through different departments and statutory authorities over the course of their careers, MAS officials are not necessarily recruited internally. Quite a large proportion of new recruits are midcareer officers.[22] The managing director has sometimes been appointed from outside the bureaucracy: the first (1971–81) was a professional banker from one of the large local banks; a merchant banker was appointed after the reorganization in 1981; and three politicians served briefly in the early 1980s. Except for the first managing director, who appears to have been selected entirely on professional merit demonstrated in the private sector, all these other outsiders were firmly within the circuit encompassed by Singapore's informal governing institutions.[23] Richard Hu, for example, was brought onto the board in the early 1970s while still a career executive with Shell Oil. In the mid-1980s he was briefly made MAS managing director before moving into the cabinet, soon to take up the position of finance minister and chairman of the MAS (*Straits Times*, 27 November and 24 December 1984; *Government Directory*, various issues). Two long-serving civil servants held the post of managing director between 1985 and 1998.

For managerial positions below that of managing director (who frequently holds multiple appointments in the public sector and must therefore delegate duties), the MAS generally recruits internally. Listings of senior officers in the *Government Directory* show that a reasonably high level of continuity was the norm before the 1981 reorganization, and this continuity had been more than reestablished by the 1990s. By 1997 the ten departmental or divisional heads had all been with the MAS for more than ten years. No overall retention figures are publicly available. A press estimate in 1984 was that 75 percent of the banking department staff had less than three years' work experience (*Euromoney*, September 1984), but coming after the 1981 upheaval, this is likely to be atypical. Each year in the 1990s about 10 percent of staff received awards for ten or more years' service (MAS, *Annual Report*, various issues). The outflow of MAS officers to the private sector is relatively common; however, not all of those who leave go to the private sector, nor is their departure from government service necessarily permanent.

The expertise and competence of MAS staff have rarely been questioned. Most complaints from the private sector (mostly from the foreign private sector) have been that MAS officers are not sensitive enough to their needs and overregulate the industry. Where different interests or views on banking are not at issue, however, private sector bankers acknowledge that MAS officers are highly competent. The MAS regularly has a few staff members studying for higher degrees at foreign universities, and in 1988 it reopened its undergraduate scholarship scheme.[24] Only 3 percent of the training budget goes on these scholarships. In-house training and short-term specialized courses have been much more

22. In 1996 a quarter of all new recruits were midcareer officers (MAS, *Annual Report* 1997).
23. They were Yong Pung How, Lim Kim San, and (very briefly in 1985) Goh Keng Swee. See Hamilton-Hart 2000b for biographical details.
24. This paragraph is drawn from various issues of the MAS annual report.

important. From 1979 to 1989 only four officers were sent for postgraduate degrees, compared with about twenty sent each year for short overseas courses until the mid-1980s. Since then numbers have been higher. By the 1990s over half of all staff underwent some kind of training each year, the majority in local courses. Training has thus been focused on developing skills that will be primarily recognized in-house, whereas degree courses (which are given much more emphasis by the Indonesian central bank) represent the acquisition of transferable skills.

Apart from the 1981 changes, the structure of the MAS has been stable; for the most part it has added departments only as new functions are acquired. Another indicator of organizational rationality was the very frank and methodical approach to bank supervision outlined in an inter-central bank discussion paper that systematically presented the problems faced by the MAS. The paper also described how the inspection method had changed over time, with most attention given to problem institutions and domestic institutions, and said that the MAS was regularly studying legislation "to modify and remedy . . . 'gray' areas and 'loopholes' so as to cope with the growing sophistication of the financial structure in Singapore" (MAS 1981). The general approach taken by the MAS has been preemptive. On its actions during the international debt crisis of the early 1980s, a Singapore banker said that everything it had done was "part of a carefully thought out plan" that demonstrated "extreme caution and concern for the vulnerable individual investor" (*Euromoney*, September 1984).

A cadet system under which all new recruits go through a period of rotation and intensive training in different areas has been in place since the 1980s. In 1997 the MAS reported 100 percent staff participation in Work Improvement Teams, part of the civil service–wide PS21 (Public Service in the Twenty-first Century) initiative launched in 1995. These teams are meant to promote an internal culture of flexibility, innovation, and focus on output. They may also serve to enhance an organizational ethos among staff. Interviews with former MAS officers suggest that initiative, practical effectiveness, and the ability to generate and come to grips quickly with new ideas were highly valued. Those that earned the respect of their superiors on these measures tended to advance rapidly.[25] A senior officer who rejoined the MAS in December 1997 placed a high priority on teamwork, "getting every individual in the organisation thinking" and "getting older, seasoned, experienced officers to be able to take new ideas and take criticism without feeling defensive about it" (*Business Times*, 28 March 2000).

MAS officers are under the same basic rules of conduct as civil servants. There are no publicly known cases of corrupt behavior by MAS officials. An investment officer at a spin-off organization, the Government Investment Corporation (GIC), did receive a nine-year sentence for accepting bribes in Hong Kong, but in a highly unusual ruling he successfully appealed his sentence in early 1998 (*Straits Times*,

25. The general climate in Singapore, however, would encourage these observations whether they were true or not.

16 April 1998). The only other disciplinary case to attract attention occurred in 1994, when a senior MAS officer was accused of breaching the Official Secrets Act by disclosing GDP growth estimates a few days before they were due to be released (*Straits Times*, 2 April 1994). The officer left his job, but the MAS report for the year thanked him for "dedicated service." In 1997 he was appointed to a high-level committee tasked with recommending the future course of financial policy, and he later became MAS managing director.

The Monetary Authority's Public Role and Relationship with Government
The MAS expanded its regulatory scope and public role over time. Early in the 1970s it assumed responsibility for monitoring finance companies as well as banks and merchant banks. In 1977 it took over the staff and responsibilities of the insurance commissioner's department. In the late 1970s the managing director was concurrently chair of the Securities Industry Council, and MAS staff carried out most of the work of the council, which was a joint public-private capital market watchdog (*Far Eastern Economic Review*, 3 April 1981). In 1984 the MAS took over the administration of the Securities Industry Act, thus centralizing the supervision of all financial markets.[26]

The one central bank function never formally assumed is currency issue, which remains, in theory, the province of the Currency Board. At the time the MAS was established, the retention of the board was intended to maintain confidence in the currency, but in practical terms it has not been significant. Both the MAS and the Currency Board are under the Ministry of Finance, with the minister of finance generally the chair of both organizations, which also often share other board members. The MAS actively manages the foreign exchange rate as a monetary policy instrument. Hence, although the Currency Board continues to exist, Singapore does not operate a currency-board system (Peebles and Wilson 1996, 130–32).

The MAS has not had a major role in economic planning, and its role in government finance schemes has been limited largely to the discounting of export credits. It has, however, carried out a range of functions other than financial sector regulation and policy implementation. It has used its foreign reserves to provide forward cover, reportedly at minimal cost, for the foreign currency liabilities of statutory boards (*Euromoney*, September 1984). It holds the deposits of public authorities and companies, which it has used to support monetary policy goals (Claassen 1992); allowing the MAS to accept these deposits was also thought to be a move to rein in some of the treasury managers of GLCs. In addition, the MAS has played a role in the government's policy of encouraging the development of selected financial markets. Development initiatives started with the offshore banking market in 1968 and continued with the promotion of the offshore Asian bond market. The foreign exchange, money, and futures markets were also devel-

26. Organizations such as the stock exchange also have self-regulatory bodies.

oped with input from MAS officials and tax breaks for profits on offshore business (*Straits Times*, 14 May 1987; Tan 1996).

The MAS is very much a part of the government. It is supervised by a board of directors, generally chaired by the minister of finance. In 1971 there were seven directors: the minister of finance, one of the permanent secretaries of the Ministry of Finance, the accountant general, the MAS managing director, two members from the private sector (Richard Hu and Ho Rih Wah), and an academic. For the rest of the decade the only changes were related to the rotation of the civil servant members. Since 1975 almost all board members have had a minimum of five years of public service, as civil servant, cabinet minister, or director of a statutory board (*Government Directory*, various years).

It has been the practice for cabinet ministers to take an active role in the operations of the MAS. An officer in the 1970s said that the minister of finance was prone to telephone even midlevel officers directly for information or comment (interview, Singapore, August 1997). The minister of finance and MAS chairman in the 1970s, Hon Sui Sen, reportedly chaired a Financial Assets Management Committee, which had some role in setting monetary policy and managing official reserves (*Far Eastern Economic Review*, 27 March 1981). Later, monetary policy was formulated at a weekly monetary and investment policy meeting of MAS board members (including the MAS chairman, always a cabinet minister) and senior MAS staff. Decisions were reportedly made by consensus and relayed to the MAS's monetary management division for implementation (*Business Times*, 22 March 2000).

The most dramatic demonstration of ministerial control over the MAS remains its reorganization of 1981. This began with an external review instituted by Deputy Prime Minister Goh Keng Swee after he became chairman in 1980. The review team, made up largely of officials who had worked for Goh in the Ministry of Defence, produced a critical report accusing the MAS of inefficiency and poor management of the country's reserves. Foreign press commentary at the time saw these charges as unfair, and no evidence of anything other than cautious management was advanced. Rather, it was rumored that the managing director had shown too much initiative in his push to constitute the MAS formally as a central bank. Shortly afterward, in January 1981, the managing director resigned, and by March about forty senior staff had also left, out of loyalty or as a protest (*Far Eastern Economic Review*, 6 March 1981). Later, a further sixty-one staff members were retrenched, and outsiders from both public and private sectors were brought into senior positions. Although the MAS gained the ability to match private sector salaries, it lost the task of managing at least a portion of the country's external reserves. The new Government Investment Corporation took over the management of official foreign investments. A foreign merchant bank, Rothschild in London, advised on the establishment of the GIC.

An undisclosed number of those who left the MAS in 1981 went to work in the new GIC, and in the late 1990s at least four of its most senior positions were held by former MAS officers. The GIC had 350 employees in 1996, most of them investment professionals (*Straits Times*, 15 March 1996). Its first board of directors included Lee Kuan Yew as chair, Goh Keng Swee, Lim Kim San (chair of the Port of Singapore Authority), Goh Chok Tong (then trade and industry minister, later prime minister), Tony Tan (then education minister), and Suppiah Dhanabalan (then foreign minister). In 1996 the board was still dominated by cabinet ministers—Lee Kuan Yew, Lee Hsien Loong, Tony Tan, and Richard Hu—but also included former cabinet minister Dhanabalan and the chairman of a large local bank, Lee Seng Wee (*Straits Times*, 15 March 1996; *Far Eastern Economic Review*, 27 March 1981).

Political involvement is clearly at a high level in the GIC and the MAS. In 1996 Lee Kuan Yew described the MAS deputy managing director, Koh Beng Seng, as having been "nurtured" by him and Goh Keng Swee. Earlier, Lee had supported Koh in policy differences with the managing director, who was removed. Koh's tendered resignation in 1997, rumored to be the result of policy differences with Finance Minister Hu or Deputy Prime Minister Lee Hsien Loong, prompted direct intervention by Prime Minister Goh Chok Tong, who refused to accept his resignation (*Straits Times*, 9 August 1997; *Asian Wall Street Journal*, 4 August 1997), but after initially putting his resignation on hold, Koh did resign. The ongoing political salience of the MAS was demonstrated again in 1998 when Lee Kuan Yew's son, high-flying Deputy Prime Minister Lee Hsien Loong, became chair of the organization.

Other State Organizations in the Financial Sector

The MAS has been first and foremost a regulator and a monetary authority. Other organizations in the state sector have implemented the government's developmental policies (Rodan 1989). In addition to fiscal incentives (Asher 1999), the government has used statutory authorities and GLCs to influence patterns of investment and the course of economic development in Singapore. Particularly important in the mobilization and use of financial resources are the Economic Development Board (EDB), a statutory authority, and the Development Bank of Singapore (DBS), a government-linked company.

The report that recommended the formation of the EDB cited the need for each citizen to see "further than his own direct interests, further than today, and over Singapore's frontiers" (EDB 1991). When the EDB was established in 1961, its first chairman was Hon Sui Sen, Lee Kuan Yew's "best permanent secretary," who came over from the Ministry of Finance. Some indication of the intended importance of the EDB is shown by its initial allocation of funds—$100 million over the first four years—which represented nearly 20 percent of the economic development budget for the period and was a radical increase over the allocation to its nominal predecessor, the Industrial Promotion Board (Rodan 1989, 47, 65). By the end of the year its staff had grown to eighty-one.

Its first focus was on providing infrastructure to attract foreign investment: it built roads, an industrial reservoir, housing, schools, and community centers for yet-to-be-constituted factory workers in the early 1960s. These functions have since been hived off to a separate organization, the Jurong Town Corporation. This pattern of developing core functions and spawning more specialized organizations has been typical of the EDB. Other spin-off agencies include the Singapore Institute of Management (later the base for Singapore's third university), the government-linked trading and export-promotion company Intraco, the National Productivity Board, and the Standards Institute of Singapore.

In 1968, DBS was founded to take over the development financing role of the EDB. For a while this left the EDB to concentrate on promoting inward foreign investment. More recently it has also played a role in coordinating and cofinancing Singaporean investment abroad. Its international manpower director, in San Francisco, is tasked with recruiting overseas Singaporeans to work in Singapore. By 1997 the EDB had seventeen offices abroad. It also plays a role in several governmental financial subsidy schemes. Between 1976 and 1990 the EDB was involved in schemes covering $4.1 billion in loans and financial assistance. Funds administered by the EDB in financial year 1990 came to over $714 million (Low et al. 1993, 206–7, 101). It continues to disburse a range of incentives and assistance. For example, in 1996 the EDB announced that a total of $4.3 billion would be available in loans and grants until the year 2000 (EDB, *Investment News*, February 1996). The Cluster Development Fund, established in 1994, is used by the investment arm of the EDB to take equity stakes in joint ventures, particularly in technology-intensive areas: $500 million had been invested by April 1997, at which time the fund was increased by $1 billion to reach $2 billion.

DBS played an early role in financing some of the government's industrialization initiatives, and some of its financial market activity—such as early bond issues in the Asian dollar market—were consonant with government policies to develop these markets. It also appears to function as a holding company for government assets, either directly or through subsidiaries. Mostly, however, DBS has operated as a profit-oriented commercial bank, growing to become Singapore's—and Southeast Asia's—largest local bank.

The achievements of both the EDB and DBS are impressive. DBS is profitable, innovative, and reasonably prudent. Although there was an element of subsidy in its funds in the early years, it is not considered by anyone to be a drain on the government's financial resources. In the 1970s it did engage in some lending to shipbuilding and other industries which turned out not to be successful. On the whole, however, it was from the start so meticulous a lender that some Singaporean companies were unwilling to take loans or equity from the bank because of the scrutiny of their operations that doing so would involve (Koh et al. 1973, 279–300). The role that the EDB has played in Singapore's economic development has been positive, with the organization generally receiving a lot of praise and no accusations that it has underperformed (Low et al. 1993; Schein 1996).

The organizational attributes of the EDB and DBS, as well as those of the wider state system, help explain their success. While given day-to-day managerial autonomy, managers in these organizations have little scope to deviate from their official priorities without the concurrence of senior political actors. The EDB is overseen by a board of directors drawn from public and private sectors, appointed by the minister of trade and industry for such terms as he decides. As a company in which the government maintains a controlling stake, DBS is also under substantive political control. The bank's status as a listed corporation with private sector shareholding acts as an additional mechanism to monitor its performance and, potentially, as a check on its management.

The practical supervision of these organizations is designed to minimize their responsiveness to sectional interests. Initially, private sector representatives on the EDB's board were to represent various economic and professional groups (a carryover of colonial habits), but that rule was subsequently amended. Instead, the composition of the board, explains Philip Pillai (1983, 142–45), "reflects the ad hoc reaction to changing needs, rather than a uniform principle that the Board should represent the widest spread of various interest groups." A similar shift away from the notion of representation can be seen in the composition of the DBS board, which at first included local and foreign bankers but over time has been more often composed entirely of state-sector personnel drawn from the ministries or GLCs. Local bankers left the board in early 1985, and it has had few private sector representatives since then (DBS, *Annual Report*, various issues). Stringent conflict-of-interest rules govern the activities and interests of EDB employees. The appointment of board members from the private sector means that potential conflicts of interest will occur (Pillai 1983, 146–47), but board members are expected to absent themselves from decisions that relate to their own interests.

The recruitment of staff for both organizations reflects a commitment to selectivity on the basis of prior performance, generally in related roles. When the bill establishing the EDB was drafted, its chairman and managing director were to be full-time executives: because the first managing director was to be a foreign expert, proper control required a full-time (local) chairman. This was amended in 1972 when suitable local ability to fill the managing director's position was identified (Pillai 1983, 142–45). Since Hon Sui Sen ended his tenure as chairman of the EDB in 1968, the position has been filled by other senior civil servants and EDB officers (EDB 1991; Schein 1996). The directors of DBS have included many of the senior civil servants whose names frequently crop up in other roles.[27] As far as can be judged from the bank's published lists of management staff since 1974, senior executive positions were generally filled by career DBS staff or other state-sector people until 1998. Since then, however, several foreign bankers have taken over senior positions, including that of chief executive. These are outsiders but their appointment indicates an ongoing concern to select on the basis of demonstrated professional performance. The decision to import managerial expertise may have

27. The serving attorney general has often been on the board, as well as representatives from the Ministry of Finance. Several board members since the 1970s have been career DBS officers.

been a strategic move in support of the government's policy of attracting "foreign talent" to Singapore. Or it may have been a deliberate signal to state-sector executives, some of whom were accused of poor performance during the regional financial crisis in 1997–98 (Lim 1999, 246), that they could be removed if they failed to perform.

Both organizations have gone some way to develop organizational ethos and staff commitment. Although the EDB and DBS (like all other state organizations) have been open to lateral entry and subject to midcareer staff outflows, a degree of personnel continuity has been achieved. In the early 1990s a substantial proportion of the EDB staff had been with the organization for ten years or more (Low et al. 1993, 398), and until recently, DBS appeared to recruit internally for many senior positions. Further, commitment may be generated by selective recruitment and the intensity of organizational practices. The EDB continues to attract top graduates and makes them aware of their elite status. It has created an organizational culture in which demanding workloads, a high level of delegation and participation, innovation, and a tremendous emphasis on efficiency are both routine practice and overtly espoused standards (Schein 1996). Under the Singapore Inc. scholarship scheme, the EDB has initiated a mentoring program for scholarship holders while they are still attending a university (*Straits Times*, 14 August 1997). Other moves that reflect a concern with organizational identity include the establishment in 1991 of the EDB Society by "alumni" who have moved on to other positions. It is this society that commissioned Edgar Schein's (1996) study of the EDB. DBS has produced its own anecdotal and personal history (DBS 1988).

DBS and the EDB are just two organizations that have supported the government's economic development goals. Rather than attempting to influence bank lending directly, the government has taken on the task of investment itself and provided incentives for foreign investment. Government-linked companies operate in almost all sectors of the economy and have been concentrated in areas that government policy has targeted. GLCs led early investment in heavy industries and oil processing and in the 1990s were leading the state's shift to a high-technology policy for Singapore.

GLCs and statutory boards have also supported the government's policy of encouraging the financial industry since the 1980s. The fund-management industry, for example, first benefited from tax incentives in 1983, and the surplus funds of the GLCs and statutory boards have served as a bargaining chip to attract foreign fund managers to Singapore. By the mid-1980s the government was allowing private managers to invest state funds on the condition that they managed the investments from Singapore and brought in expertise (*Straits Times*, 3 January 1987). Contracting out the management of some government funds on these terms continued in the 1990s as part of the effort to build the fund-management industry (*Straits Times*, 16 February 1995).

A second, and related, element of the government's financial sector activity has been its direct control of financial assets. Those subject to government control include the assets of DBS, the Post Office Savings Bank (POSB, merged with DBS since 1998), public sector deposits lodged with the MAS, and investments in the Central Provident Fund (CPF), the compulsory retirement savings fund. Whereas in 1960 these government-controlled financial assets made up 11 percent of total financial assets in Singapore, since 1985 they have accounted for at least 45 percent.[28]

CPF contribution rates vary in accordance with changing economic conditions and thus serve as a macroeconomic policy lever. In periods of strong growth, contribution rates have been fixed at 20 percent of salary for both employee and employer (Tan 1996, 361). In the 1960s and 1970s, CPF and post office savings were invested almost entirely in government securities, providing the government with a low-cost source of noninflationary finance. After fiscal surpluses eliminated the need for this kind of funding, account holders were authorized to take more direct control over their CPF savings: since the 1980s they have been allowed to allocate a proportion to housing or welfare needs and, since the 1990s, to investment in financial markets, either privately or through approved fund managers (Tan 1996, 362–83). While decreasing the government's direct control over how these assets are used, these new freedoms support the government's welfare policy and its policy of encouraging the financial services industry.

Government and the Private Financial Sector

Quite apart from the role it plays in mediating savings, the financial sector is an important industry in its own right in Singapore. Finance is also an important business sector for Singapore's local, mostly ethnic Chinese, business class. Local entrepreneurs ventured into banking in the first half of the twentieth century, building on prior success in trade and Malayan resource industries, chiefly rubber (Lee 1974, 70–80; Paix 1993; Huff 1994, 208–35). The Chinese banks established before 1950 make up three of the "big four" local banks, the fourth being government-linked DBS; they are the Oversea-Chinese Banking Corporation (OCBC), Overseas Union Bank (OUB), and United Overseas Bank (UOB). Other entrants to the banking market after 1950 almost all disappeared as independent institutions in the 1970s and 1980s, absorbed by the large local banks. The two that remained into the 1990s, government-controlled Keppel Bank and Tat Lee Bank, merged in 1998.

The personal ties that link public and private actors in Singapore are particularly evident in the financial sector. Tat Lee Bank's founder, Goh Tjoei Kok, served on the boards of many GLCs in the 1970s, and at this time his bank was sufficiently linked with Lee Kuan Yew's family (a brother held a board position and was a minority shareholder) to prompt allegations in 1978 that the law firm connected with Lee Kuan Yew had intervened with the MAS to support Tat Lee Bank's acquisition of a license. The allegations were denied (*Straits Times*, 20 October 1994). The founder and major shareholder of OUB, Lien Ying Chow, served as Singapore's high commissioner to Malaysia in the 1960s (Lien 1992).

---

28. Based on official figures. See Hamilton-Hart 1999, 488, for further details.

Several of the bank's senior managers are well integrated in the Singaporean system of movement between public and private sectors (see, e.g., Owyang 1996). OCBC's connections with the public sector have been even more numerous and sustained. In 1996 a former long-term director of OCBC was a cabinet minister and another was the chief justice; four of nine board members had had senior appointments in the civil service or statutory authorities (the MAS and EDB); another (Michael Fam) had been associated with various GLCs; and one of the bank's substantial shareholders was a director of the Government Investment Corporation.

UOB's ties with government actors are also close. In 1980 the bank's managing director and major owner, Wee Cho Yaw, was reported to be "good friends with Lee [Kuan Yew] and other politicos"; the same article quoted a rival banker that there was "no question that Wee is a business statesman. The question is whether he should fulfill that role to a greater degree or look after his own interests more. It is the eternal philosophical conflict between public and private interest" (*Insight*, May 1980). As well as involving industry-wide joint bodies, ties between the bank and the state include partnerships with DBS and personnel overlap. In 1979, Wee appointed parliamentarian Tan Eng Liang as the general manager of a conglomerate partly owned by UOB. Francis Yeo was a senior MAS officer in the 1970s and a senior UOB manager in the 1980s and 1990s. Koh Beng Seng, the very senior MAS manager who resigned in 1997, joined UOB in 2000. Lim Chong Yah, who had held a number of public appointments and whose daughter married Lee Kuan Yew's second son, was a director of UOB. Lim Kim San, who served briefly as managing director of the MAS in the early 1980s and in many other public roles from the 1960s onward, was also involved with the bank in its early years.

Although relations between the local banks and the state sector are close, there are few signs that political favoritism has determined bank performance or hindered policy implementation. Given the relative performance of Singapore banks in Table 4.1, the bank that has most improved its position over time is the government-controlled DBS, established in 1968. Private banks have faced keen competition from DBS and the Post Office Savings Bank (Schulze 1990). Although the decision not to convert POSB into a full commercial bank followed protests from the local banks, the locals have not always been so successful; innovative moves by DBS in the early 1980s, for example, were unsuccessfully criticized as unfair (*Far Eastern Economic Review*, 8 February 1980). In 1998, POSB was absorbed by DBS, increasing the government bank's share of the banking market.

UOB also grew rapidly, relative to the other private banks, until 1980. Otherwise, the relative size of these banks' assets has been stable. Can UOB's growth be explained by its connections to state actors? There is no direct evidence of intervention in support of the bank, but in the Singaporean context such evidence would be extraordinarily difficult for outsiders to discover.[29] UOB's rapid expan-

29. One former MAS official did say that he knew of bankers who had asked politicians to intervene on their behalf, but he maintained that these instances were rare (interview, Singapore, July 1997).

Table 4.1. Singapore: Ranking of Local Banks

	1964		1972		1980		1995	
	$	No.	$	No.	$	No.	$	No.
DBS	—		0.95	3	7.0	2	72	1
OCBC	0.51	1	1.28	2	5.1	3	62	2
UOB	0.09	3	1.52	1	7.5	1	59	3
OUB	0.23	2	0.72	4	4.1	4	28	4
TLB	—		—	—	1.1	6	12	5

Sources: SGV-Goh Tan, *A Study of Commercial Banks in Singapore* (various years); Systems and Resource Management, *Comparative Survey of Commercial Banks in Singapore* (various years); annual reports of the banks.
Note: Ranking based on total assets in billions of dollars, excludes nonbank subsidiaries 1964–85 and group figures for 1995, except Tat Lee Bank.

sion in the early 1970s was mainly due to its acquisition of Chung Khiaw Bank in 1971 and Lee Wah Bank in 1973. Chung Khiaw's assets were larger than UOB's, but UOB, with capital and reserves nearly three times those of Chung Khiaw (UOB 1985, 53), was, objectively, the stronger bank. Its acquisitions were entirely consistent with the government policy of strengthening local banks and rationalizing the banking sector.

Another indicator that government favoritism has not played a large role in determining bank growth is the record of OCBC. Lee Kuan Yew's animosity toward OCBC's chairman (until 1983), Tan Chin Tuan, was reported to be "an open secret"—and the reason behind the preservation order placed on Raffles Hotel after it was bought by Tan, who had intended to use the site for development (*Insight*, January 1979). OCBC did lose ground to UOB during the 1970s, but OCBC was known as a particularly conservative bank at this time (Gill 1987). It has since maintained its position and, like UOB, acquired smaller banks.

The overall condition of the banking sector is another sign of consistent policy implementation. As the MAS has developed its regulatory role, the banks have been held to increasingly strict standards. They have had a low level of non-performing loans and high capital adequacy ratios. No local bank has failed outright in the postindependence period, nor have public funds been used to rescue banks in trouble—a notable achievement anywhere and a record that stands in contrast to that of most other countries in the region. The relative resilience of the local banks in the wake of the regional crisis of 1997–98 was noticeable in comparison with the severe problems experienced by other banks in Southeast Asia. The local banks did sustain losses, largely because of direct exposure to distressed markets in Asia, but the temporary losses or declines in profitability felt by the banks themselves had no significant public repercussions.

The financial policy regime under which Singapore banks operated before the regional crisis had evolved over time. The establishment of the MAS in 1971 centralized control over banks and other financial institutions. Given that most banks in Singapore are part of diversified financial sector business groups (many of which are linked to nonfinancial businesses as well), this centralization gave regulators a comprehensive view of the groups' operations and reduced the scope for financial firms to evade regulatory scrutiny. The MAS also acted early to increase reserve requirements, under which banks must keep a portion of their deposits in specified liquid assets such as government bills or cash balances with the MAS. Although reserve requirements are potentially monetary policy levers if varied, they were in fact set at around 18 percent from the 1970s to the late 1990s (Tan 1996, 38). They have thus mostly served prudential purposes, as well as being a moderate tax on financial intermediation.

The MAS tightened prudential controls in 1981, after former Finance Minister Goh Keng Swee became chairman. Under his leadership the MAS was seen by the banks as much more intrusive, even before the comprehensive Banking Act of 1984. The new act laid down further regulatory standards and provided the MAS with extensive discretionary powers. Amendments in 1993 increased capital requirements and changed bank secrecy laws to allow the authorities greater scope for inquiries and to let banks exchange credit information. Some restrictions have been further loosened since 1997 but only (as shown in Chapter 7) in conjunction with increased requirements relating to divestment of nonfinancial businesses and disclosure.

The financial policy implemented by the MAS has promoted rationalization of the banking sector since the 1970s. Unlike the proliferation seen in other developing countries, the number of banks in Singapore has been controlled. If groups are taken into account, the official figure of twelve local banks falls to six by the mid-1980s and five by 1998. The government, through the MAS, promoted many the mergers (see, e.g., Oei 1991, 86–97). Increasing the size of local banks through mergers was justified on the grounds that large banks are more resilient and more able to compete with foreign banks.

A similar policy of controlling entry and exit has held for other areas of the financial sector. The number of finance companies was reduced from ninety-six in 1965 to thirty-six in 1970 and then to twenty-seven by 1995. Informal financial institutions such as chit funds were practically eliminated in the early 1970s (MAS, *Annual Report*, 1972). The 1985 stock exchange crisis resulted in consolidation when, under MAS guidance, the local banks moved in to take over a fragmented brokerage system (MAS, *Annual Report*, 1985–86). Finally, discount houses, established under the auspices of the MAS in 1972 (Tan 1996, 190), were closed when changes to the government securities market in 1987 made them redundant.

Its pattern of interaction with the banks provides some indication of how the MAS was able to be an effective regulator. One factor that structured this interaction was the seriousness with which the MAS pursued its regulatory role. Its departments with regulatory and supervisory functions have always been allocated a significant share of the organization's human resources (in numbers, training, and prestige), rather than being subsidiary to its monetary policy functions and macroeconomists. A practical concern with regulation was probably also promoted by separating the MAS's regulatory role from the industrial policy role of the EDB. This meant that the MAS was never in the position of having simultaneously to nurture an industry through preferential credit schemes and to hold it to performance requirements—though the official shift, since 1998, to a more promotional role regarding the financial-services industry does introduce this kind of conflict.

Between 1981 and 1997 the MAS took its regulatory role seriously because its internal climate promoted an understanding of banking as an industry that needs controls even in good times. By its own account, its approach to regulation was anticipatory, seeking to nip problems in the bud and ensure that banks had adequate provisions and internal safety processes before problems arose (MAS 1981). Goh Keng Swee's reorganization of the MAS in 1981 marked a deliberate shift to more formalized relations with the banks. "We had been too chummy [with the banks] in the past," Goh explained. "I myself believe that a Central Bank, which is what the MAS is to the commercial banks, should keep a certain distance from commercial banks." The risk that the commercial banks might profit from information conveyed in informal contacts was "a good reason for not fraternising too much with bankers." He added that bankers were "not a protected or endangered species" (qtd. in *Straits Times*, 1 August 1982).

In the years after 1981, financial policy did not necessarily accord with the preferences of the financial sector. According to later Finance Minister Richard Hu, strengthened prudential regulations introduced from 1981 onward were "highly unpopular" (*Straits Times*, 13 April 1985). Enforcing these regulations frequently involved taking action that imposed costs on private sector actors. For example, in 1983 the MAS rejected the long-standing application for a banking license by the Hong Leong Finance group, the largest in Singapore and also a major property developer. The MAS also occasionally removed company directors—including one from Overseas Union Finance, a subsidiary of one of the "big four" banks—for violations of the law. Ng Quee Lam's wealth and position as the owner of Far Eastern Bank did not prevent his removal for misuse of the bank's funds and its takeover by UOB in the 1980s (*Straits Times*, 27 September 1986). Other disciplinary actions taken by the MAS have included imposing fines and requiring erring foreign bankers to leave the country (Tan 1996, 39). Local banks did not escape investigation of their property loans in the early 1980s and reportedly suffered along with the foreign banks after the MAS made banks increase their provisions. Domestic institutions were generally the focus of its prudential investigation but not to the exclusion of foreign banks (MAS 1981). Press commentary in 1984 that "few central banks in the world are viewed with the mixture of fear and dislike that the MAS has aroused among foreign bankers" (*Euromoney*, September 1984) was not that different from the views echoed in my interviews with foreign bankers in 1996 and 1997—all of whom requested anonymity to avoid appearing to criticize the MAS.

This kind of reputation not only confirms that the MAS was a strong regulator but also helps explain why this continued to be the case well after Goh Keng Swee, the principal force behind the stricter regulatory style after 1981, ceased to play an active role. That is, frequent demonstrations of official willingness to enforce standards would have contributed to establishing precedents for action by MAS officers. Rather than requiring the exceptional courage needed to undertake distinctly abnormal action, tough action conformed with accepted understandings of what the regulator's job involved. In addition, this kind of precedent is a deterrent to the violation of official standards: its threats were credible because the MAS repeatedly signaled that infractions were not likely to be tolerated.

Consequently, the considerable discretion accorded to the MAS has been a resource for the organization. Laws governing the financial sector make many activities subject to its approval. In the 1990s, for example, loan limits to individuals, the $5 million limit on Singapore dollar loans overseas, and limits on bank investments in other companies could all be exceeded if approved by the MAS (Tan 1996, 39–41). Such discretion has not provided banks with a means of extending their operations beyond the intent of regulators. Rather, it has produced a tendency among banks to ask for specific approval before developing new products or practices.[30]

A final element in the pattern of interaction between the MAS and the financial sector since the mid-1980s has been the practice of organized, industry-wide consultation through many committees and formal bodies. Although many of these structures existed earlier (and some are still similar to colonial arrangements), in 1985 the government formally committed itself to including the private sector in policy formulation and established a set of committees for this purpose. The Banking and Finance Subcommittee, a product of this initiative, has provided substantive financial policy inputs to government and the MAS. Thus, although the MAS gained a reputation for being an uncompromising regulator, it did consult with the financial sector. For example, it took note of the objections voiced by Stock Exchange of Singapore (SES) members to its draft bill for the securities industry in 1985 and "thus deferred the Bill pending further consultation with the SES" (MAS, *Annual Report*, 1985–86). The watchdog Supervisory Committee set up at this time comprised both MAS officers and bank and SES representatives (*Straits Times*, 5 December 1985). The MAS has also worked with the private sector in other supervisory bodies such as the Foreign Exchange and Money Market Practices Committee, which has regulatory and market development functions. Most recently, the various financial policy panels established by the government since 1997 have included more private sector than state representatives.

30. Interview, private bank, August 1997. See also Peebles and Wilson 1996, 153.

It is not clear how much the private sector exercises independent policy influence through these mechanisms. For an understanding of why the MAS has implemented policy according to its intent, however, the public nature and substantive agendas of these consultative groups may be important: they potentially constrain any tendency for personal ties between state and private actors to develop into favoritism or forbearance with regard to any particular bank. The visible and inclusive structure of industry representation on formal committees works against private collusion.[31]

Singapore's economic success since the 1960s—financial stability, high rates of per capita economic growth, high and increasing savings, low inflation, and rapid industrialization—may or may not be due to the government's active intervention in the economy. What is certain is that the Singapore government has used a variety of levers to intervene in the mobilization and allocation of financial assets. These levers have changed over time, but the degree of government control over financial resources and financial sector firms has not significantly decreased.[32] The fact that this government activity has been consistent with sustained positive economic outcomes demonstrates the wide area of potential policy choice available to the Singapore government.

The scope and success of financial policies and strategies in Singapore rest on the attributes of Singapore's state organizations. Government organizations developed norms of formality and legalism early in the colonial era and, later in the colonial period, a distinct bureaucratic identity and rationalized disciplinary systems. The transition to independence allowed for considerable administrative continuity and was followed by efforts to centralize political power and further strengthen government organizations. The governing system has not replicated Weber's prescription for rational-legal authority, but a strong concern with discipline, formal rewards, and selectivity is entrenched in both formal government organizations and the institutions that link public and private sectors. Their capacity to structure the behavior of individual officeholders is crucial to an understanding of why policy has been implemented according to its intent. This capacity has been at least as important as the specific policy choices themselves in accounting for Singapore's record of financial stability and economic growth.

31. Bodies such as the Banking and Finance Subcommittee scrupulously involve representatives from all the local banks and many foreign ones. Again, names, positions, and recommendations are on record.
32. Although a shift in policy is clear, much of the apparent decline in the government's presence in the economy since 1990 is the product of recategorizing certain sources of revenue and public sector assets. See Hamilton-Hart 1999, 183–86, 196–99.

5.

Malaysia: Partial Discipline

In 1999 a large billboard in Kuala Lumpur proclaimed, in Malay, English, and Chinese, "Foreign Interference Threatens National Stability." The sign was posted in the dilapidated inner-city area of Chow Kit, the scene of violent racial riots in 1969, and not far from where demonstrations against the government had taken place in 1998. The billboard both located outside Malaysia the source of recent internal disturbances—presumably in the form of foreign currency speculators and outspoken American officials—and invoked an enduring national trauma: political contention that had spiraled into serious violence and ushered in a massive thirty-year program of interethnic redistribution. The message could easily be interpreted as yet another attempt by the Malaysian government to use foreigners and the specter of instability as means of managing internal dissent. What is less readily explained is why the tactic has worked so well in Malaysia.

To say that it has worked is of course a relative judgment. Yet in its own terms the government's pursuit of stability through an ethnically based political economy has been remarkably successful, managing troublesome communal relations in such a way that Malaysia, since 1969, has avoided the violence and instability often associated with ethnically fragmented polities (Tilman 1961, 191; Esman 1994). It engineered a significant redistribution of economic assets while maintaining, overall, exceptionally high rates of economic growth. It used financial resources, including control over the banking system, as a major instrument of economic policy while maintaining financial stability most of the time.

Sheer luck no doubt played a role in these achievements, but they also rest on identifiable attributes of Malaysia's public sector. Although the Malaysian state that emerged after independence was, like its colonial predecessor, quite a long way from Weber's rational-legal ideal type, particular organizations had structures, routines, and norms that distinguished them from their institutional environment. Malaysia's central bank was one of the more rationalized organizations, and its governing capacity was a significant factor behind the success of the country's financial policies. Other state organizations always displayed mixed tendencies. In addition, the deliberate erosion of bureaucratic structures and an increasingly blurred distinction between public and private spheres in the 1980s tended to undermine the capacity of state organizations to implement certain policies in a consistent, rule-abiding way. This aspect of Malaysia's state organizations helps explain why, in addition to policy successes, there have been many undoubted cases of failure, when policy goals were either not achieved or achieved at great cost.

STATE AND FINANCE IN THE COLONIAL ERA

The territory of present-day Malaysia does not correspond with a single administrative or political unit from the colonial era. From the end of the eighteenth century, British influence in the area expanded slowly and ambiguously with regard to territorial scope, legal sovereignty, and functional authority. Colonial rule also took on a variety of institutional forms in different places, resulting in a fragmented structure of government which solidified inside the borders of modern Malaysia only in 1965. In 1874, four states on the Malay peninsula, Selangor, Pahang, Perak, and Negri Sembilan (yet to take shape as a single unit), came under British "protection" through treaties with local rulers. They were formally constituted as the Federated Malay States (FMS) in 1896. The government in Singapore posted advisers known as residents to these states and exercised increasingly direct authority in them. In contrast, the five Unfederated Malay States (UMS), which made up the rest of the Malay peninsula, retained varying degrees of autonomy until 1919. Siamese suzerainty coexisted with informal British influence and local authority in the UMS until 1909. The extent of Siamese involvement in these states was more symbolic than practical for most of the time, and following an agreement with the British in 1902, the "Siamese Adviser" to the ruler of Kelantan was actually one of Siam's British civil servants (Gullick 1992, 144). The states that now make up East Malaysia, Sabah and Sarawak, remained subject to semiprivate colonial rule long after the end of company rule elsewhere, being governed by a trading company and a British family, respectively. The crown later took over responsibility for these territories, and they merged with the Malayan states only with the formation of Malaysia in 1963.

The Malay states were closely connected to Singapore, the administrative and commercial center of an area that came to be known as Malaya. Johor in particular, well before its formal incorporation into the colonial system from 1910, came within the sphere of British influence as a result of its physical, social, and economic proximity to Singapore and the intimate dealings between the rulers of Johor and the government of Singapore (Trocki 1990).[1] Government in the Malay states did not develop along entirely the same lines as in Singapore, but the transformation of state and finance in Singapore was an essential part of developments on the peninsula. In the area of money and finance there was virtually no distinction to be made: as the somewhat vague boundaries of Malaya extended outward from Singapore, so the banks, coinages, and systems for financial governance centered on Singapore spread out over a single financial system.

---

1. Although the Anglo-Johor Treaty of 1885 provided for the appointment of a British agent in an advisory role, no adviser was actually appointed until 1910. See Gullick 1992, 111–16.

The Colonial State
In the first decades of the residential system, limited financial and administrative resources prevented residents from expanding their role. Until the early twentieth century they relied on the same revenue-farming systems that the Malay rulers had used and, in consequence, were forced to carry on local government through the same system of local Malay headmen. The Chinese communities, which bore the brunt of taxation, were governed in practice by Chinese revenue farmers. The early residents were a mixed bag. According to Heussler (1981, 40–45), Perak's resident was the colonial secretary, "who had come from the Royal Navy via Ceylon; Selangor got a prominent Straits lawyer; Sungei Ujong, an army officer. One Assistant Resident was a free-booter and the other a Straits Settlements cadet on secondment." They governed in an atmosphere of improvisation and local discretion, with few European officials (about fifty by the 1890s). Recruitment continued to be haphazard, and "eccentric methods of entry remained possible," with planters and personal friends of serving officials joining government service. Appointments could still be made on the strength of letters from leading merchants, and in 1895 the patronage system was still operating more or less unchanged in the Malay states.

Rules concerning nonsalary income changed more slowly in the Malay states than in Singapore. In 1874 the British Colonial Office considered a potential resident questionable because of his business connections, but the governor in Singapore supported him on the grounds that his personal ties to powerful Malay aristocrats would make him effective. The idea of limiting residents' commercial activity was raised in 1888, but several officials argued that commercial ventures were necessary, given their "minuscule salaries." Frank Swettenham, who had served in Malaya since 1870 and was later to become governor, argued that land dealings were common and not prejudicial to the public interest. He himself was involved in many land transactions—which were recorded under his wife's name, at the suggestion of the governor (Heussler 1981, 43). In 1904, just after his retirement, Swettenham acquired a large land grant from the Sultan of Johor. The deal reportedly scandalized the Colonial Office, but Swettenham's later honors and role as a government adviser suggest that the taint was minimal (Gullick 1992, 129–32, 369).

By 1900 it was "understood that officers could not take part in the running of businesses and could not invest in companies with which they dealt in the course of their official duties," but this understanding was not strictly enforced. When the resident of Perak was investigated in 1907 for promotional activity on behalf of a mining company, the Colonial Office found that the man, "who was popular with the business community, had often come under fire from his superior for laxity of this kind. As governor of North Borneo, a quasi-commercial position, he had accepted a piece of land and a house in return for some tin-bearing land wanted by his benefactor. Against regulations, he had allowed two government doctors to continue inspecting brothels for private remuneration" (Heussler 1981, 128–29). Despite Colonial Office disapproval, the resident remained in his post until his scheduled retirement in 1910, after which he was knighted. By the 1930s, rules prohibiting officers from speculation or the ownership of assets that might create a conflict of interest with their duties were, according to a later report, taken to mean all interests in commercial undertakings in Malaya and strictly enforced. Until then, however, they were applied more liberally (Commissioners' Report 1955, app.).

Other moves to rationalize government organizations were made around the turn of the century but took hold only over the next two decades. In 1895 the government decided that all officers should be recruited by examination, a move that was regretted by many senior officials, who believed that the different nature of government in the Malay states meant that more experienced, versatile managers were required. In rural areas officials continued to be multifunctional administrators and magistrates right into the inter–World War years. One district officer who retired only in the 1920s built up intimate local bonds over twenty-seven years of "arbitrary personal rule" in Perak. "What he had created by then was a self-contained feudal satrapy, leisurely in its pace of life, traditional, and rural, ignorant of and indifferent to the humming, interracial society to the south" (Heussler 1981, 42–48, 124–26). He was, however, the last of a dying breed. Officials recruited in the 1920s would still be responsible for large and remote areas, might continue to dispense summary justice, and simultaneously occupy several functional positions (Gilmour 1974, 55, 38–41), but regular rotation and changing rules left open no possibility of personal fiefdoms.

One change was simply in the size and scope of government. The Colonial Office, conceded that Malaya's increasing prosperity both created a need for a larger administration, and produced revenues to maintain one. With the support of members of the commercial community, salaries were increased in the early 1920s. Before then, junior salaries were insufficient, in the eyes of contemporaries, to support "normal" family life, and officials had been leaving to join the business sector. After the increases the civil service in Malaya moved from being the least sought colonial service to one of the most popular (Tilman 1964, 47; Heussler 1981, 269). The change in salaries and conditions were later cited as a reason for the relative lack of corruption at the middle and senior levels of the service (Commissioners' Report 1955).[2]

The growth of business in the first decades of the twentieth century, therefore, supported an extension of government activity and a change in governing style. As "the atmosphere that officers worked in became steadily more commercial, the government grew more and more bureaucratic" (Heussler 1981, 135, 126). Internal organizational concerns and records multiplied. The pre–World War II Malayan Civil List, for example, minutely recorded each officer's career (Gilmour 1974, 28). The practice of file annotation in which every report had to make its

2. According to the report, most corruption was confined to petty incidents among clerks of the railway and customs services.

way through each level of the hierarchy, receiving the appropriate initials at each stage, was a well-known and sometimes notorious feature of the system (Tilman 1964). An increase in morale among officials saw the end of an earlier sense of inferiority (Heussler 1981, 115–18).

These conditions provided the basis for the colonial administration's pursuit of goals that were independent of those of the British business community. It was, however, frequently thwarted in achieving these goals by its own lack of resources and by business opposition (White 1996). Individuals could take energetic action against European interests but also recognized limits to how much annoyance they could cause. For example, one official recalled seizing consignments of rubber from an estate in the 1930s and auctioning the goods to pay wages owed to the estate's laborers, but another official did not have to courage to charge the largest rubber estate in the district for failing to provide its workers with adequate facilities (Gilmour 1974, 38, 86).

Elements of the local population and local systems of rule were not fully subsumed by the emerging colonial state. The fragmented political systems on the Malay peninsula onto which the British grafted colonial institutions consisted of units with loosely defined borders and, to European eyes, hardly any government (Gullick 1958). These polities were centered on and defined by the person of the ruler, the Raja, who held a monopoly on the granting of social status. Government was largely ceremonial; politics, in the sense of activity that requires the development of a public sphere differentiated from private concerns, was unknown until the nineteenth century and developed only in the early twentieth (Milner 1995).

Because of the ambiguities of the residential system and the status of the UMS, "traditional" authority existed alongside the colonial state yet had changed even before the formalization of colonial rule. Commerce, intellectual exchange, and the changing nature of colonial government altered the relationship between Malay rulers and subjects (Jomo 1986; Milner 1995). The residential system from 1874 broke the ties that had existed between Malay rulers and local Chinese revenue farmers, with the rulers increasingly turning to Western banks to supplement their official salaries (Gullick 1992, 372–75). Members of the Malay aristocracy began to be remunerated through fixed salaries, compensation for their loss of traditional influence (Heussler 1981, 129).

The rulers in the UMS reacted to the extension of colonial authority in the FMS by developing their own government systems: authority was still personal, exercised by the ruler or influential aristocrats, but entirely new bureaucracies and legal institutions emerged before the consolidation of colonial rule (Gullick 1992, 138–63). Although these government organizations became less personalized over time, the changes were often slow and contested. In Trengganu, for example, the first British agent arrived in 1909, but despite seizing on the local court system as a target of reform, not until the 1930s were he and his successors able to bring the local justice system into line with norms prevailing elsewhere in Malaya (Sutherland 1980).

Malays were drawn into the colonial bureaucracy in increasingly formal ways from the early twentieth century. By 1915 there were twenty-five in the civil service outside the Malay Administrative Service, and during the war years a shortage of European personnel meant that more Malays were drawn into colonial government (Heussler 1981, 131–35). The Malay Administrative Service, however, became the focus of attempts to develop Malay bureaucrats after 1910.[3] Junior to the mainly European Malayan Civil Service, it was nonetheless prestigious. Many recruits were trained at the Malay College, established as an elite institution supposedly along the lines of an English public school, whose main function was to socialize and educate boys for the civil service. Many of the students came from aristocratic or royal backgrounds, and the college worked hard at instilling in them a sense of pride and tradition. It was an intensive experience, involving (for some) several years of residence and round-the-clock supervision. Forming a common background for many Malay civil servants from both the FMS and UMS, it may have given them a shared identity. The Malay College, the Malay Administrative Service, and other areas of government in which Malays worked were part of the increasingly rationalized colonial state. The college emphasized legal and administrative training, including the niceties of drafting memos, taking minutes, and filing. Malay civil servants, even on lower levels of pay than Europeans, were able to live in a manner closer to the European population than most locals. Salary schemes were designed to avoid the personal indebtedness of government employees.

On the other hand, the training and treatment of Malay administrators reflected a mixed set of standards. The Malay College, for example, was at least as concerned with the development of its students' characters as with their practical skills. Low academic standards meant that passing the British school-leaving exams often took several attempts—the cause of some hand-wringing but at least partially reflecting the aims of the officials involved in establishing the college. One stipulated that a prospective teacher for the Malay College should "above all be fond of and used to boys. Previous training in teaching is not necessary. A considerable proportion of the master's work will be out of school. He should be athletic, a University man and a gentleman. . . . the school is one where Malays, generally of good birth are being instructed in the English language and the English notions of honour and duty, so as to fit them to take part in the administration of their country, and they [the Crown Agents] should be requested to pay more attention to the manners, bearing and personality of the selected candidates than to [their] scholastic attainments" (qtd. in Khasnor 1984, 30).

In other respects too, the standards of a rational-legal bureaucracy did not fully apply to the colonial government's incorporation of Malays. There was the obvious compromise of meritocratic principles in the reluctance to promote Malay officers, although the notion of merit had pervaded the system enough that it was fre-

---

3. This account of the Malay College and Malay Administrative Service draws on Khasnor 1984.

quently used by some as a reason for treating Malay officers in a more nearly equal fashion—and by others for not doing so. In addition there was a confusion of purpose in what the Malay official was meant to represent. Malay administrators were valuable intermediaries with Malay rulers, but residual ties to traditional authority systems could put them in ambiguous positions: the status that aristocratic birth or honors conferred by a Malay ruler entitled them to could conflict with their official position. Increasingly, their official status won out: although the Malay Administrative Service inherited some traditions of the ruling class, "it was more obviously a professional civil service cadre associated with the colonial regime and imbued with its ethos," according to J. M. Gullick (1992, 106).

Overall, by the end of the colonial period, government had developed into a rule-based system of administration with formally delineated functional organizations that emphasized correct procedure, written regulations, and systematized personnel management. It was held to be reasonably efficient and coherent, if focused on a narrow set of concerns: law and order, internal administration, and road building (Jones 1953). The transformation of government organizations in the colonial era was drawn out over many decades, however, and rational-legal Weberian standards contended with personalized practices and ascriptive principles until late in the colonial period.

Money and Banking: A System Centered on Singapore
Malaya's financial system was an offshoot of that of the Straits Settlements, and Singapore, the administrative center, remained the center of the Malayan financial system. The changing regulation of money in Singapore, described in Chapter 4, determined the situation in Malaya. Almost all institutions for managing the financial system were based in Singapore, from the banks' own systems to the gradual assumption of government responsibility for money. The Currency Board's notes, issued from 1899, circulated in the rest of Malaya and in Borneo. In 1938, peninsula Malaya was formally incorporated into the currency area overseen by the board, followed in 1950 by Brunei, Sarawak, and North Borneo. These territories thereby gained representation on the board and received a share in its profits (Lee 1990, 15–18, 278).

The local needs of a larger, more remote territory meant that the limits of Singapore's liberal system were felt more strongly in the rest of Malaya. In the 1880s the threat of a government note issue was used to encourage the extension of banking facilities from Penang to Perak and other native states. The Hongkong Bank, however, did not move onto the peninsula until much later, and the other major bank, the Chartered Bank, could only be induced to move into Perak in 1889, explains Frank King, only "if the Government granted it a number of 'compensations' for the losses it expected to sustain in the 'public service,' a policy which would be accepted many years later when banks were reluctant to move into the less-developed East-coast states. Six years later the Chartered Bank decided that in Perak, 'apart from the convenience to the Government, there is no field for banking operations,' and closed down its agency." The absence of banking facilities in the Malay states also prompted some vague consideration of establishing state banks to operate there as early as 1884. The acting governor, however, dismissed the idea as expensive and useless (King 1987, 348–49).

The British banks operating in Singapore dominated banking activity in the rest of Malaya. Their branches remained restricted to the major commercial centers, largely on the west coast, and their regional headquarters were in Singapore. Chinese banks became increasingly important over time, and by the late 1950s the Oversea-Chinese Banking Corporation had more branches on the peninsula than the largest British-owned bank. The biggest Chinese banks also had their headquarters in Singapore. This devolution of responsibility for banking-system stability to Singapore eliminated the need for prudential regulation by government in Kuala Lumpur. There, government relations with the major commercial banks were friendly, with bank managers drawn into government social functions and government business accounting for a large proportion of the banks' activity. In the case of the Chartered Bank, for example, government deposits could make up as much as 30 percent of its total deposits (Singh 1984, 30). Government officials were involved in managing private financial resources only through the post office savings system, itself an institution with origins in Singapore.

STATE ORGANIZATIONS IN INDEPENDENT MALAYSIA

Malaya's transition to independence in 1957 occurred in conditions that were conducive to the development of state organizations. Whereas Indonesian nationalism and social mobilization made the continuation of colonial rule after World War II impossible in the Indies, Malaya's sultans marshaled popular support behind their demands for constitutional arrangements that protected their prerogatives. Independence took a back seat to their conservative agenda and came a full twelve years after the end of World War II, in circumstances of economic stability. As well as stabilization, significant political centralization and state development occurred in this period. An active communist insurgency gave the central government the rationale it needed to increase its authority over the state governments and to expand the personnel and practical reach of its bureaucratic organizations (Stubbs 1997).

Independence itself was a bureaucratic process in which new governing arrangements came into being through a structured process of committees and commissions, which generated a heavy paper flow of reports and recommendations. The concentration of educated Malays in the bureaucracy meant that Malay participants in these preparations included many serving or former civil servants. The organization of government departments and ministries, their traditions, hierarchies, filing systems, and routines, persisted with apparently little change into the 1960s (Tilman 1964). Of nonexpatriate senior civil servants in 1960, all but one had entered government service between 1941 and 1952 (Tilman 1961, 196). Expatriate officials were phased out slowly, allowing time for further training of lower-level bureaucrats and sponsored university education for school leavers (Federation of Malaya 1956a, 1956b). The last expatriates were not replaced until the late 1960s (Crouch 1996, 131).

The senior bureaucracy was "thoroughly permeated by an appreciation of the necessity of empirical observation, deliberation and rational decision-making," wrote Robert Tilman (1964, 132). The service had internal norms of formality and discipline. Recruitment and promotions were made largely on merit-based criteria by a central Public Service Commission (Tilman 1961). Negligible numbers of officials had aristocratic connections.[4] Rather, the high status of bureaucratic positions was due to relatively high salaries and the historical association with the Malay aristocracy (Kahar 1973, 144).

The main ascriptive standard affecting recruitment was the requirement that the ratio of Malays to non-Malays be four-to-one and three-to-one in the elite Malayan Civil Service and Foreign Service respectively. Nevertheless, the distribution of senior positions shows that ethnic Malays were not overwhelmingly favored (Tilman 1964, 69–70). In later years, Chinese and Indian Malaysians continued to hold very senior public sector positions, especially in the technical departments, but having the generalist Malay officers of the MCS (later known as the home and foreign service) oversee these departments was cited as a cause of internal friction and inefficiency (Esman 1972, 78).

Some efforts were made to transmit traditions to the new generation of civil servants. A speech by a Malay official to a group of new recruits referred to the MCS as "a service with great traditions which has produced many important figures in this country." To uphold its standards, the recruits were told, "you will have to choose your friends carefully so that no one can say that you are in a position to show favour to them in your official capacity. While there is every reason that you should be civil and on good terms with members of the general public it is certainly not desirable that you should always be seen in the company of towkays [Chinese businessmen] and business officials" (qtd. in Tilman 1964, 112–13).

The structures and norms of the bureaucracy meant that the personnel of the higher civil service constituted a "solidary group of people" with a sense of "belonging together to a corporate body which is structurally and organizationally placed in authority roles of great importance," wrote A. Kahar Bador (1973, 145). At the end of the 1960s the prestige and pay offered by government service were still attractive, and there was a perception that government was able to recruit the best and brightest (Esman 1972, 7–8, 68–70). Through the 1970s the civil service

4. Several civil servants from modest backgrounds rose to very senior positions. See, e.g., Doh 1985.

grew rapidly in numbers and distributed increasing amounts of government revenue.[5]

Senior bureaucrats were influential, but the political leadership was firmly in control of the bureaucracy (Puthucheary 1978, 44–45; Esman 1972, 135). One factor masking the extent of political influence was the close alignment of elite bureaucrats and the first generation of ruling politicians. Normal civil service rules on bureaucratic neutrality were waived for the preindependence United Malays Nationalist Organization (UMNO) leadership, which included serving bureaucrats.[6] All dominant groups had gone through the same process of socialization and had an interest in the same rules. It was only in the context of a consensus among elites that one could speak of the bureaucratic neutrality (in the Weberian sense) of the MCS (Tilman 1964, 118–20). Adding to the image of a bureaucratic elite, the Malayanization of the bureaucracy reduced the close intermingling of bureaucrats and businessmen in social settings. Relationships between them were far from unknown, however, and retired civil servants did take up positions as directors in private firms and banks.

Nonetheless, the links between business and government tended to be mediated by politicians. This became increasingly obvious after 1969, when the politics of ethnicity became institutionalized in a massive expansion of the state apparatus. Malaysia had inherited an ethnically fragmented society in which the three main groups, Indian, Chinese, and Malay, tended to occupy separate economic and social positions. Commerce, finance, and industry were largely in Chinese or European hands. When the politically privileged position held by Malays appeared to be threatened by the results of the 1969 general election, intercommunal relations broke down in a period of rioting and violence in Kuala Lumpur.

The events of 1969 prompted a serious reappraisal of economic and political arrangements, resulting in a long-term program known as the National Economic Policy or NEP.[7] Its aims were to eradicate poverty and to restructure society so as to eliminate the identification of race with economic position. The NEP thus aimed at the virtual creation of a *Bumiputera*, or indigenous Malaysian, business class.[8] Given the lack of wealth and business expertise among *Bumiputeras*, the public sector accumulated and managed economic assets on their behalf. This was explicit in the trusteeship element of the NEP—which created large holding companies and investment schemes (Mehmet 1986)—and implicit in most of the other initiatives that expanded state economic activity after 1970.

The reorientation of public policy left its imprint on state organizations, which were seized on as instruments of the new political economy. Ultimately, this left

---

5. From 60,500 in 1950 the bureaucracy expanded to 522,000 in 1983 (Mehmet 1986, 9; Evers 1987, 672).
6. The UMNO is the dominant party in the coalition governments that have ruled Malaysia since independence.
7. On the political economy of the NEP, see Jesudason 1989; and Bowie 1991.
8. *Bumiputera* refers to "indigenous Malaysians"; it includes other groups as well as Malays, but Malays dominate the category, so I use the terms interchangeably.

many parts of the bureaucracy weaker and less able to implement policy consistently. Initially, however, the successes of the NEP were made possible by preexisting bureaucratic capacities. The NEP itself was in a sense a product of Malaysia's bureaucracy: when the violence of 1969 led to the suspension of parliamentary government, senior officials were "the indispensable steel frame which . . . held this precarious state together even when the political processes failed," wrote Milton Esman (1972, v). Political leadership and political institutions were also critical. The suspension of Parliament was temporary, and Malaysia returned to its previous party-based governing system within two years. These parties proved to be enduring institutions, able to survive generational and leadership changes.

Against the backdrop of a relatively institutionalized political system, the nature of Malaysia's state organizations both enabled a substantial part of the NEP and placed limits on it. The bureaucracy asked to carry out much of its policy was disciplined and effective when it came to such tasks as revenue-gathering and data-collecting; however, contemporaries perceived it to be insufficiently responsive, flexible, or oriented toward developmental goals. Consequently, the most interventionist initiatives associated with the NEP were carried on outside the core bureaucracy, by agencies or state-owned enterprises that were less subject to central auditing or civil service rules. Some of these managed to develop reasonable standards of efficiency and discipline, but recurrent scandals and high costs dogged many (Bowie 1991; Jomo 1995).

Over the longer term, the ability of public sector organizations to implement interventionist policies consistently was constrained by the private goals of the NEP and personalized links between political and business spheres. Not only was the public sector to be a major player in the economy; it was also intended, by some at least, to be the personal training ground of *Bumiputera* entrepreneurs, the avenue whereby they would advance to positions of power and wealth. Significantly, this view was held by Mahathir Mohamad, prime minister from 1981 onward, who wrote that "Malays must be made to realize that work with the Government is merely a stepping stone to better things" (1970, 107). The orientation of state organizations to private interests was thus a feature of the shift toward a state-led economy. Later, it provided the foundation for a shift to policies of privatization.

Ties between political and business actors were a mixture of formally recognized public connections and informal relations. From the early years of independence, Chinese political parties were more or less explicit voices for Chinese business interests. UMNO and the Malaysian Chinese Association or MCA (the main Chinese party in the ruling coalition) made their own forays into business in the late 1940s. Significant party businesses were established in the 1970s and rapidly grew into large corporate groups (Gomez 1994). Informal intervention by political actors was important for advancing the interests of Malay individuals through state enterprises and contracts (Gale 1981; Gomez and Jomo 1997). Prominent Malay politicians were also in business on their own account by the

1970s, although at this stage their numbers were small. Both Malay and Chinese politicians developed relationships with business actors which combined patronage, joint ventures between state and private firms, commercial exchanges, and political party funding (Heng 1992; Gomez 1999). These links became increasingly important after 1970, as Chinese businesspeople sought to protect their interests in response to the ethnic bias in public policy and as *Bumiputera* individuals seized on opportunities for easy profits opened by the NEP.[9]

Although the seeds of change had been planted much earlier, developments in the 1980s altered the capacities of some state organizations. The high proportion of politicians and UMNO members with extensive business involvement was a development of the 1980s (Doh 1985, 109–15; Leigh 1992). The major public policy initiative of the decade, the privatization of many state assets and functions, was the primary means by which this close identity of political and business interests occurred. The NEP, which had brought about the preceding increase in state economic activity, had always been intended to create a class of Malay entrepreneurs. The beneficiaries of "state" activism and retreat were thus identical, with many of the individuals who profited from privatizations in the 1980s having been nurtured in state projects in the 1970s.[10]

Given the preexisting mechanisms that allowed politicians to intervene in the affairs of state organizations, this change increased intervention in policy implementation. There had been a perceived rise in corruption during the 1970s, much of it associated with the agencies established to advance *Bumiputera* interests outside the core civil service (Mansoor 1979; Gale 1981; Mehmet 1986). As the number of entrepreneurs whose businesses depended on government favor increased, so did the number of people with an interest in exploiting this avenue of influence. Later, the divestment of party assets to trusted individuals moved political party business interests further from the public domain and made them subject to more opaque, informal processes: ownership, control, and influence all became harder to verify but open to wide-ranging speculation.

Concurrent with policies of privatization, Mahathir aimed to make the civil service more responsive to the private sector (Root 1996, 65–89). Reforms in the 1980s moved the pay and career structure away from the security of a career system, creating further scope for political influence and decreasing the salience of intraorganizational reward and disciplinary systems. Think tanks and consultants began to carry out some of the studies formerly the province of the civil service. Declining salaries, status, and influence, combined with increased opportunities in the private sector, reduced civil service attractiveness as a career choice. Anecdotal reports suggest that the problem of recruiting and retaining skilled personnel increased significantly from this time. The concurrent concentration of power in the hands of the prime minister gave Mahathir the means to drive

---

9. See, e.g., Yoshihara 1988, 93; and Jesudason 1989, 152.
10. On the move from state to "privatized patronage," see Jomo 1995; and Gomez and Jomo 1997.

these changes through and defend his position within UMNO (Means 1991, 215–19).

Alternative arenas of policy formulation grew out of Mahathir's initiatives to bring public and private sectors together under the concept of "Malaysia Inc." The Malaysian Business Council (MBC) became the major institutional expression of the amalgamation of political, business, and civil service spheres.[11] MBC reports repeatedly asserted a common interest and partnership between government and business, but the principles on which this partnership was structured were mixed: a regularized, organizational notion of interest concentrated in the official sector competed with systems of collaboration based on individual relationships, particularistic gains, and ascriptive principles. At the 1993 MBC meeting, discussion of a paper on Malaysia Inc. included the call to give the business sector access to permanent officials, thereby "minimising the involvement of elected officials"—possibly an acknowledgment of political influence-peddling. There was also a call for decisions to follow standardized rules rather than allowing for discretion. The May 1995 meeting recognized that retention in the civil service was a serious problem but did not advance a solution. An MBC paper on meeting international challenges expressed a vision of general rather than sectorally specific goals and (the paper was based on input by officials) contrasted them critically with the private sector focus on "short-term benefits rather than long-term interests" (MBC 1995).

In contrast to Singaporean practices, the pattern of public-private collaboration in Malaysia reveals a low priority given to performance-based criteria. Mahathir frequently argued that privileges were granted on the basis of ability, but many government contracts were not allocated on the basis of demonstrated expertise (see, e.g., Gomez 1994, 92–93). And most of those who fell from grace did so for political reasons or because of the involvement of foreign regulators, not because they failed to implement the projects they were tasked with. People such as Eric Chia, associated with financial irregularities and serious problems at a large state-owned enterprise, continued to attend MBC meetings. Successful prosecutions of prominent people by the Anti-Corruption Agency (ACA) were rare.[12] It was wryly suggested that a rule-based system of government would emerge when Malaysian prison wardens started morning assemblies with the greeting "Datuk-Datuk dan Tan Sri–Tan Sri."[13]

Even so, the normalization of corruption and toleration of underperformance in return for political loyalty was not completely pervasive. In comparative surveys of corruption carried out in the 1980s and early 1990s, Malaysia was consistently

---

11. The MBC has met regularly since 1991 and has a number of semipermanent working groups on different sectoral issues. See MBC 1996; and Root 1996, 82–84.

12. The ACA was reduced to proposing that top government posts be reserved for those with strong religious values (*Straits Times*, 7 July 1997).

13. Professor Jomo K. S., reported in *Straits Times*, 15 July 1997. Datuk and Tan Sri are honorific titles awarded to almost all successful politicians and businesspeople. The greeting could be translated as "Honored Sirs."

in the middle ranks, among countries such as Japan and South Korea (Root 1996, xv). Patronage-based links between business and political actors were common but were not the only ways of structuring private-sector activity. Many cases demonstrated the scope for more rule-based entrepreneurship and institutionalized modes of influence. The Malaysian environment supported both patterns (Gomez 1999; Searle 1999). Pockets of rationalized administration and institutionalized representation endured in some bureaucratic organizations and in the formal structures of interethnic accommodation.

BANK NEGARA MALAYSIA AND THE FINANCIAL SYSTEM

Bank Negara Malaysia (BNM) was established as the central bank in 1959. It had a planned and carefully structured birth and assumed responsibilities gradually (Lee 1987). Currency issue was left to the Currency Board in Singapore until 1967, and fixed exchange rates and exchangeability at par with the Singapore currency until 1973 meant that no active monetary policy was attempted until the 1970s. Thus the new central bank had more than a decade to concentrate on internal organization and the regulation and development of the banking system.

The Central Bank: Establishment and Internal Organization
Bank Negara quickly established a reputation for high levels of staff expertise.[14] In the 1960s the central bank was the source of most authoritative economic reporting in (or outside) government, and its staff and assessments were often used in other departments. BNM also made use of outside expertise: the first governor (1959–62) came from the Commonwealth Bank of Australia and other staff came from Reserve Banks of Australia and India. Two advisers from the IMF were also present in 1970. After this, although ad hoc consultants were employed, BNM did not host the kind of semipermanent advisers that remained at the Indonesian central bank in the 1980s.

Since BNM was established outside formal civil service structures, pay rates were higher, and it was able to attract top graduates in economics and accounting. It awarded scholarships for secondary and tertiary education from 1961, sponsored postgraduate training abroad for employees, and opened an internal training institute in 1971. From 1970 the bank's scholarship scheme was open to Malaysians of all races, a significant concession to merit over ethnicity in the Malaysian context. A regular system of postentry training for policy and support staff was in place early on, and Bank Negara was the prime mover behind the establishment of the Southeast Asian Central Bank training center in Kuala Lumpur in the early 1970s.

---

14. Unless otherwise identified, the BNM material is taken from Singh 1984, the annual reports of the central bank, and interviews with former staff carried out in 1996.

New departments were added as the central bank acquired new responsibilities. In addition, major reorganization (with less obvious rationale) occurred in the early 1970s, mid-1980s, and 1990s. After increasing steadily, staff numbers were reduced following a review process started in early 1995.[15] Most of the retrenchments were due to the closure of six of the twelve branches and increasing computerization. There was no loss of graduate-stream officers, and the review involved nothing like the upheaval that the Monetary Authority of Singapore went through in 1981. The number of staff receiving long-service awards each year increased over time. At senior levels, long incumbency in some positions and a lack of rotation were cited in internal reviews of 1980 and 1981 as a problem (BNM 1981a).

Bank Negara's status owed a lot to its first Malaysian governor, Tun Ismail Mohamed Ali (1962–80). His competence, attention to detail, and demands for meticulous work and conduct were legendary. Tun Ismail was reportedly held in high respect, if not fear, by most of the banks. Friendship with the finance minister in the early 1960s and family connections with other members of Malaysia's political elite added to the central bank's influence. Although Tun Ismail's management style was formal and suggested nothing of the fatherly patron, Bank Negara's authority was in some ways dependent on him. His tendency toward micromanagement and the use of consultants was, according to a former employee, damaging to staff morale and commitment.

On the other hand, BNM was concerned about the morale and commitment of its staff. Internal reviews in the early 1980s suggesting that morale was a problem prompted moves to open up communication channels and improve the assessment system (BNM 1981b). Bank Negara was much more conscious of itself as an organization than either Bank Indonesia or the Monetary Authority of Singapore. Unlike those central banks, BNM published a number of commemorative volumes, a collection of speeches by bank officials, and a commissioned history of the central bank that focuses on its organization and people rather than financial policy (Singh 1984; BNM 1989). The bank also had internal practices that may have been attempts to inculcate identification with the organization, from a song ("BNM Forever") to induction courses aimed at generating commitment (BNM 1981a). Also in contrast to the reports of the Indonesian central bank, Bank Negara's annual reports would note staff movements, comment on changes in directors, and give an account of "housekeeping" developments such as progress on new buildings, training schemes, staff welfare initiatives, and the award of public honors to staff. The commemorative history was prominently displayed and available for sale at the bank.

Tun Ismail believed in the importance of developing organizational traditions, saying in a speech that "my chief role and responsibility, as head of the Central Bank in these early years of its existence, is to attempt to build up a body of traditions in the Bank: a tradition of absolute integrity, a tradition of competency,

---

15. See Appendix 5 for staff numbers and indicators of turnover.

... a tradition of efficiency even to the point of ruthlessness, ... and above all, a tradition of being able readily to recognise and accept absolutely the dictates of the national interests, as against the interests of the individual or particular groups either within or outside the Bank" (BNM 1989, 41).

As to internal rationality, considerations of merit combined with attention to ethnicity in appointments and promotions. Officially, the bank gave priority to merit and was thus unlike some government agencies that had a policy of promoting Malays. Although the number of Malays in senior positions increased markedly, the proportion of non-Malays remained higher than in most government organizations.[16] A formal system for staff assessment was in place at least by the 1970s, with clear guidelines for performance criteria (BNM 1971). A common complaint among employees was that seniority was more important than merit (BNM 1981a), but seniority at least does not depend on personal relationships.

The bank is a career service except for the positions of governor and deputy governor, which are political appointments that have increasingly gone to outsiders since 1985; before that, internal appointments were the norm. Tun Ismail's appointment could be considered an internal promotion in that he came from a civil service background, and BNM had been established for only three years. His successor had spent most of his career with the bank. The next two governors came from government-linked commercial banks and the third from the prime minister's department; the fourth was an internal appointment. Deputy governors were generally career officers and often Chinese. Lateral entry became more common after 1985.[17]

Bank Negara always had some outflow of personnel to the private sector, mostly the commercial banks. Several people who served in BNM in the 1960s, 1970s, and early 1980s later held positions outside the government.[18] These people left before the bank was considered to have a turnover problem. According to some interviewees, many new recruits in the 1990s saw employment with Bank Negara as a training ground for subsequent work in commercial banks.[19] In 1997, BNM investigated the issue of staff retention and comparability with private sector salaries, leading to new salaries by July 1997 (BNM, *Annual Report* 1997, 171).

Internal discipline was a priority under Tun Ismail, who was intolerant of staff he considered to be underperforming or "not suited" to central bank work (interview, Tun Ismail, Kuala Lumpur, October 1996). Private moneymaking ventures were strongly discouraged: Tun Ismail regarded stock ownership as a sacking offense, and the next governor, Tan Sri Aziz Taha, confirmed that stock ownership and business activity were not allowed during his time at the bank (interview, Kuala Lumpur, October 1996). This attitude subsequently relaxed. The shift in public culture since the 1980s encouraged people to get involved in business,

16. See Appendix 5.
17. On some lateral entrants since the 1980s, see *New Straits Times*, 2 March 1996.
18. See Singh 1984, 223–25, 323, for examples.
19. As a common route to a commercial bank position, a central bank officer might serve with a non-banking affiliate for three months before joining the commercial bank itself.

develop closer relations with businesspeople, and prioritize wealth acquisition. One source said that the "atmosphere" since the 1980s meant that officers in the central bank (and other key agencies such as the Economic Planning Unit) would be showing "extraordinary restraint" if they did not trade stock tips and share allocations for some kind of quid pro quo.[20] In early 1999, an anonymous article on the antigovernment "freeMalaysia" website accused BNM's former deputy governor of covert share ownership. Another former BNM official was officially charged in September 1999 for failing to declare RM 24 million in assets (*Asian Wall Street Journal*, 29–30 October 1999).[21]

Bank Negara remains relatively untainted by allegations of outright corruption, although the governor appointed from the Economic Planning Unit (EPU) in 1998 was later accused of improper conduct there.[22] Opportunities for corruption by staff were potentially available: the bank's regulatory role created incentives for bribery by the commercial banks, and BNM operated a branch network, subsidized rediscounting schemes, administered development funds, and took temporary control of some commercial banks in the 1980s. Yet apart from one case of internal embezzlement by clerical staff (later prosecuted), these opportunities do not appear to have been taken.

The major failure associated with the bank's internal operations was its large losses in foreign exchange trading in 1993, which led to the resignation of the governor and a senior official (Lim 1994), but these losses were the result of mismanagement rather than corruption. A profit-oriented strategy of aggressive foreign-currency trading had been brought in after 1985 by the new governor, who came from a commercial bank. This mission was also openly encouraged by Mahathir and his post-1985 finance minister, himself one of Malaysia's wealthiest entrepreneurs. For several years, BNM did realize large trading profits; however, as well as being a reckless strategy that was abandoned after 1993, former employees said that the new profit mission resulted in less attention and status being given to other departments in the bank.

Bank Negara's Public Role and Relations with Government
In the conventional definition of central bank independence, Bank Negara has never been independent. In any serious dispute with the minister of finance it can take its case to Parliament, but the likelihood of that is exceedingly remote. Bank Negara has always expressly functioned as part of the government. Tun Ismail held that "the central bank is too important, too powerful, to be operating in complete independence" (BNM 1989, 92). Central bank directors have always included

---

20. Interview, Kuala Lumpur, October 1996. Former BNM officers, although mostly not prepared to make allegations of improper conduct, did concur that the mid-1980s marked a significant change in public norms regarding officials' involvement in moneymaking ventures.
21. Action against this official, closely linked to former Finance Minister Anwar Ibrahim, came at a time when associates of the jailed former minister were being removed from government and corporate positions.
22. He allegedly had large sums of money in his office. The former head of the ACA later said that Mahathir shut down the agency's investigation of the matter (*Straits Times*, 14 June 2000).

the BNM governor, his deputy, and the top official at the Finance Ministry. Other directors tend to be prominent individuals, often nonexecutive directors of commercial banks or blue chip companies.

The bank carved out a policy role for itself through the personal stature of Tun Ismail and the competence of its economic analysis. Tun Ismail was represented on the main public-policy planning committee, and the bank's Economic Department staff were frequently tasked with analysis by other government departments. According to a former EPU officer, communication between the planning agency and the central bank was frequent and substantive (interview, Kuala Lumpur, September 1996). Both during and after his governorship of BNM, Tun Ismail oversaw a large government-controlled investment company, Permodalan Nasional Berhad (PNB). As of 1996 the central bank governor was a director of Khazanah Nasional, the government's main investment company, and was a member of the MBC.

Bank Negara served the government as a source of revenue and as the sometime owner of businesses such as a shipping line, airline, and telephone company. It was also tasked with cleaning up private and state sector institutions not then under central bank supervision. This included involvement in the aftermath of a corruption and mismanagement scandal at a state development bank in 1978, a series of failed deposit-taking companies and problem banks in the mid-1980s, and the insurance industry in the late 1980s. In each case, Bank Negara carried out effective damage control: the financial problems of the banks under its temporary management were resolved, in contrast to ongoing deterioration of banks under the management of Indonesia's central bank.

Bank Negara was subject to informal political pressure, especially from the 1980s. In 1985 its third governor was forced to resign, reportedly because of disagreements with the recently appointed Finance Minister Daim Zainuddin (*Asian Wall Street Journal*, 4 March 1985).[23] Daim was the most prominent of the *Bumiputera* businessmen who made enormous fortunes while closely involved with the ruling political party. He was also known as a sponsor of a younger generation of *Bumiputera* entrepreneurs and was the owner of a commercial bank at the time he was appointed finance minister.[24] As well as replacing the BNM governor with a commercial banker and pushing BNM to adopt its aggressive foreign exchange trading practices, Daim also removed the powerful Capital Issues Committee from central bank control, a move that may have inadvertently insulated the bank from irregular political influence.[25]

23. That year, an unusual number of staff resigned.
24. Daim's involvement with this bank, UMBC, is discussed below.
25. The committee was responsible for overseeing new issues on the stock exchange and thus played a crucial role in Malaysia's privatization policy and the redistribution of wealth associated with the NEP. Access to underpriced issues was a major route to securing personal wealth, and the beneficiaries were often close relatives or friends of politicians. See, e.g., *Asian Wall Street Journal*, 19 June 1995. Government-controlled investment funds also used preferential subscription rights to acquire large portfolios.

Apart from the governors, a few central bank officers had personal relationships with politicians. Among senior BNM officials in the 1980s or 1990s, one was married to a cabinet minister, and another was closely associated with the prime minister. An assistant governor was rumored in 1996 to be personally linked to Finance Minister Anwar Ibrahim. His resignation six months after Anwar was deposed and arrested in September 1998 tends to confirm the association. In his statutory declaration made around the time of Anwar's trial for sodomy and corruption in 1999, he admitted to having acted as a conduit for Anwar's fund-raising activity and, on Anwar's instructions, as an intermediary for some of Anwar's associates (*Asian Wall Street Journal*, 29–30 October 1999).

Malaysia's most interventionist financial policies did not involve the central bank. BNM did run or oversee some special loan funds to support lending to particular sectors or groups from the 1970s, but at the end of 1996 total credit approvals under these schemes amounted to only RM 3.6 billion. Until 1998, BNM also ran an export credit refinancing scheme for rediscounting export lending by banks. Direct government transfers and lending were much more significant, however (Kanapathy and Ismail 1994, 107; Zainal et al. 1994, 287). Other government interventions in the financial system took the form of compulsory savings in a central pension fund, subsidized voluntary savings schemes, and the creation of state-owned banks. Largely through these mechanisms, government control of financial assets rose from 37 percent of total financial system assets in 1960 to peak at 64 percent in 1980, moderating thereafter to 43 percent in 1995.[26]

The main area in which Bank Negara was involved with other state organizations in the financial sector was its regulation of state-owned banks. Government ownership in the banking sector began with the establishment of Bank Bumiputera in 1966 and the partial takeover of Malayan Banking (following a run on that bank) in 1967. These two banks subsequently became the largest in Malaysia. The government had a substantial interest also in two other banks, and the military pension fund controlled still another. Malayan Banking (also called Maybank) grew steadily after 1967 and was profitable, whereas Bank Bumiputera required repeated bailouts. This mixed record among state-owned banks is consistent with the variegated nature of state organizations in Malaysia, some maintaining much higher standards of internal discipline and insulation than others.

The history of Bank Bumiputera shows how a state organization established to further collective *Bumiputera* interests operated mainly to advance the interests of individuals. A scandal involving a finance company subsidiary in the early 1980s brought to light enough of the detail necessary to understand the bank's operations and its interaction with the central bank. The finance company, Bumiputera Malaysia Finance (BMF), was established in 1977 as a subsidiary in Hong Kong. When its losses were disclosed, the government blamed the affair on a few "wicked" individuals who had been able to deceive Bank Bumiputera, the central

26. See Hamilton-Hart 1999, 495–96, for a breakdown of these estimates and sources.

bank, and the government itself; however, the internal routines of the bank, the structure of supervision, and the way government players related to the bank all created scope for such abuses.[27]

By 1979, BMF had become involved in lending to a group of companies associated with a Hong Kong businessman, George Tan. Tan's meteoric rise was something of a mystery in Hong Kong, and so was the identity of his financial backers (Gill 1985). After his companies began to collapse in late 1982, his major creditor was revealed to be BMF, which had channeled almost all its lending to Tan's enterprises. George Tan was finally convicted in Hong Kong in September 1996 of illegal financial dealings. BMF officers were accused of receiving payoffs and of being involved in his other fraudulent practices. One was convicted in the mid-1980s, another in 1993. BMF's losses were absorbed by its parent bank, which in turn was rescued by the state oil company. Losses to the Malaysian taxpayer came to about RM 2.5 billion.

Several aspects of Bank Negara's supervision in this case are worth noting. First, it did not investigate the many irregularities in the transfer of funds from Bank Bumiputera to BMF, even though exchange control reporting requirements would have shown up the large transfers (BCE 1986, 39). Second, the central bank did not use its powers to inspect BMF until July 1982, even though overexposure to George Tan had been queried by auditors in their interim report on the bank to mid-1980 (BCE 1986, 213–14). Bank Negara also missed an opportunity to investigate when it wrote to Hong Kong regulators in April 1981 that it did not object to the parent bank's issuing a guarantee to BMF (Lim 1986, 33). The governor later said that Bank Negara had been looking into BMF loans since 1981 (*New Straits Times*, 11 April 1982), yet no mission to Hong Kong resulted until well into 1982.

Third, Bank Negara was late in using its powers to remove directors of either BMF or Bank Bumiputera. Virtually the same Bank Bumiputera supervisory board was allowed to manage the issue after the central bank had become involved. Transfers to Hong Kong continued during this time. Considering that Bank Negara's on-site inspection in mid-1982 uncovered evidence of serious mismanagement and concealment, an immediate change of all management would have been warranted (BCE 1986, 529). As it was, most of those implicated did not resign until well into 1983, and one not until the end of 1984.

Fourth, the scandal showed the scope for pursuing private interests in and through Bank Bumiputera. Documents seized in Hong Kong revealed regular personal trading by BMF officials (Gill 1985; BCE 1986, 270–90). Other Bank Bumiputera officers were involved in business in Malaysia; one was associated with nearly one hundred companies, including one of which Mahathir was a director (Gomez 1990, 33). Testimony at the Hong Kong trials on what constituted standard office practice at BMF showed that its officials had ample scope for abusing the company's resources: records were not properly kept or filed, and bank officers were

---

27. The main source used here is BCE 1986, a detailed report by independent investigators.

known to be actively involved on their own account in business dealings with their major client. Supervision by Bank Bumiputera was entirely inadequate, even after the parent bank received notice of the extreme overconcentration of the BMF loan portfolio and the inadequacy of its collateral as early as 1980 (*Star*, 3 December 1993).

Finally, the affair shows the close involvement between a state business and politicians. Bank Bumiputera had been chaired by Razaleigh Hamzah before he became finance minister in 1976, and many board members in the early 1980s were people with whom he had had long-standing relations. Malaysian politicians (including Razaleigh) and UMNO's main holding company either had documented interests in companies associated with BMF officers and George Tan or had received loans from them (BCE 1986, 430–45). One of the officers later convicted in Hong Kong alleged that Razaleigh was behind the association with Tan and that Tan had supported Razaleigh financially in return (*New Straits Times*, 17 October 1990). Razaleigh denied any impropriety and maintained that he had never met Tan, or even heard of him (*Business Times*, 18 December 1994). Since George Tan was a well-known figure in Hong Kong at the time (Gill 1985) and Razaleigh had business there (and visited frequently), the claim not to have heard of him lacks credibility.

Overall, the BMF affair was consistent with a pattern of permissiveness by the central bank when interests close to leading politicians were involved. The use of Bank Bumiputera as a vehicle for the advancement of the personal interests of its employees was entirely accepted: open personal enrichment did not provoke countermeasures until the failure of the project (and the costs this would impose on the state) were well in the open.

Bank Bumiputera's record shows that the BMF scandal was far from being its only problem. The bank was set up to increase the *Bumiputera* community's access to finance and also to provide a way for *Bumiputeras* to gain working experience in the financial sector, which at the time was entirely in the hands of foreigners and Malaysian Chinese. Given these goals, lower profitability compared with other banks might be expected; however, the failure to maintain organizational discipline meant that costs far exceeded those that were inherent in the policy itself. Bank Bumiputera financed government initiatives such as the costly attempt to corner the world tin market in the early 1980s (*Asian Wall Street Journal*, 22 September 1986). It was also known for financing many Malay business interests but repeatedly failing to enforce loan repayments. Even the bank's own unreliable financial accounts reveal a poor financial record. After it was rescued from its Hong Kong losses, it again received a large bailout (RM 1.15 billion) in 1989 (*Far Eastern Economic Review*, 19 October 1989). When Malaysia was hit by the regional financial crisis of 1998, Bank Bumiputera was one of three financial institutions accounting for the greater part of the entire bad debt of the financial sector (Danaharta 2000, app. 1). Again, the serving finance minister, Anwar Ibrahim, initially denied any serious problem (*Business Times*, 18 March 1998). After these bad loans were taken off its books, the bank was finally privatized.

The Central Bank and the Private Financial Sector

Bank Negara's regulatory role was a priority early on. Unlike the Indonesian central bank, which was almost always preoccupied with monetary policy, BNM did not assume responsibility for currency issue until 1967. This allowed organizational attention to be turned toward the financial sector. By the end of the 1980s, BNM was responsible for regulation and supervision of all finance companies, merchant banks, and insurance companies as well as commercial banks.

One of the central bank's early regulatory moves was to impose substantial reserve ratios on banks and other financial institutions, requiring them to hold a portion of their liabilities in the form of government debt instruments. It also imposed a new obligation on commercial banks to produce regular financial reports (Siew 1960). BNM placed an early priority on the development of the banking system and the mobilization of savings (Lee 1981, 1987). Until the late 1960s, BNM used exhortation and some material incentives to influence the spread of commercial bank branches (Singh 1984; BNM 1989, 18). The number of banking offices more than doubled between 1959 and 1963, and the resulting distribution of bank branches reduced their previous concentration in major urban centers (Lee 1981, 38–41; BNM 1994, 518). The central bank also played a role in the development of foreign exchange and stock and money markets, such the offshore financial center in Labuan.

The central bank never made much use of interest-rate controls or credit directives. It did set all interest rates until they were liberalized between 1972 and 1978; however, mandated interest rates on deposits were maximum rates to prevent "excess competition" among banks—mainly to prevent foreign banks from outbidding local banks (Lee 1981, 67). Similarly, lending rates were mostly minimum rates (Emery 1970, 279). BNM reinstituted partial interest-rate controls during the 1980s, when banks were required to publish their base lending rates. These were determined in relation to the cost of funds, and specified types of loans were not to deviate more than a set amount from the base rate. This system continued until 1991 (Zainal et al. 1994).

Banks were not subject to the kind of credit directives used to support industrial policy in countries such as Korea. The central bank urged banks to limit lending for property development and shares and to increase lending to *Bumiputeras*, industry, and agriculture. These informal requests were implicitly acknowledged to be ineffective when, in 1975, a formal requirement to direct 20 percent of bank lending to *Bumiputeras* was brought in. By the late 1980s, bank lending to *Bumiputeras* well exceeded this minimum. Lending to manufacturing increased from less than 3 percent of bank loans in the 1960s to more than 20 percent in the 1980s and 1990s but was never compulsory.[28]

---

28. On the distribution of bank lending, see BNM 1994, 506; and BNM, *Quarterly Bulletin* (various issues).

The 1989 revision of the banking and financial institutions law consolidated earlier policies to liberalize the financial sector by allowing banks more freedom to set prices and develop products.[29] It also marked the formalization and strengthening of prudential controls such as limits on lending to directors, reporting requirements, and provisions aimed at diluting the ownership structure of banks. It set limits on lending to the property sector and lending to purchase shares, a response to the banking instability in the mid-1980s caused by overexposure to these sectors. Lending to the broad property sector subsequently declined slightly: in the decade before the 1989 act, property-related lending averaged 32.5 percent of bank lending; in the first half of the 1990s it averaged 30.5 percent.

Bank Negara's style of policy implementation changed over time. Its early approach to dealing with the banks through friendly cooperation rather than legal measures (Siew 1960, 123) gave way to a more formal, mandatory style. Relying on moral suasion would have to wait until an "appropriate" banking culture developed (BNM 1989, 85). On some issues, such as branching, Bank Negara extended its influence over the banks beyond its 1960s statutory purview (Lee 1981, 42). On several occasions it was able to exercise its powers with little regard to the costs it imposed on bank owners. For example, Bank Negara intervened when Malayan Banking experienced a depositor run in 1966, with the result that government agencies became the bank's largest shareholders. Malayan Banking had been established in 1960 by a Singapore-based banker, Khoo Teck Puat, with the active support of ruling coalition politicians—who received donations in return (Gill 1987, 11–12, 24). Bank Negara was also able to bring about management changes and force the recapitalization of the private banks that were in trouble in the 1980s.

On the other hand, BNM at times had less influence over bank decisions and practices than its legal powers provided for. Bank Negara already had the legal powers to deal with most of the banking abuses that were uncovered in the wake of the 1985 recession: limits on loans to related interests and directors, for example, had been tightened in 1982, and uncollateralized loans to directors had always been subject to regulatory controls.[30] Bank Negara did generally put a stop to irregular practices but only after those responsible had realized substantial gains. Moreover, it frequently used its discretionary power to waive prudential regulations, with the approval of the minister of finance. For example, it often disregarded the requirement that a single shareholder (or related group of shareholders) not control more than 20 percent of a commercial bank. That legislation did not apply to bank owners who already held larger shares, but when a bank changed hands, ownership was meant to be diluted. Yet several mergers

29. Zainal et al. 1994 provides an overview of financial policy changes.
30. On the development of Bank Negara's authority to the mid-1980s, see Lee 1987.

or transfers of banking licenses in the 1990s were apparently exempt from this rule.[31]

This inconsistent enforcement of declared policy can be traced to the nature of ties between politicians and bankers more than to the direct relationship between Bank Negara and the financial industry. Particularly until the 1980s, BNM had distant and formal relations with most banks. There was little consultation prior to the introduction of new legislation or regulatory controls. The central bank initiated regular meetings with the banks early in the 1960s, but accounts of such meetings suggest that they were not opportunities for bankers to express their views frankly until at least the mid-1980s. Instead, the meetings were mostly ceremonial occasions for lecturing by the central bank governor (Singh 1984, 222–58; interview, former BNM official, Kuala Lumpur, November 1996).

More consultation was said to have been brought in with the new governor in 1985. The president of a commercial bank referred to the governor's "kitchen cabinet," a group of bankers from the larger banks (interview, Kuala Lumpur, October 1996). Others would not admit to knowing of such a group, which suggests that its membership was very restricted or that it was not considered a regular channel of communication. The financial policy-working group of the Malaysian Business Council may have been a channel of communication, since it included several bankers as well as the central bank's governor, his deputy, and the finance minister.

Informal contacts between central bankers and private bankers increased from the mid-1980s, as the outflow of Bank Negara officials to the financial industry increased and some senior positions at Bank Negara (including the governorship) were given to commercial bankers. Nonetheless, the weight of evidence suggests that inconsistencies in Bank Negara's enforcement of official rules was mainly due to the involvement of powerful political actors, notably the prime minster and minister of finance. Abdul Murad Khalid, the former BNM official associated with Anwar Ibrahim when he was finance minister, later said that Anwar had instructed him to help settle the debts of two individuals and to help a business associate in a corporate takeover.[32] In the latter case, his "help" involved his meeting with Maybank officers to secure a loan to fund the takeover. He also said that Tong Kooi Ong, the controlling shareholder of PhileoAllied Bank, told him about a bank account from which financial contributions in support of Anwar's interests could be made. He estimated that at least twenty similar accounts with total funds of RM 3 billion had been established for Anwar.

---

31. These involved EON bank, DCB-RHB, UMBC-Sime, PhileoAllied Bank, Arab-Malaysian Bank, and Hong Leong Bank.
32. His testimony needs to be interpreted in the context of the many claims and counter-claims of corruption and abuse of office involving Daim and Mahathir, as well as Anwar, which were made during and after the trial. One witness for the prosecution later recanted his statement. See *New Straits Times*, 19 June 1999; *Straits Times*, 21 June 1999; *Asian Wall Street Journal*, 25 and 29–30 October 1999.

Table 5.1. Malaysia: Ranking of Local Banks

	1980		1985		1995	
	Assets[a]	Rank	Assets[a]	Rank	Assets[a]	Rank
Bumiputero	12.82	1	24.97	1	36.46	2
Maybank	9.26	2	24.11	2	66.91	1
UMBC	2.82	3	8.02	3	13.05	7
UAB[b]	2.19	4	5.10	5		
Public	1.61	5	6.13	4	23.26	3
DCB	1.237	6	4.48	6	17.55	4
Commerce	0.22	15	0.90	16	14.62	5

Sources: Arab-Malaysian Merchant Bank, *Bankers' Directory* (various issues); *Malaysian Business*, 16 January 1997.
[a] In billions of ringgit.
[b] United Asian Bank merged with the Bank of Commerce in 1991.

In many cases politicians had no need to use central bank officials as intermediaries to influence lending. The bank loans that financed Malaysia's privatization policy may have been made out of a belief that recipients of privatization projects would not be allowed to fail.[33] Given the known political connections of those involved, such guarantees would not have needed to be made explicit. Mahathir, however, was said to have personally intervened to help a Malay businessman obtain the large syndicated loan he needed to support the privatization of the national airline (interview, financial analyst, October 1996). A loan of RM 3 billion, syndicated by four Malaysian banks to support the takeover of a Philippine steel plant by a Hong Kong–registered firm associated with one of Daim's *Bumiputera* protégés, was also reportedly made at Mahathir's behest. The loan was later completely written off (*Business Times*, 17 March 1999).

In such cases, even favored bank owners could suffer from "national service" obligations. More often, however, they benefited from their political relationships. Most inconsistencies in Bank Negara's policy implementation involved bank owners known to have patronage-based relations with politicians. For example, the bank mergers or takeovers in the 1990s that breached the 20 percent maximum shareholding limit all involved owners closely related to the then minister of finance, the prime minister, or his close adviser and former minister of finance, Daim Zainuddin. The rise and fall of several Malaysian banks can also be related to levels of personal access to political powerholders. There is not, however, so complete a correspondence between private access and success as in Indonesia's banking industry.

Table 5.1 summarizes the positions over time of Malaysia's largest domestic banks. The slower growth of state-owned Bank Bumiputera from the early 1980s

33. An acknowledged RM 5.1 billion in soft loans had also been given out to support privatization projects by 1996. See *New Straits Times*, 30 October 1996.

suggests that it was somewhat restricted after its disastrous Hong Kong venture. Its preeminent position was taken by Maybank, also state controlled but with diversified private shareholding. Public Bank has fared well without personal ties to politicians. Its major owner, Teh Hong Piow, has been independent of ties to the political elite since his acquisition of a banking license in the 1960s. Rather than developing personal ties to power-holders, he made a point of studying NEP policy guidelines, limiting diversification into other sectors, and steering clear of controversy (Gomez 1999, 39, 79–81). Public Bank weathered the financial crisis of 1998 without difficulty: it was not among the ten banks requiring recapitalization funds from the government, and it transferred a very small amount of nonperforming loans to the national asset management company (Danaharta 2000, app. 1).

The rise and fall of other banks, as well as the profits bank owners have realized, are related to the personal favor enjoyed by the owners. UMBC's performance declined, but its owners realized large gains. When Daim Zainuddin was required to divest his interest in the bank after becoming finance minister, it was sold to what was then a state-owned company, Pernas.[34] The nature of Daim's use of UMBC may be assessed by Pernas's reluctance to take on the bank because of its poor condition. Later, a small company allegedly connected to influential *Bumiputera* interests acquired a major interest in UMBC. Suspected irregularities at the bank eventually led Bank Negara to force its sale, but with large gains for those divesting. It was bought by a conglomerate, Sime Darby, partially owned by a government-controlled investment fund. Again, its performance was dismal: along with Bank Bumiputera, it had the worst level of nonperforming loans among Malaysian banks in 1998 (Danaharta 2000, app. 1).

The growth of the Bank of Commerce and the Development and Commercial Bank (DCB; now Rashid Hussain Bank, RHB) is also consistent with their political links (Gomez and Jomo 1997, 61–62). Other major changes in position not shown in the table include the rise of Arab-Malaysian Bank from twenty-ninth rank in 1994 to seventeenth rank in 1995. It is owned by a well-known Malay merchant banker, Azman Hashim, also with links to UMNO. Another change in position is that of MUI Bank, which stagnated in the second half of the 1980s when the owner refused repeated requests to expand its operations. The bank was then owned by a Khoo Kay Peng, a supporter of Razaleigh Hamzah, who had failed in his attempt to oust Mahathir from the leadership of UMNO in 1987. Khoo eventually sold his bank to Quek Leng Chan of the Hong Leong group, a finance sector tycoon allied with then Finance Minister Anwar Ibrahim.[35]

---

34. For details of Daim's involvement with the bank, its sale, and its subsequent performance, see *Asian Wall Street Journal*, 30 April 1986, 18 July and 1 August 1994; *Business Times*, 1 July 1992; *Star*, 11 March 1995. The later owner, Datuk Keramat Holdings, bought its share in the bank in 1993 for RM 600 million and sold it for an estimated RM 1.2 billion in 1995 (*Business Times*, 11 November 1995).
35. Quek bought the bank in 1993 for about RM 700 million. He soon received permission to open twenty-five new branches and to list on the exchange, where it was valued at RM 3.3 billion (*Far Eastern Economic Review*, 22 June 1995).

The impact of such politically mediated intervention in the regulation of the banking sector did not completely undermine the central bank's regulatory effectiveness. Bank Negara was for the most part respected for its technical competence and the integrity of its officers. In the absence of political intervention, it had a demonstrated ability to force compliance with its rulings, which led to its gradually assuming regulatory control over different areas relating to finance as they became exposed to instability. Before the financial crisis of 1997, interviewees from the financial sector and the press almost all agreed that the banking system was more regularized than it had been in the 1980s—with better lending practices, more rigorous auditing, and fewer dubious intrabusiness group loans—under the more effective and watchful supervision of Bank Negara. The problems that emerged later show that this picture was overly rosy. During the crisis, Bank Negara's apparent favoritism in enforcing the banking law was again criticized (*Business Times*, 7 March 1998).

The problems of Malaysian banks in 1998 were not, however, anything like as severe as those of Indonesian or Thai banks. Malaysia's banking sector in 1998 had lower overall public costs, and its problems were largely concentrated in a few banks. Before the crisis, Malaysia had not had a high level of banking distress when compared with other developing countries, even counting the banking instability of the 1980s, and in earlier years its record was exceptional. Political intervention sometimes prevented Bank Negara from enforcing its regulatory standards consistently, but the immediate interests of politically influential actors did not always prevail.

This mixed record of success and failure in maintaining financial stability in the context of a moderately interventionist financial policy, a rapidly growing financial sector, and increasing rates of private saving is consonant with the organizational features of the central bank and other state organizations in Malaysia. The bureaucracy underwent considerable rationalization in the colonial era, and a high level of continuity over the transition to independence meant that many of these characteristics were maintained well into the postindependence period. Several new organizations, including the central bank, benefited from careful planning processes and efforts at state-building in the 1950s and 1960s. Bank Negara also moved early to establish its regulatory role. It made data collection a priority and developed the organizational skills to evaluate and use information. The effectiveness with which these routine tasks were carried out would serve the bank well in later years. Its internal discipline was relatively high, which was congruent with elements of its internal structures and norms: particularly in the twenty-five years before 1985, it was largely a career service that paid attention to developing a strong organizational culture, including an explicit standard of maintaining distance from business interests.

There were limits to Bank Negara's effectiveness, reflected not only in the instances when it failed to enforce regulation but also in the kinds of financial policy that it never attempted. The most interventionist projects associated with

Malaysia's industrial policy and its program of interethnic redistribution were deliberately implemented through agencies that would be less conservative and restrained than the central bank and the core civil service. A former EPU and BNM official said that Malaysia had never adopted Korean-style industrial policy lending through the banks because it did not want to subject the banking system to such "abuse" (interview, Kuala Lumpur, September 1996). The influential Tun Ismail, Bank Negara's longest-serving governor, was also known to have a conservative view of central banking. Beyond the matter of intellectual predisposition, however, the Malaysian context meant that it was hard to pursue a more developmental strategy: to remain disciplined, agencies such as the central bank had to restrict their range of activity.

6.

Governing Open Economies

The protesters who disrupted the World Trade Organization meeting in Seattle in 1999 and, over the next year, demonstrated against World Bank and IMF conferences in Washington and Prague took to the streets with a variety of agendas. Almost all, however, expressed a concern with "globalization" and its presumed consequences: a world in which finance is unfettered and corporations rule. The curiosity of middle-class Americans smashing the windows of an international coffee retailer in the name of the world's poor was not lost on many onlookers. Perhaps more curiously, however, many of the fears voiced at these protests resonated with a broad range of academic and policy-oriented studies of capital mobility, international trade, and global capitalism.[1] What connects these studies with street-level protests against globalization is a common focus on whether an economy that is global in scope can be controlled by national governments—and, if so, in whose interest?[2]

The debate over globalization raises a significant question for this book. If finance is global, does it make state organizations obsolete? We have reasons to believe that capital mobility complicates the task of governing. Independent macroeconomic policy, for example, is likely to involve significant policy trade-offs, and financial markets may be more unstable. Far from being irrelevant in a world of mobile finance, however, the governing capacity of state organizations helps determine how countries manage these challenges. Because many strategies to cope with the political and economic pressures associated with capital mobility are administratively demanding, some states lack the organizational attributes to deal with an internationalized economy. Others, however, are much less restricted.

The preceding chapters have already shown the differences among a group of Southeast Asian countries in their ability to govern the financial sector. Different degrees of capital mobility cannot explain these intercountry differences, because all countries in Southeast Asia inherited internationalized economies from the colonial period and, in consequence, have operated in conditions of relatively high capital mobility since the 1950s. The viability of the specific strategies for governing an open economy adopted by these countries, however, is contingent on particular state attributes.

1. Among the more notable, see Berger and Dore 1996; Hirst and Thompson 1996; Strange 1996; Pauly 1997; and Baker, Epstein, and Pollin 1998.
2. The title of Cohen 1986.

CAPITAL MOBILITY: REGIONAL AND INTERNATIONAL LINKAGES

Most Southeast Asian countries have had internationalized economies since the 1950s. Capital has been able to flow relatively easily across national borders; external markets have been important for economic growth; and foreigners have been a significant source of investment. Although these countries have become more economically open since the 1980s, there was no sudden movement from closed to open economies, nor has the process been a linear one. Singapore and Malaysia in particular were operating in environments of high capital mobility in the 1960s and 1970s—periods when their governments pursued ambitious and successful financial policies.

The Regional Dimension

One reason why most Southeast Asian countries always had relatively open economies was their location in a wider regional area of trade and exchange. This meant that the entrepreneurs, bankers, and traders who made up the local business class often had significant friendships, family relations, commercial ties, and investments abroad. Consequently, a substantial portion of domestic capital was internationally mobile regardless of government policy. By the 1990s these transnational ties had become more visible, and the increasing intraregional flow of investment and trade began to attract attention.

The transnational ties underlying the highly visible economic regionalization of the 1990s had concrete, and remarkably resilient, historical foundations. In the nineteenth century the flow of goods, money, and people between China and India coexisted with the intensification of Western colonialism and ensured that a type of economic regionalism existed in Asia (Hamashita 1997). The rise of Chinese nationalism and the commercial rivalry associated with Japanese expansion in first decades of the twentieth century saw these economic linkages gain a new political dimension by the 1930s (Sugiyama and Guerrero 1994). By the middle of the twentieth century, depression, war, nationalist policies, and the global cold war had reduced levels of regional interdependence (Katzenstein et al. 2000, 118–21). Yet despite this overall trend, there was a degree of continuity in regional economic ties. Focal points such as Singapore and Hong Kong were at the center of areas of trade and financial exchange throughout the twentieth century. The continuity in regional economic linkages was often direct and personal, as many of those who led the highly visible regionalization of banking and business activity in the 1990s were families with transregional friendships and business contacts dating from the 1930s.

Much of the regional activity of ethnic Chinese entrepreneurs continued after the war, when transnational, diversified business groups grew rapidly.[3] The Jack

3. In the case of Singapore, see Paix 1993. Ho 1991 describes an internationalized firm in the 1950s and 1960s. For further details on the international orientation of business and banking in twentieth-century Asia, see Katzenstein et al. 2000.

Chia group of companies, the Aw family, and Robert Kuok were among those to have significant overseas operations as early as the 1950s.[4] Robert Kuok (Kuok Hock Nien) headed one of the largest commercial groups based in Hong Kong in the 1990s but had started business as an international commodities trader in Malaya and London in the 1950s. From the late 1950s his operations extended to Indonesia, Thailand, China, and Cuba. He established a brokerage, among other companies, in Hong Kong in 1963 and based himself in Hong Kong from 1976. His foreign ties included a close relationship with Sino-Indonesian businessman Liem Sioe Liong, who helped Kuok gain a virtual monopoly in refined sugar imports to Indonesia.

The wealthiest local business actors were frequently involved in banking, and the international operations of their banks illustrate the regional cast to their connections. A major ethnic Chinese bank to expand in the region at this time was the Thai-based Bangkok Bank, founded in December 1944. It opened its first international branch in Hong Kong in 1954, followed by one in Tokyo in 1955, and by the early 1980s foreign operations accounted for about 40 percent of its profits. The principal figure associated with the Bangkok Bank was Sino-Thai entrepreneur Chin Sophonpanich (Tan Piak Chin), who had close ties with a number of regional businessmen.[5] Chin had been involved in trade with Hong Kong, Singapore, and the Netherlands East Indies before and during the war. He left Thailand to live in Hong Kong from 1958 until 1963 and built up an interest in three banks there. Among the prominent Asian operators who were directors or shareholders of these banks were Robin Loh, who was originally from Indonesia, Malaysia's Lim Goh Tong, Hong Kong's Tsao family, and the Mitsubishi Bank. Chin had a well-known relationship with Liem Sioe Liong of Indonesia and Robert Kuok. His Japanese ties also included the Tokai Bank and Nomura Securities. Chin met Zhou Enlai in 1972 during a visit by a Thai sporting team to China; Chin, acting as the team's "adviser," helped to reopen relations between China and Thailand (Hewison 1989, 196).

Friendly relations and business ties in the region provided opportunities for pooling capital, business contacts, and mutual support. An example of the support that could be extended dates from the late 1940s: when the Bangkok Bank was having trouble finding premises for a branch in Singapore, Singapore-based Lien Ying Chow (who already had the idea of establishing his own bank) provided one of his properties, free of charge, for about a year. Lien described this as a "gesture of friendship which we people from China want to extend to each other in Southeast Asia. We always like to cooperate with each other" (Lien 1992, 107).

Banks established in Singapore set about restoring and developing regional ties soon after the war. Overseas Union Bank (OUB), founded in 1949, illustrates the process. Lien Ying Chow, its founder, came to Singapore as a teenager and became

4. On Jack Chia, see *Singapore Trade and Industry*, June 1973, January 1974; on Kuok, see *Insight*, August 1978; on the Aw family, see *Singapore Trade*, July 1961.
5. Hewison 1989, 196–201, is the main source for this paragraph.

established in commerce in the 1930s. He maintained ties with family members in Thailand and China, spending time during the war in the Chinese wartime capital of Chongqing, where he established not only a bank but contacts among both nationalist and communist leaders, including Chiang Kai-shek and Zhou Enlai.[6] As a representative of China he went to London during the war, where he made contact with a number of British companies that had interests in the Far East. After the war Lien's bank in China closed, and he did not take up business there again until 1978, when he started negotiations to build a hotel in Beijing. This was built some time later with the help of the Bank of China. Lien raised the initial deposits and capital for OUB from friends and relations in Thailand, Hong Kong, and Vietnam. In 1966 he served as Singapore's high commissioner to Malaysia, where he and then Prime Minister Tunku Abdul Rahman were described as "old chums" since before the war. Lien also had close relations with the Sultan of Johor, Thai royalty, and a number of Thai prime ministers.

Lien's international orientation was mirrored by that of OUB's senior staff and directors. Chi Owyang, Lien's long-serving manager (1947–68), had personal ties and banking experience in China, Hong Kong, and Thailand. Chi Owyang was also able to develop OUB's relationship in new areas, such as in Burma from the 1950s onward. Through the State Commercial Bank there, OUB handled all the Burmese business in Singapore at that time, and later on in Hong Kong as well (Owyang 1996, 87). The general manager in the early 1970s had thirty years of banking experience in Hong Kong and Thailand before joining OUB as the Penang branch manager in 1958. Many of OUB's early directors were China-born and almost all came to the bank with business interests in a number of different countries (OUB 1974).

Another Singapore-based bank, Oversea-Chinese Banking Corporation (OCBC), had had extensive regional business links in the prewar period (Wilson 1972, 25–50). By the 1960s it had lost many of these regional branches, but its association with Malaysian businesses and political figures increased. One of its directors from 1932 to 1959 was Tan Cheng Lock, a plantation owner whose son, Tan Siew Sin, was Malaysia's finance minister from 1959 until 1974 (Wilson 1972, 123; Yoshihara 1988, 77, 210). Tan Siew Sin owned considerable corporate stock in Malaysia and served as a director of many companies (Gomez 1994, 180). The bank was also closely connected with businessmen based in Hong Kong: for example, the tycoon Runme Shaw was a director of OCBC from 1962 until 1982; he and his brother owned entertainment outlets across Asia in the 1960s and 1970s. Another director of OCBC (1978–83) was Lamson Kwok, the China-educated chair of Hong Kong's Wing On Life Ltd. (associated with OCBC since 1974) and a prominent business leader in Hong Kong (OCBC, *Annual Report* 1978).

Regional banking operations continued to link economies that were becoming more closed during the 1960s. For example, Malayan Banking, now Malaysia's

---

6. This section is drawn from Lien 1992, particularly 34–48, 101–8.

largest bank and substantially state controlled, was established by a Singapore-based banker, with the support of some of Malaysia's ruling politicians.[7] Its founding investors also included two Singapore-based Chinese entrepreneurs with Indonesian connections, Oei Tjong Ie and Goh Tjoei Kok (Gill 1987, 12). The relative closure of mainland China after 1949 presented more of a break with the past. The Bank of China opted to serve the new regime in 1949, as did the Singaporean, Malayan, and Indonesian branches (the Australian, New York, and Thai branches stayed with the Chiang Kai-shek government).[8] The Malayan government consequently closed its branches in Penang and Kuala Lumpur in 1959.[9] In 1964 the Indonesian offices were closed (the bank had already been substantially taken over), leaving the Singapore branch as the only one in Southeast Asia. In the early 1970s the bank played an important role in Singapore-China trade, but its regional presence was diminished. Even then, however, this "communist" bank was an accepted member of the Hong Kong banking fraternity (*Insight*, August 1973). China also maintained overseas economic ties through government-linked companies based in Hong Kong and through the overseas operations of Chinese firms.[10]

Ethnic Chinese entrepreneurs and bankers operating in the region at this time included almost all those who would become prominent in the 1980s and 1990s. Many were able to make use of friendships formed during the years they had spent at school in China before or during the war, as it was common for relatively affluent Chinese living in Southeast Asia to send their sons to China for education.[11] In a few cases, Southeast Asian Chinese continued this practice after the war. Notably, Peter Oei Hong Leong, of the Sino-Indonesian Oei family—which owns the major resource-based conglomerate Sinar Mas and Bank International Indonesia—was educated in China and remained there from 1960 until 1969, reportedly forging contacts with Communist Party cadres.[12] The Oei family, which had overseas business interests in Asia from the late 1960s on, emerged in the 1990s as one of the two largest overseas Chinese investors in China, where Peter Oei was said to have capitalized on relationships formed during the 1960s. The family also had investments in the United States, and Eka Tjipta Widjaya (Peter Oei's father, Oei Ek Tjhong) was named Emerging Markets CEO of the Year in 1996—an honor on which he was congratulated by President Bill Clinton.[13]

Regional interests and relationships thus included individuals from Indonesia, despite that country's restrictive policy from the 1950s. In 1969, Indonesia was

7. The banker was Khoo Teck Puat, later to gain fame for his spectacular rise on the financial scene in London, followed by notoriety with the collapse in 1987 of his bank in Brunei. See Gill 1987.
8. This paragraph is drawn from *Singapore Trade and Industry*, April 1972.
9. The Bank of China returned to Malaysia at the end of 1999.
10. Firms such as China Ocean Shipping Company were operating overseas before 1978.
11. See, e.g., Ho 1991; and Tabalujan 1995.
12. The sources for this section are *Singapore Business*, August 1990; *Asia Inc.*, August 1993; and DFAT 1995, 242–43.
13. The letter from Clinton was reproduced in *Inni Yu Dongxie* (Indonesia and ASEAN) in November 1996. I am grateful to Edwin Yang Tsung-Rong for bringing the item to my attention.

Singapore's second largest source of tourists, and Indonesians were significant property buyers in Singapore from at least the early 1970s (*Singapore Trade and Industry*, July 1970, September 1971; *Singapore Business*, August 1977). Even before capital controls ended in 1970, Indonesian names often occurred among the principal capital subscribers of companies registered in Singapore.[14] Sino-Indonesians such as Liem Sioe Liong, who would later gain notoriety as President Suharto's leading business partner and emerge as one of the region's wealthiest individuals, began investing in Singapore at least as early as 1968. In 1975 he founded a finance company in Hong Kong with fellow Indonesian banker Mochtar Riady. By the end of the decade he had large trading companies in Singapore and Hong Kong and was well known in Asian business circles, with ties to Robert Kuok and the Koo family of Taiwan as well as early support from the Bangkok Bank, reportedly on the recommendation of its chairman, Chin Sophonpanich (Chin was said to be indebted to Liem for secretly covering a $20 million shortfall on his foreign exchange dealings in the mid-1970s). Liem renewed ties with China (where his first wife remained) after being approached by Chinese officials in 1975 to import cloves from China into Indonesia (*Insight*, April and May 1978). By the early 1990s, overseas operations accounted for about 35 percent of total revenues for Salim group, then the country's largest conglomerate (*Asian Wall Street Journal*, 25–26 February 1994).

Liem's business partner, Mochtar Riady, had on his own account built up foreign business interests by the end of the 1970s. The Riady family's investments later formed part of a large conglomerate, the Lippo group, which channeled many investments through holding companies in Hong Kong (DFAT 1995, 177). Mochtar Riady made rather controversial attempts to buy into American banks in the 1970s (*Insight*, September 1978), and Lippo, although concentrating on Asia, eventually took over a Chinese-run bank in California in 1984. Also in 1984 the Riadys bought into an Arkansas bank in partnership with an American investment banker, Jackson Stephens, with whom they had established ties through a Hong Kong company in the 1970s. Lippo would later gain minor notoriety in the United States when the family was the subject of investigations into political party funding in 1997.

Another Indonesian businessman whose ties and operations were transnational before the 1980s was Robin Loh.[15] His group of companies was, by the late 1970s, based in Hong Kong, where Loh also had an interest in Chin Sophonpanich's Commercial Bank of Hong Kong, but his oil and real estate interests were managed from Singapore, and he also had a presence in Tokyo, Taipei, and elsewhere. Loh was born in Indonesia in 1929, moved to Singapore in 1947, and for the next twenty years traveled back and forth between those countries. He received financial backing in the early 1960s from Singapore-based OCBC and the Thai-based

14. *Singapore Trade* (later *Singapore Trade and Industry*, then *Singapore Business*) intermittently prints a monthly list of companies registered in Singapore.
15. This paragraph is drawn from *Insight*, March 1978.

Bangkok Bank. He also had a "great friend and ally" in Ibnu Sutowo, the head of Indonesia's state oil company.

Many Indonesian Chinese left the country. Singapore was a destination for the wealthier individuals, and thousands more went to China and later to Hong Kong (DFAT 1995, 181–82). Those going to Singapore very often retained family or business connections in Indonesia. Goh Tjoei Kok, for example, left in 1954 for Singapore, where he established Tat Lee Bank in 1974. But before that, his rubber-trading business meant that he maintained ties with Indonesian producers and merchants. He later formed a joint venture bank in Indonesia with one of these associates. Ng Quee Lam was a China-born, Singapore-based rubber trader with close ties to Indonesian businesses (*Singapore Trade and Industry*, June 1972). He also founded Far Eastern Bank in 1959 and had interests in shipping and real estate. Ong Tjoe Kim was another Sino-Indonesian who left Indonesia in 1957 to found a retail business in Singapore. Again, ties to Indonesia were maintained, including those by marriage into an Indonesian family that owned a chain of department shops in which Ong invested in the 1990s.

Singapore-based individuals also renewed or established contact with Indonesian officials and traders. In 1963, Indonesia's opposition to the formation of Malaysia resulted in the prohibition of Indonesia-Malaysia trade, severely affecting the foreign exchange business of Singapore banks. Consequently, businessmen from both countries by passed the economic blockade by trading through third countries. UOB, now one of Singapore's largest banks, established a branch in Hong Kong mainly to circumvent the Indonesian economic boycott (UOB 1985, 35–39). The combined effect of these interests and relationships was that although Indonesia's trade and capital-account regulations remained restrictive until 1970, the economy was already linked to regional markets and financial centers.[16]

Another aspect of the regionalization of business activity that contributed to levels of capital mobility was the postwar spread of Japanese investment in Southeast Asia, extending Japanese banking activity in the region as relationships established in Japan moved overseas. Japanese businesses not only started to return to Southeast Asia as part of an American-supported policy of economic cooperation (Shiraishi 1997b, 176–78) but also resurrected relationships formed during the Japanese occupation, particularly in Indonesia (Nishihara 1975). Outward investments in manufacturing and natural resources in Southeast Asia were well under way by the mid-1970s, sustained by the provision of credit, often through the Japanese trading houses (Doner 1997, 207–8).

Japanese banks were restricted in their retail branching in the region but provided finance through representative offices and locally based joint venture merchant banks (Yoshihara 1978, 10–12; Tokunaga 1992, 153–89). Some of these were long-term relationships. In Indonesia, for example, Liem Sioe Liong's Bank

16. In the 1960s there were active (unofficial) foreign-exchange markets for the rupiah in Hong Kong as well as Jakarta. See *Singapore Trade*, December 1961; and Mackie 1996, 343–44.

Central Asia (BCA), and the Long Term Credit Bank (LTCB) of Japan jointly established a finance company in 1975—and when joint venture commercial banks were permitted in 1989, BCA and LTCB were among the first to establish one.[17] Japanese banks moved early into the Singapore offshore market which directed the largest part of its funds (52 percent of lending in 1975) to Asian countries (MAS, *Annual Report*, 1976, 90). In addition, Japanese foreign aid funds and organizations were important for many outward investment projects (Doner 1997, 204–5).

In summary, the mobility of private capital in Southeast Asia was initially based on the transnational dispersion of contacts and interests of the ethnic Chinese who made up a significant part of the modern business sector. Many of their banks developed on the basis of prior success in inherently international, trade-based ventures. Despite a retreat from regional operations during World War II and the early postwar years, the regional ties of many bank-related business groups were never entirely broken. Through Singapore and Hong Kong in particular, relations with the relatively closed economies of Indonesia and China were maintained. As financial centers, these two cities also provided an outlet for regional capital seeking overseas investment opportunities (*Singapore Trade and Industry*, January 1972).

Country Experiences of Internationalization

Aggregate measures of economic internationalization show that although Singapore and Malaysia were more open than Indonesia, all three were significantly open. As a small island state, Singapore has always been heavily dependent on external markets. Merchandise exports were about the same in the 1990s as in the early 1960s—over 130 percent of GDP. Exports of merchandise and services rose in the 1970s from the already high level of 120 percent of GDP in the early 1970s to around 190 percent from 1980 onward.[18] A high level of foreign ownership in the economy meant that most of the largest businesses had ties to foreign financial centers right from 1960 (Puthucheary 1960). Foreigners' share in the domestic economy averaged 20 percent of GDP in the 1970s and 32 percent in the 1990s.

With a few exceptions, capital inflows and outflows have been uninhibited. Singapore's capital account was not fully liberalized until 1978, but because Sterling Area transactions were not controlled, a liberal regime applied to most capital transactions once self-government was granted in 1959. Transfers were freely permitted between Singapore and the "Scheduled Territories" of the Commonwealth (Ministry of Finance 1963), and the free movement of funds by foreign investors was assured. Family remittances to China were also permitted, although demo-

---

17. LTCB closed its Indonesian offices in 1999.
18. Unless otherwise stated, all statistical data (such as balance-of-payments figures, national income estimates, bank assets, and government revenue) used in this chapter come from figures provided in official reports issued by the country concerned: Department of Statistics (Singapore), *Yearbook of Statistics*; Monetary Authority of Singapore, *Annual Report*; Bank Indonesia, *Indonesian Financial Statistics, Report for the Financial Year*; Bank Negara Malaysia, *Annual Report, Monthly Bulletin of Statistics*; and BNM 1994. A more detailed summary of levels of economic internationalization and the government's economic position in each country is given in Hamilton-Hart 1999, 475–97.

graphic and immigration trends saw the amounts decline from the 1950s. Access by Singaporeans to the offshore market, established in 1968, was restricted, but significant exemptions were made in 1973 and 1976 before decontrol in 1978 (*Singapore Banking and Finance*, 1979). Banks operating in the offshore market are still limited as to the Singapore dollar loans they can make, but since residents were always free to access the London market, these restrictions never prevented Singaporeans from investing overseas. Liberalization in 1978 may have added to the ease of transactions but was not a significant turningpoint.

The banking sector was always internationalized. Foreign exposure of the banking system reached a low point in the 1970s, when overseas assets made up 16 percent of total assets, and overseas liabilities 17 percent of total liabilities. Foreign liabilities rose from the 1980s on, but overseas assets were only marginally higher in the first half of the 1990s than they had been in 1960, rising from an average of 24 percent of total assets to 26 percent. At independence, the largest banks were all British-owned multinational businesses, and by the early 1970s all local banks had branches in the world's major international financial centers.[19]

Capital flows have always been important, facilitated by Singapore's relatively developed financial system. The stock exchange was active from the 1960s and periodically attracted large inflows of foreign capital.[20] Although long-term capital inflows increased in the 1960s to remain at about 10 percent of GDP from 1970 onward, as measured by the savings-to-investment ratio, capital inflows were most critical in the early 1960s. Since the mid-1980s, Singapore has had a net excess of national savings, and so, although capital inflows remain important for reasons such as technology transmission, reliance on foreign capital to finance domestic investment has decreased. The relative importance of short-term capital—which is more potentially destabilizing—appears to have declined over time. In 1994, portfolio capital was only 3 percent of total investment, a lower proportion than for either Malaysia or Indonesia at the same time (Department of Statistics n.d., 1995).

Malaysia's economy and financial sector have not, in most respects, been as highly internationalized as Singapore's. Nonetheless, capital mobility and economic internationalization in Malaysia have always been at high levels, in part because of a colonial legacy that linked it to Singapore and London. Even though some capital-account restrictions on non–Sterling Area transactions were in place until the 1970s and a requirement to remit export earnings continued until the 1990s, the capital account was largely permissive, especially for foreign investors. Further, Malaysia's high level of trade dependence must always have limited the enforcement of capital-account regulations. From 1960 to the mid-1980s, exports of goods and services were generally around 50 percent of GNP, rising to 90 percent in the 1990s. As in many other postcolonial countries, foreign companies dominated the Malaysian economy for over a decade after independence

19. For details of bank operations overseas, see Hamilton-Hart 1999, 175–79.
20. Foreign capital was behind the boom markets in the early and mid-1970s. See *Singapore Trade and Industry*, December 1971.

(Jesudason 1989, 56–60). Overall, foreigners owned 63 percent of share capital in 1970, a proportion that was reduced to 25 percent in 1990 and 28 percent in 1995.[21]

Malaysia's banking sector has been moderately internationalized at all times since 1960. The proportion of foreign assets and liabilities of the banking system decreased after the 1960s because of central bank regulation. Since then, there has been little variation in the percentage of assets or liabilities held abroad: foreign assets remain at around 6 percent of the total, liabilities at around 8 percent. As discussed below, government policy gradually reduced the dominance of foreign banks in the early postindependence period. Local banks have been chiefly oriented to the domestic market, although some inherited branches in Singapore, and most established offices in the major foreign financial centers in the 1960s or 1970s. In the 1990s, some banks increased their overseas operations, largely in Asia.[22]

Capital flows have been consistently significant for Malaysia. Total net inflows were higher in the first half of the 1990s, when they averaged 11 percent of GNP, than in the 1960s, when they averaged 1 percent (as they did also in the late 1980s). Net inflows reached an all-time high of 24 percent of GNP in 1993. A noticeable change over time was the shift to net inflows of short-term capital, until the major reversals in 1997. From 1960 to 1985, the net balance of short-term capital always represented an outflow of funds, with the one exceptional year of 1974. As for many other regional countries (but not Singapore), portfolio flows increased to extraordinarily high levels in both absolute and relative terms during the first half of the 1990s. These inflows were related to the rapid development of the financial sector from the 1980s. Malaysia already had a comparatively developed financial sector in 1980, when total financial assets were 139 percent of GDP, but the massive increase in stock market capitalization from the late 1980s was to a great extent fueled by foreign funds that turned their attention to the region.

Indonesia's economy until the 1990s was in most respects the least internationalized among these countries. The foreign-exchange regime was, in theory, highly restrictive before it was progressively simplified after 1967 and almost completely liberalized in 1970 (Cole and Slade 1996, 42–44). Even before 1970, however, foreign-exchange controls were only partially effective as a means of controlling private access to foreign exchange or ensuring the repatriation of export proceeds. There were exemptions for oil companies under the let-alone agreement negotiated with the Dutch (Oey 1991, 58–59). More significantly, the controls were not implemented consistently. Evidence of effective capital mobility before 1970 is the wide divergence between official foreign exchange rates and the unofficial free-market rates quoted in both Jakarta and Hong Kong (Emery 1970, 154; Oey 1991, 375).

On most other measures of internationalization, economic openness declined in the mid-1950s and increased in the late 1960s and after the mid-1980s. Export

---

21. Official figures, as cited in Gomez 1999, 2.
22. Information on branching comes from the annual reports of the banks themselves.

ratios have never been high by regional standards, but the export sector has been important. Exports rose from 12 percent of GNP in 1970 to 30 percent in 1980 and fluctuated thereafter between 24 and 30 percent. For most of the 1950s and 1960s, exports sank from 19 percent of GNP in 1951 to around 10 percent; however, trade figures for that period are an underestimation because of smuggling and misreporting (Simkin 1970).

Foreign ownership of domestic assets has followed a similar trend, decreasing after the mid-1950s until the 1980s. As of 1985, foreign companies accounted for 20 percent of the paid-up capital of major companies (Sato 1994, 110). The situation before 1966 is not clear. A fairly extensive survey concluded that much of the modern sector was in foreign hands in the early 1950s, although even by then the Indonesian government owned significant commercial assets that had been in the hands of the colonial government (Allen and Donnithorne 1957, 60). By the late 1950s, foreign ownership had been reduced by the nationalization of Dutch enterprises, which had constituted the largest part of the foreign-owned sector. In the early 1950s, capital inflows of all types were low, particularly long-term loans and foreign direct investment (FDI) which frequently registered a net outflow. After the change of regime in 1966, capital inflows increased to average 5 percent of GDP until 1974, slightly higher than the 4 percent recorded in the first half of the 1990s, which does not, however, include the large, unrecorded foreign liabilities of Indonesian firms in the 1990s.

Since the nationalization of most foreign banks in the 1950s, Indonesia has in some ways had a less internationalized banking sector than Malaysia or Singapore, with a smaller part of the domestic market going to foreign banks and less overseas branching by local banks. On the other hand, the international exposure of the banking system has often been high. For example, foreign currency liabilities averaged 19 percent of total liabilities in the early 1970s and 21 percent in the first half of the 1990s. Currency substitution has been significant since the early 1970s (Arndt and Suwidjana 1982).

Indonesia's currency has always been vulnerable to pressure, suffering frequent devaluations through the 1950s and 1960s and two major devaluations in the 1980s. None of these episodes of currency instability, however, even approached the level of real devaluation experienced in the 1998 currency crisis.[23] A sharp increase in inflows of short-term capital preceded this crisis, as foreign investors responded to capital-market deregulation in Indonesia in the late 1980s. Partly in consequence, financial development (the ratio of financial assets to GDP) increased rapidly over the same period. At independence, Indonesia had a much less developed financial system than either Malaysia or Singapore; the internationalized foreign banks of the 1950s were a small enclave in an economy that made very little use of banks or formal financial markets. The rapid growth in financial assets from the late 1980s, therefore, marked a revolutionary change in the financial system

---

23. See Appendix 1 for currency values.

(Cole and Slade 1996, 14). The stock exchange did not become active until the late 1980s, when foreign purchasers led its spectacular revival.[24]

In summary, on most measures of economic openness and capital mobility, Malaysia and Singapore have had highly internationalized economies since the 1960s. For Malaysia, short-term capital inflows assumed a new importance in the early 1990s, but in most other respects these two countries did not suddenly acquire internationalized economies in the late 1980s; they already had internationalized economies. In Indonesia, by contrast, there was a definite trend over time toward higher levels of economic internationalization and capital mobility. Nonetheless, the transnational ties and trading interests of many Indonesian entrepreneurs meant that the potential for outflows of capital from Indonesia always existed.

GOVERNMENT CAPACITY AND MANAGEMENT STRATEGIES

The different attributes and capacities of state organizations in Singapore, Malaysia, and Indonesia resulted in different responses to four challenges related to capital mobility and economic internationalization: managing local capital outflows, reducing foreign dominance in the banking sector, maintaining macroeconomic stability, and monitoring the capital account. These responses determined how much political control over the economy would be sustainable and influenced how vulnerable each country would be to financial instability.

Managing Capital Outflows

No Southeast Asian government has been in a position to prevent outward investment by its nationals. Faced with the same potential for capital outflows, however, different governments managed the situation differently. This meant that capital outflows had qualitatively different implications for the domestic economy and the reach of government policy. In Singapore, the government used internationalization as part of its activist approach to managing economic change. Regional investment as a comprehensive strategy was actualized only from the 1990s, but there were antecedents for the policy. With the establishment of the Asian dollar market in 1968 and development of telecommunications infrastructure at the same time, the idea of Singapore as a regional services hub was already being pursued. In the 1970s the government gave tax incentives for investment in Malaysia and Indonesia (*Singapore Trade and Industry*, December 1970, February 1972, September 1973).

In the mid-1980s, when outward investment had picked up independent of any government strategy, the government stepped in to provide leadership and man-

---

24. Stock market capitalization increased from 100 billion rupiah in 1987 to 215 trillion in 1996. Over this period, domestic investors became more active, but foreigners (or at least those classified as such) remained significant players. In 1996, trading transactions involving only domestic parties accounted for 24 percent of the total, while transactions involving only foreign parties accounted for 45 percent (Jakarta Stock Exchange, *JSX Statistics 1996*).

agement. It offered some support for regional investment in the mid-1980s and launched a concerted regionalization policy in the 1990s.[25] The aim was to use outward investment as a strategy to bring about structural change in the domestic economy and to expand the economy geographically (Rodan 1993a, 225). Along with the domestic economy, much of the government's managerial role was externalized. Two mechanisms supported the outward investment strategy: facilities and coordination offered as government incentives to private Singapore firms, and the government's role as a lead investor.

The Economic Development Board (EDB), one of the government agencies tasked with a facilitation role, launched a range of incentive schemes aimed at transforming local enterprises into Singaporean multinationals. The government led a number of missions to target countries such as China and formed an investment zone with Indonesia and Malaysia, known as the growth triangle (Toh and Low 1993). The government also initiated conferences with the business community to provide a two-way flow of information on the needs of Singapore business and the objectives of the regionalization policy (*Business Times*, 9 November 1992; *Straits Times*, 30 May 1993). A joint public-private sector committee provided economic policy analysis and looked at a range of second-tier concerns, from the provision of schooling to the establishment of social groups for Singaporeans posted overseas.[26]

In support of the regionalization policy, government-linked companies, statutory authorities, and holding companies became regional investors (Rodan 1993a, 240; Hamilton-Hart 1999, 253–55). Through their activities, these organizations provided material support and leadership for private Singaporean investment. In part, this was done through the provision of infrastructure overseas in a way that replicated the activity of the EDB and other development agencies at home. According to the EDB chairman, some of its overseas investment was a "symbolic move to build confidence" and might, according to the EDB managing director, be used to "bring about a certain desirable activity" (qtd. in *Business Times*, 30 July 1991).

Although private Singapore businesses had long-standing overseas operations, the government's outward investment policy was an attempt to bring those ventures under the wing of formal and informal Singaporean systems of coordination. One study of ethnic Chinese investment in the region concluded that the substantial amounts of Singaporean investment in China were not structured along ethnic lines or based on traditional personal networks (DFAT 1995, 188–89, 239–41). Instead, investment was the product of government-to-government cooperation and the creation of Singaporean enclaves of regular management and reliable infrastructure in China.

As with the other aspects of Singapore's economic policy, core features of the state system provided the institutional base on which policy stands: the attention to

25. Tax incentives were provided in 1986 and 1988, and in 1988 the EDB set up its International Direct Investment program and a China Focus unit (*Straits Times*, 30 May 1993).
26. See Committee to Promote Overseas Investment 1993a and 1993b.

performance-based measures of success, the maintenance of disciplinary mechanisms, and the development of rationalized public sector organizations with strong monitoring capacities. There was recognition that the regionalization policy should not be an excuse for handing out tax breaks and subsidized finance. The minister of trade and industry stressed the importance of safeguarding public assets and stated that spin-offs for Singapore were a condition of government aid (*Straits Times*, 23 May and 4 September 1993). Not all overseas investments have been profitable, particularly those in China, but they were continually monitored, and some unprofitable ventures were sold. The Government Investment Corporation measured its returns in Singapore dollars, which, given the appreciation of the currency to 1997, made its task more challenging (*Straits Times*, 2 December 1995).

The governments of Malaysia and Indonesia each reacted rather differently to the reality of capital outflows. In Malaysia, official policy began to encourage outward investment in 1991, declaring repatriated income from approved investments to be tax exempt. Tax exemptions were extended in 1995. This "reverse investment" initiative spawned a low-profile Reverse Investment Committee under the Ministry of International Trade and Industry to vet applications for approved investment status. A Malaysian Business Council paper discussed rationales and means for supporting reverse investment (MBC 1995). The increase in outward investment in the 1990s, however, occurred with minimal government coordination or stewardship.

Government involvement was largely limited to trade- and investment-promotion missions abroad and some investment by state-owned companies. The government supported "growth triangles" to both the south and the north but had limited influence over developments. The Singapore-Johor-Riau triangle mainly supported outward investment by Singapore, with the Johor-Riau leg almost non-existent (Toh and Low 1993, xviii). One reason for this may have been the government's pre-1992 policy: an assessment of the prospects for a growth triangle involving Malaysia, Indonesia, and Thailand noted that since "only companies without borrowings can invest in other countries," investments from Malaysia "tend to be in the informal sector" (EPU-ISIS 1991, 2). In fact, this rule was not enforced in any meaningful sense, since few Malaysian companies operating overseas would have had no domestic debt.

This issue illustrates the ambiguity in official policies regarding outward investment, which hampered government stewardship. Given that domestic investment outstripped domestic savings, official support for outward investment was bound to be problematic. Politicians occasionally stated that Malaysian companies should focus on Malaysia's investment needs and invest abroad using only funds raised abroad (*Malaysian Business*, 16 October 1997). The MBC paper on reverse investment did not mention Malaysia's savings-investment gap; therefore, though it identified the outward investment policies of Singapore and Taiwan as worthy of emulation, it did not address Malaysia's structural differences with these economies. Despite a policy of encouraging only certain types of outward investment, much Malaysian investment abroad has in fact gone into property development and financial services, ventures that do not serve to pick up the strain felt by labor-intensive manufacturing in Malaysia.[27]

A major reason for the limited effectiveness of Malaysia's outward internationalization policy is the absence of a state agency with attributes suited to administering incentive schemes that require disciplined, rule-based discrimination among Malaysian companies. Without this ability in the domestic context, the chances of consistently implementing discretionary policy abroad are almost nonexistent. The mixed records of Malaysia's state-owned enterprises also make it risky to pursue a role comparable to that taken by Singapore's government-linked companies. Nonetheless, the limited support that the government extended to outward investment is significant. Ending the vague official disapproval of investment outflows was a step toward closing the gap between rhetoric and reality. This change in attitude should therefore have increased the government's ability to monitor outward flows because it would not have forced investors to hide their activity. Given that many of the Malaysians with the resources to make significant overseas investments were ethnic Chinese, the change in official policy on outward investment reduced the perceived vulnerability of an important section of domestic capital. It also reduced the need for those most able to invest abroad to forge personal relationships with government actors in order to do so.

Indonesia's ethnic Chinese investors, operating in the context of a very different state system, employed different strategies. The capital-account regime they operated under was restrictive before 1970, but controls were subject to high rates of evasion and manipulation: political patronage and corruption around the granting of import licenses and allocations of foreign exchange were common, as were foreign-exchange scandals in the 1950s and 1960s. Further, the controls encouraged informal and barter trade as well as smuggling, a perennial problem for Indonesia (Higgins 1957, 27–35; Simkin 1970). The policy of controlling capital outflows before 1970, therefore, was never effectively enforced. A former Bank Indonesia governor joked that capital flight before 1970 meant that all liquid assets had left the country before capital controls were lifted (interview, Rachmat Saleh, Jakarta, April 1997).

After substantially liberalizing the capital account in 1970, the government introduced a regulation in 1974 restricting transfers of equity abroad. The scope of this regulation was vague, and no machinery to implement it was put in place. In the mid-1970s the government did deny permission for an Indonesian banker, Mochtar Riady, to open a bank office abroad (*Insight*, September 1978), but such restrictions were extremely rare—and Riady did open an office abroad shortly afterward.

27. The other two criteria for approved investment status, as listed in MBC 1995, app. 1, were that the project should supply the inputs required by domestic industry in Malaysia, or contribute to "South-South co-operation." According to Bank Negara Malaysia's *1995 Survey on Residents' Exposure*, 41 percent of investment abroad was channeled through offshore financial centers.

Indonesians invested abroad in part simply because of the commercial opportunities available to them. In this, they were no different from investors from countries such as Hong Kong, where the burden of economic regulation was very light and local investors were not politically vulnerable. In Indonesia, however, the political insecurity of ethnic Chinese Indonesians was an additional factor motivating outward investment (Robison 1986, 310–11). Anecdotal reports about outward investment by Sino-Indonesians confirm what might be expected from a home environment that has frequently been hostile, sometimes violently so, to ethnic Chinese: outward investment is an insurance policy against any sudden deterioration in political conditions.

This motivation for outward investment is quite different from capital outflow caused by official restrictions which make local business activity less profitable. Government policy in Malaysia in the 1970s, for example, prompted some outward investment by Malaysian Chinese businesses that were materially affected by new rules requiring *Bumiputera* participation (Jesudason 1989, 131–39, 154). This kind of capital outflow, a reaction to reduced profit opportunities at home, is likely to be reversed when policy in the home country changes: when Malaysia liberalized its foreign investment rules in response to recession in 1985, some of the subsequent "foreign" investment was believed to represent local Chinese investors. In contrast, the capital for outward investment by many Indonesian firms came from the profits that accrued to them as a result of special privileges. Liem Sioe Liong's overseas activity is probably the clearest example of how monopoly rents earned in Indonesia supported outward investment (Robison 1986, 296–315).

In these circumstances, the 1974 regulation restricting transfers of equity abroad served as a source of discretionary leverage over Sino-Indonesian investors. Keeping a vague regulation on the books but not enforcing it reinforced a more generalized gap between policy and practice. In addition, the residual scope for ad hoc enforcement encouraged many Sino-Indonesians to avoid official controls and scrutiny by establishing foreign-incorporated companies that were, on paper, quite separate from their Indonesian interests. The perception that these maneuvers were covert or based on collusion and special privilege was almost inevitable, given the way business and government interacted. Outward investment by Sino-Indonesians was therefore seen as "capital flight," evidence of disloyalty and grounds for discrimination against "Chinese" business.[28]

This climate reinforces the sense of political vulnerability that motivates strategies of international asset diversification in the first place. Government actions systematically created an environment in which Sino-Indonesians depended on personal connections and collusive arrangements. The exclusion of ethnic Chinese from public roles in the New Order effectively removed the option of organized,

28. Indonesian businessmen who defended themselves against accusations of capital flight in 1991 were again subject to accusations of capital flight and tax evasion when Indonesian-linked companies restructured assets on the Singapore exchange in 1996 and 1997. See *Straits Times*, 9 February 1991, 31 July 1997; *Asian Wall Street Journal*, 22 August 1996.

open political activity and denied Sino-Indonesians a recognized place in the polity. In this, Indonesian anti-Sinicism has been very different from Malaysia's ethnically biased political economy, in which Malaysian Chinese have always had legitimate public positions. The origins of anti-Sinicism in Indonesia can be traced to growing perceptions of local Chinese as predatory and sinister in the early twentieth century. By the late 1910s, with the assurance that "anti-Sinicism would henceforth be firmly in place in the native mind," the colonial government could make economic concessions to the Chinese with confidence, since the new form of anti-Sinicism reduced the Chinese to "pariahs—no longer part of the regime, without any real power to threaten the Dutch, and vulnerable to popular native antagonism," writes Takashi Shiraishi (1997a, 205).

This politically expedient strategy was as useful to the New Order as it had been to the Dutch. The colonial government, however, did not rely on politically marginalized and vulnerable ethnic Chinese businesses to run the modern sectors of the economy; that phenomenon of the postindependence period reached its height in the New Order. What made it workable, for a time, was the particular nature of Indonesian state organizations: because they had incorporated personalized interventions and ways of circumventing formal rules and procedures into their organizational routines, they could sustain informal alliances with Sino-Indonesian entrepreneurs in the context of broader discrimination.

Managing Foreign Banks

In the newly independent states of Southeast Asia, popular aspirations and economic nationalism led to demands for colonial patterns of ownership to change. In both Malaysia, and Indonesia, overt political pressure resulted in policies of reducing foreign ownership: in Indonesia in the 1950s, in Malaysia from the late 1960s (Glassburner 1971; Jesudason 1989). Banks were a particular target of policies to alter the distribution of assets among different political groups and economic sectors. Singapore, Malaysia, and Indonesia all reduced the role played by foreign banks in the domestic market, but the outcomes of this policy were rather different in each case.

When Singapore assumed self-government, the banking market was dominated by foreign banks, which accounted for twenty-seven of the thirty-four banks operating in 1959 (Ministry of Finance 1963). In the combined Singapore-Malaya banking market, local banks accounted for 32 percent of bank credit in 1959 (Lee 1974, 88). Over the next decades the relative positions of local and foreign banks were reversed. The high share of total bank assets (always over 60 percent) that continued to be held by foreign banks in Singapore was due to their offshore operations. Their exclusion from the much more profitable domestic market was evident in the decline in the foreign share of total banking profits, which fell from 49 percent in 1974 to 28 percent in 1995 (SGV; SRMS).

A similar reversal occurred in Malaysia. In 1959 there were eighteen foreign and four local banks. Foreign banks accounted for 89 percent of all branch offices, and the largest local bank, Kwong Yik, accounted for 2 percent of all bank credit in the Malaya-Singapore market (Lee 1974, 88; Singh 1984, 26). By the mid-1970s, local banks had achieved parity with foreign banks in terms of assets. By 1995, foreign banks held only 10 percent of banking offices and 22 percent of total banking assets (Bank Negara Malaysia, *Quarterly Bulletin*).

In Indonesia the decline of foreign banks was more dramatic. In the immediate postwar period the largest banks operating in Indonesia were Dutch. By 1951, however, several Indonesian banks had been established, and the new state banks grew rapidly. By 1960 most foreign banks were effectively nationalized (Bank Indonesia, *Report for the Financial Year 1959–60*). Foreign banks were readmitted in 1968, but their share of domestic bank assets, even at its highest (about 13 percent in the late 1960s and early 1970s), remained much lower than in either Singapore or Malaysia.

Reducing the role played by foreign banks required political will but no particular administrative capacity, since local ownership could be achieved simply by nationalization and subsidy. The organizational capacity to implement policy in a consistent and disciplined way, however, is necessary if this policy is not to be extremely costly. It is a demanding task to replace established and relatively efficient foreign banks with inexperienced domestic banks without prompting a loss of confidence in the banking system or seriously constraining its development. It requires regulatory capacity and, particularly if state-owned banks play a large role, self-discipline in state agencies. If the process is gradual (as in Malaysia and Singapore), it requires that foreign banks be convinced that it is worthwhile to stay and collect a smaller share of the pie. These challenges were explicitly recognized by a former governor of Malaysia's central bank, who identified the organization's most urgent priorities in its early years as the interrelated objectives of increasing domestic ownership in the banking system and establishing the central bank as an authoritative and respected institution (interview, Tun Ismail, Kuala Lumpur, October 1996). Given these challenges and considering what is known about the nature of state organizations in Singapore, Malaysia, and Indonesia, it should be predictable that the economic consequences of reducing foreign dominance in the banking sector would be different in each case. And indeed, the costs in terms of financial sector efficiency, stability, and savings mobilization were absent or relatively low in Singapore and Malaysia but significant in Indonesia.

Managing the Macroeconomy

By extending the range of viable policy options, governing capacity can reduce the trade-offs associated with maintaining national macroeconomic goals under conditions of capital mobility.[29] Government appropriation of financial assets provides some alternative to monetary policy as a macroeconomic lever, avoids the con-

---

29. See Chapter 2.

straints that can arise from reliance on foreign borrowing, and reduces the proportion of domestic financial assets sensitive to differentials between foreign and domestic interest rates. Temporary controls on short-term capital flows can lessen capital mobility, providing an alternative way of avoiding the trade-off between monetary autonomy and exchange-rate stability. Other regulatory controls, from restrictions on real estate speculation to ad hoc limits on credit card or margin lending, can reduce the need to use monetary policy to maintain domestic price stability. All these strategies, however, are administratively demanding and have the potential to be very costly if not implemented with discipline.

Singapore's record suggests that states with high governing capacity can employ a range of strategies to manage the macroeconomy. One mechanism was an early and concerted move to increase government appropriation of financial assets, both through the tax system and through financial institutions. Government revenues escalated from the 1960s, from 16 percent of GDP in the first half of the 1960s to 29 percent in the second half of the 1980s (total public sector revenues were significantly higher from the 1970s). The government also tapped compulsory and voluntary savings through institutions such as the Central Provident Fund, the Post Office Savings Bank, and the commercial banks, which were required to hold a proportion of their assets in government securities.

One consequence was that the Singapore government met virtually all its financing requirements domestically—at mildly concessionary rates. The CPF alone held over 80 percent of government debt until 1982, after which official figures on holders of public debt were discontinued. Even at its peak, external government debt never accounted for more than 13 percent of the total. As public sector surpluses since the 1980s removed the need for this type of financing, CPF funds supported other policy goals: home ownership, welfare substitution, and capital-market development. The CPF was also used to complement monetary and fiscal policies. For example, employer contribution rates were halved to support economic recovery after the 1985 recession, raised during the period of strong economic growth that followed, and halved again in response to the economic downturn of 1998. Like the public sector fiscal surpluses, the CPF has a contractionary effect on money supply, for which it is often criticized. But a built-in bias to contractionary policy allows the MAS to concentrate on injecting liquidity as required, an advantage during periods of capital inflow.

The ability to ensure a positive return on members' contributions by containing inflation was a background condition of the CPF system. More directly, it required the capacity to enforce contributions and run the CPF efficiently and incorruptly. The contributor base expanded until the early 1980s, and administration costs were low (Asher 1994, 45, 70). Relatively high income levels and an urban environment made it easier to limit administration costs and monitor compliance. Nonetheless, considerable effort went into enforcing contributions in the early years of the scheme: CPF officers conducted intensive field checks on employers, imposed penalties on those evading contributions, and successfully prosecuted recalcitrant employers.[30]

Although the government was able to influence monetary conditions, Singapore could not avoid the trade-off between exchange-rate stability and monetary autonomy. From the 1950s the openness of the financial system meant that interest rates (set by a bank cartel until 1975) followed those in London. Senior policymakers believed that there was little prospect for an independent monetary policy, given the high import content of domestic consumption and the need to reassure foreign investors (*Singapore Trade and Industry*, January 1970; Lee 1990, 53–62).

In 1980, exchange rate targeting was adopted as the main monetary policy tool.[31] This enabled domestic interest rates to remain significantly lower than U.S. rates without any large outflow of funds. With recession in the mid-1980s, interest rates were reduced to about 3 percentage points lower than rates in the offshore market. After 1988, with full recovery, the exchange rate was appreciated more aggressively to contain domestic inflation. At this time, the government also introduced a variable requirement for the surplus funds of government-linked companies and statutory authorities to be deposited with the MAS, thereby centralizing a sizable portion of financial assets. In addition, the government in the 1990s used ad hoc regulatory controls such as taxes on property speculation and restrictions on credit cards to contain asset price inflation and dampen domestic liquidity. Despite its open financial system, therefore, Singapore has generally been successful in maintaining enough macroeconomic discretion to achieve its goals of stability and high economic growth. Notably, it was able to avoid the self-defeating monetary policies of Malaysia and Indonesia in the years before 1997.

Malaysia employed many of the same strategies as Singapore to achieve its macroeconomic goals. An important element was government appropriation of financial assets through relatively high public sector revenues, a centralized compulsory savings fund, and compulsory purchases of government debt by financial institutions. The compulsory retirement savings fund, the Employees Provident Fund, remains a key institution. The EPF steadily built up its contributor base, and as of 1993 its membership covered 89 percent of the workforce and it held 77 percent of the provident, pension, and insurance funds in Malaysia (BNM 1994, 248). EPF balances accounted for a substantial percentage of private savings (Kanapathy and Ismail 1994, 75, 96). The EPF generally held about half of the government's domestic debt, and compulsory holdings by other financial institutions have accounted for around 30 percent since 1965. The government has raised most of its debt domestically.[32]

The administrative ability to collect and manage funds is a condition of such appropriation. An effective tax collection infrastructure raised government rev-

---

30. See the annual CPF *Report to Parliament* for the 1960s.
31. The main sources for this paragraph are Claassen 1992; Peebles and Wilson 1996, 145–54, 175–83; and *Asian Wall Street Journal*, 2 July 1997.
32. Foreign borrowing did rise in the early 1980s but did not present a servicing problem.

enues from a relatively high (by developing country standards) 19 percent of GDP in the second half of the 1960s to 27 percent or more since the early 1980s (as for Singapore, total public-sector revenues are higher). The EPF's administration costs are higher than those of Singapore's CPF, but if Malaysia's lower level of per capita wealth and larger physical area are considered, administrative costs have not been high (Asher 1994). To enforce contributions, the EPF developed an active field inspection staff in its early years and published information on defaulting employers. The 7,236 prosecutions of employers between 1990 and 1994 (EPF, *Annual Report* 1994) suggests vigorous enforcement. Questions have been raised about periodic attempts by the political leadership to engage EPF funds for risky projects (Gomez 1994, 60). The EPF has been protected to some extent, however, both by the high level of public interest in its performance (and consequently the very heavy political price that would be paid for abuses) and by other control mechanisms. Central bank and Finance Ministry officials, as well as academic advisers, generally hold positions on the fund's investment panel. It is audited by the auditor general's office, which has a reputation for independence (Doh 1985). The EPF Act was amended in 1991 with the aim of giving the fund a new role in capital-market development by allowing it to invest in the stock market (BNM 1994, 249–55). Although it suffered large losses when the local stock market collapsed in 1998, the EPF has been relatively adept at its new asset management role.[33]

Monetary policy has been constrained by the openness of Malaysia's financial markets. In the 1960s the central bank frequently referred to the need to maintain rough parity with rates in London. The desire for greater monetary autonomy was part of the reason that Malaysia ended the Currency Board system shared with Singapore and Brunei in 1967 and moved toward more flexible exchange rates in 1973 (Lee 1974, 222–42). Periodic recourse to regulatory controls has also allowed Malaysia some leeway in its monetary policy, even in the early 1990s (Brouwer 1997). Other means of maintaining stability, such as the centralization of public sector financial assets, were less effective in Malaysia than in Singapore (Claassen 1992). Similarly, the central bank's attempt to use regulatory controls, such as tightened limits on bank lending for share purchases in 1997, came too late to be effective in dampening Malaysia's booming financial markets.

When macroeconomic goals were most under pressure in the years before the regional financial crisis of 1997, Malaysia relied chiefly on conventional monetary levers. The attempt was largely counterproductive. Extremely large inflows of capital aggravated excess domestic liquidity and incipient inflationary pressure. Because of a desire not to increase an already significant current account deficit, however, little currency appreciation was permitted. The ringgit remained under-

33. The head of investments for the EPF said that its investment managers outperform contracted asset managers from the private sector, whose main function is to provide a performance measure (interview, Kuala Lumpur, November 1996).

valued in 1996.[34] The central bank attempted to deal with the situation by raising interest rates and engaging in massive sterilization, with the result that official foreign reserves increased 55 percent in 1992 and 62 percent in 1993. The direct costs of this kind of sterilization are likely to have been significant (Khan and Reinhart 1995, 27). Further, the expectation of eventual appreciation added to the incentives for capital inflow, compounding the effect of the continued high interest rates that were due to sterilization.

The attempt to apply closed economy monetary policy is difficult to explain, especially since the central bank clearly recognized the real dilemmas it faced (Zeti 1997). In particular, one must ask why the central bank only briefly, in 1994, pursued the alternative policy of taxing short-term capital inflows. An assistant governor of the central bank in 1994 explained later that bank officials had been worried about maintaining financial market confidence; in addition, "the IMF did not like such distortions" (interview, Kuala Lumpur, October 1996). Before accepting this explanation, however, one must consider at least three other possibilities.[35] One involves the political gains deriving from Malaysia's rapidly rising stock market, which was stimulated by capital inflows; not only did this yield benefits to important constituents of the ruling party, but members of the ruling party may have used the stock market to fund political campaigns (Gomez 1996). A second possibility is that, as noted earlier, the central bank in the early 1990s was distracted by its pursuit of foreign-exchange trading profits and the subsequent scandal around the trading losses; less coherent central-bank policy might be an expected result. Third, the increasingly close relations and identity of outlook between government and bankers may have made officials reluctant to pursue a policy that was both unorthodox and against the interests of the financial industry.

Nevertheless, the fact that the controls *were* implemented, albeit briefly, suggests that they were a realistic policy option for Malaysia. They did not lead to a decline in inflows of direct foreign investment, nor, according to foreign bankers and securities firms interviewed in Kuala Lumpur, did they contribute to a sense of country risk about Malaysia.[36] Specific and temporary, they did not touch long-term capital, convertibility, or repatriation. Malaysia's later record of implementing a much more ambitious set of controls, including restrictions on outflows in 1998, provides an additional reason for believing that "market forces" were not the reason for Malaysia's reluctance to restrict inflows before then.

---

34. The IMF's managing director was among those to hold this view. A Morgan Stanley report predicted in 1994 that the ringgit should trade at RM 2.00 to the U.S. dollar by 1996. See Ong 1996, 10; and Zeti 1997.

35. Another former central bank official was adamant that neither market nor IMF pressure could explain why the capital controls were imposed late and removed quickly (interview, Kuala Lumpur, October 1996).

36. This was the consensus among foreigners in Malaysia in 1996. In Singapore, American investment firms saw the controls much more negatively (interview, *Asian Wall Street Journal* journalist, Singapore, August 1997).

If Malaysia found it harder to realize macroeconomic goals than Singapore, Indonesia was most constrained. One reason is that Indonesia was never able to exercise the same degree of direct control over financial resources. Until well into the 1980s, the government relied on aid, oil, debt, or the printing press to fund a large part of its expenditure. The vulnerabilities these strategies create are fairly obvious. Disorganization and private diversion impeded the government's tax collection, and domestic revenues remained low: while increasing from 11 percent of GDP in the 1950s (Azhari 1965, 73–78), they remained around 18 percent even after tax reform in the 1980s. Since the 1970s, oil receipts have made up a large proportion, generally over 30 percent, of total government revenues, and foreign aid accounted for 24 percent of total revenues in the second half of the 1980s.

Unlike Malaysia and Singapore, Indonesia found that raising domestic debt was a risky proposition, one that its technocrats and foreign donors thought best to remove as an option after the change of regime in 1966. Given the abuses suffered by the relatively small pension and savings fund for government employees, the prospects for a Malaysian-style centralized pension fund were poor. In the Indonesian context, it was inconceivable that any such fund would not be seen as yet another source of easy money for the well-connected (interview, Mari Pangestu, Jakarta, March 1997). Similarly, Indonesia found that the compulsory purchase of government debt by financial institutions was incompatible with financial sector development. Financial deregulation in the 1980s involved slashing the commercial banks' reserve ratios and therefore removed a potential source of government funding. Again, Indonesian state organizations, not the policy of required reserves itself, was at issue: Malaysia and Singapore both required financial institutions to hold government debt, but rates of financial intermediation did not suffer as a result.

Indonesia, then, had a more limited set of policy options available when, for the first time, it faced large private-capital inflows, excess domestic liquidity, and upward pressure on the exchange rate in the first half of the 1990s. To maintain export competitiveness, the exchange rate was gradually depreciated and thus could not absorb any of the macroeconomic pressures created by inflows. The reserve ratio imposed on banks was increased, but only from 2 to 3 percent of deposits. The central bank also announced annual ceilings on new credit by commercial banks but failed to enforce them. Rather, the main mechanism for dealing with the situation was a monetary one: issuing central bank bonds at rates of interest attractive enough to mop up excess financial-market liquidity. As a result, real interest rates in Indonesia remained high; incentives for offshore borrowing increased; and capital inflows, although fluctuating, remained high right up to the massive reversals experienced in 1997 and 1998.

Managing the Capital Account

Effective government monitoring of the capital account is an important part of financial management in an open economy. It is a prerequisite for controls on capital flows, and a necessary adjunct to macroeconomic management and financial policy more generally, if basic economic indicators are to be useful sources of information. Reliably monitoring the capital account and tracking the foreign assets and liabilities of domestic firms are administratively demanding tasks. Intensive monitoring also opens the door to many potential abuses of power by state officials and hence may be particularly resisted in countries that do not have records of implementing policy consistently. The different approaches to capital-account monitoring taken by Singapore, Malaysia, and Indonesia confirm the potential difficulties it presents for state organizations with limited governing capacity.

As a financial center and safe haven, Singapore had an interest in releasing little information about the source and destination of capital inflows and outflows. Until the regional crisis prompted greater disclosure to the Bank for International Settlements in 1998, it did not reveal the geographic distribution of loans or deposits made through its offshore market. There is evidence, however, that Singapore did engage in extensive capital-account monitoring well before this time: until the mid-1970s the Monetary Authority's annual reports indicate, in broad terms, where money in the offshore market came from and where it went; in the 1990s, surveys by the Department of Statistics reveal the ability to collect detailed information at the firm level and to collate this information; and after 1998, when for the first time there was effective demand for disclosure on the geographic distribution of bank assets and national foreign debt, the government had the figures readily available.[37]

Malaysia has been consistently more transparent, and the information generated by the central bank and the Department of Statistics reveals a concerted monitoring effort. The government has surveyed the foreign assets and liabilities of Malaysian companies since the 1980s.[38] In 1991 the central bank introduced a more comprehensive balance-of-payments reporting system, which details gross capital inflows and outflows under different categories, and an annual survey of selected companies provides information on the country's foreign assets and liabilities.[39] The central bank is therefore able to generate a profile of Malaysian outward investment, including the geographic distribution of portfolio investment. The central bank also monitors the immediate source of portfolio capital inflows. With this kind of monitoring capacity, Malaysia was well placed to implement restrictions on foreign currency debt acquisition by Malaysian companies, which received more attention in the wake of the regional financial crisis (Bank Negara Malaysia, *Annual Report* 1997, 192–93).

Indonesia's very limited capital-account monitoring was brought dramatically to light in 1998, when private estimates of the foreign liabilities of Indonesian com-

---

37. See, e.g., MAS, *Annual Report 1976*; Department of Statistics n.d., 1995, 1997, and 1998; and official statements regarding Singapore banks' regional lending in *Business Times*, 15 and 28 January 1998.
38. Reported in Department of Statistics, *Report on the Financial Survey of Limited Companies* (various issues).
39. This *Survey of Residents' Exposure* has had a relatively high rate of response (rising from 76 percent in 1992 to 93 percent in 1995).

panies dwarfed official figures. The immediate cause of the massive information deficit was the government's policy of imposing only minimal reporting requirements on the private sector. This was not a simple policy oversight; the central bank was aware, before the crisis, that the absence of a systematic monitoring system was a potential problem. According to a central bank officer, however, Bank Indonesia staff were largely reduced to scanning the financial press to track the overseas fund-raising activity of Indonesian firms (interview, Jakarta, April 1997). Officials knew enough to be uneasy but, in the absence of concrete information, could not even make the case for reining in the foreign borrowing of Indonesian companies. When asked why the bank did not impose reporting requirements, a senior central bank official replied that "we do not dare" (interview, Jakarta, March 1997).

Financial industry professionals and Jakarta-based commentators interviewed in 1996 and 1997 (before the onset of the crisis) explained the very limited monitoring by the central bank as a result of Indonesia's commitment to an open capital-account regime. Many interviewees asserted that any move by Indonesian authorities to impose reporting requirements, let alone controls on capital inflows, would seriously damage the economy by sending "the wrong message" to investors. The head of a foreign securities house said that it would "go against everything Bank Indonesia stands for, everything they've been saying since 1988," and the government would lose all credibility (interview, Jakarta, April 1997). In a sense, Indonesia's government had already lost credibility. The central bank's demonstrated failure to implement other financial policies in a consistent, efficient, or rule-abiding way created a suspicion of any policy that entailed an active enforcement role for government agencies. But Malaysia's ability to implement a rigorous capital-account monitoring regime indicates that monitoring per se was not the issue. As in other areas, Indonesia's range of viable policy options was constrained by the nature of its state organizations.

The different governing strategies employed by Singapore, Malaysia, and Indonesia left them in very different positions when they faced the wave of financial market turmoil that washed out from Thailand in the middle of 1997. These strategies were partly the result of politically generated policy choices; in addition, however, the way the state is organized influences the way it manages the political and economic risks arising from economic openness and capital mobility. Different states are more or less able to cope with these challenges because responding to them effectively entails complex tasks with the potential to create costly side effects if they are not implemented consistently. The political, economic, and administrative challenges of managing an open economy change over time, however, and so do states themselves, as shown by the strategies adopted in response to the crisis of 1998 and the ways in which state organizational attributes may be changing.

7.

After the Crisis: Convergence?

Actually there is not going to be much of a future for Asia, at least a future
that is distinctly Asian. In the globalised, deregulated world the future of
Asia will be so closely inter-twined and interlinked with that of the rest of
the world that it cannot be distinguished from the world's future.

—MAHATHIR MOHAMAD,
speech at the *Nihon Keizei
Shimbun* International
Conference on
The Future of Asia,
Tokyo, 4 June 1998

Financial and economic crises in Asia, Latin America, and Russia in 1997 and 1998
were unprecedented in scale and largely unexpected. As governments, international institutions, banks, and ordinary citizens struggled to cope with the consequences, contending views over what the whole episode represented began to
emerge. Many took up the idea that events in Asia marked the collision of fundamentally incompatible economic and political systems—a "clash of capitalisms"—
involving deep-seated social as well as economic arrangements (Chalmers Johnson
1998; Wade and Veneroso 1998). As the former miracle economies of Korea,
Thailand, and Indonesia collapsed and Japan remained mired in its own economic
swamp, there seemed very little doubt about which type of capitalism was going
to have to give way. Asia would have to adopt policies and institutions more like
those of the West: free markets, open financial systems, shareholder-oriented
corporate governance regimes, and independent central banks. To make all these
work, reform would also have to replace Asian "cronyism" with Anglo-American
"governance"—the rule of law, transparency, and external checks on government.
At the international level, a "new financial architecture" (see Eichengreen 2000;
Kahler 2000) would promote international regulatory standards and strengthen
agencies such as the International Monetary Fund.

The forces arrayed in support of such a reform agenda appeared compelling.
First, there was the need to regain the confidence of investors, which seemed to
imply a shift toward more liberal economies. Also urging liberalizing reforms were
two external actors with considerable clout: the IMF and the United States gov-

ernment. The blueprint for reform in crisis-hit countries was largely drawn up in Washington and imposed through conditions attached to the IMF's rescue packages for Thailand, Indonesia, and Korea, as well as direct pressure from the United States (Bello 1998; Feldstein 1998). A third source of pressure was domestic: consumers, anticorruption activists, businesspeople, and policymakers in many countries were frequently on the side of "reform." While no one expected an overnight transformation, several analyses (e.g., Haggard 2000) argued that these pressures would set countries in Asia on a path toward fundamental change in their policies and public institutions.

Other scenarios for post-crisis Asia suggest that countries are likely to follow significantly different paths. Groups that might support a liberal reform agenda remain weak in countries such as the Philippines and Indonesia, where much of the domestic business class is either politically disorganized or dependent on special favors (Robison 1998; Hutchcroft 1999). Alternatively, broad social coalitions rather than narrow sectional interests might reject IMF-style reforms. Many Thai activists, for example, see the good-governance agenda as "part of the plot to make Thailand a safe place for foreign capital" (Pasuk 1999, 7). More generally, reforms that conflict with legitimate national interests and values are likely to be resented—and jettisoned as soon as possible in favor of national or regional alternatives (Higgott 1998).

Even if economic and political pressure for reform brings about change, it will not necessarily be in the direction of greater rationalization in government or stability in financial markets. After all, certain elements of the reform package purveyed by the IMF and its supporters were implicated in the crisis itself: not only the largely unmodified commitment to international capital mobility but also the continuing influence of the same "Wall Street–Treasury–IMF complex" that promoted financial liberalization in Asia before the crisis (Bhagwati 1998; Rodrik 1999; Cohen 2000). Further, the cronyism that Asian governments were charged with after the crisis may survive liberalization. In the eyes of some critics of the Washington agencies, the prescribed reforms would substitute one kind of privilege for another. Malaysia's Prime Minister Mahathir, for example, remarked that if Malaysia accepts IMF-style reforms, "there will not be any giant Bumiputera companies. And we will be happy as there will not be any more Bumiputera 'billionaires' and 'millionaires' with their Mercedes, private jets and luxury yachts. All those who are accused of being political leaders' cronies will be got rid [of]. . . . The foreign workers will earn high wages. They will in turn be the millionaires and billionaires with the Mercedes, private aircrafts and luxury boats" (Mahathir 1998, 61).

There is no one category into which recent reforms and policy changes in Asia fit. Taken together, the national strategies of the high- or moderately high-capacity states of Taiwan, Singapore, Hong Kong, Malaysia, and Korea show the variety of policy responses that were viable in the post-crisis environment. They were compelled to react to the crisis, but the way each did so reflected primarily national priorities. In contrast, the lower-capacity states of Thailand, Indonesia, and the Philippines were more constrained in their policy choices. These countries were under significant pressure to remake themselves, in both policy and institutional terms. They also showed a remarkable ability to frustrate both domestic and foreign reformers. Although the language used is different today, parallels can be drawn with a much earlier period of internationalized business and vastly more powerful pressures for reform. As Carl Trocki has written (1992, 81), "The high tide of European colonialism was characterized by compromise, qualification, half-measures, and inevitably frustrating results. The gap between aims and achievements was usually blamed on the 'laziness,' the 'incompetence' and presumed racial, cultural and moral inferiority of the indigenous peoples. Despite the failure of stated European objectives, however, fundamental change was effected although it was often entirely unintended and sometimes contrary to the initial purpose."

A VARIETY OF CRISES

Almost all countries in Asia suffered from the currency and financial crises that followed the collapse of the Thai baht in July 1997. The debate over causes continues, but it is clear that the combination of factors accounting for financial instability in 1997 and 1998 was different for each country. The politics of crisis management also varied across the region (Pempel 1999; Haggard 2000; Noble and Ravenhill 2000; Robison et al. 2000). The governing capacity of state organizations can account for some of the variation in how vulnerable national financial systems were, and differences among regional countries are ongoing in their most recent experiences of financial crisis, economic recession, and recovery.

Table 7.1 shows that all countries except for Hong Kong, Singapore, and Taiwan experienced the severe initial shock of currency devaluation, with Indonesia by far the worst affected. Most regional currencies subsequently recovered from their lows against the U.S. dollar, but only the Singapore dollar, along with the pegged currencies of Hong Kong and Malaysia, remained stable over 2000. Table 7.2 shows that economic growth profiles are similar insofar as, again, Indonesia (trailed by Thailand) stands out for the depth of its recession in 1998 and slow recovery. Another similarity is that Taiwan and Singapore fared better than most in avoiding a sharp contraction in 1998. If serious problems in their domestic banking systems over this period are taken into account, the non-crisis countries are Singapore, Taiwan, Hong Kong, and the Philippines. Of the crisis countries, Malaysia and Korea recovered noticeably faster than Thailand and Indonesia. The long-term public costs of banking system bailouts in these countries are likely to be lowest in Malaysia and highest in Indonesia.[1] The govern-

---

1. One source puts bank recapitalization funds disbursed and remaining fiscal costs of rescue at 10 percent of GDP for Malaysia, 17 percent for Korea, 22 percent for Thailand, and 59 percent for Indonesia (Haggard 2000, 145). Other estimates of total bailout costs vary widely but generally rank the countries' relative public costs in the same order.

Table 7.1. Exchange Rates

	Local Currency Units per U.S. Dollar[a]					Change (%)	
	1997	1998	1999	2000	2001	1997–1998[b]	2000[c]
Singapore	1.41	1.76	1.69	1.68	1.73	−11.6	−2.9
Hong Kong	7.74	7.74	7.75	7.78	7.80	0	−0.2
Taiwan	27.44	33.71	32.35	30.81	32.57	−13.8	−5.4
Malaysia	2.49	4.50	3.80	3.80	3.80	−33.6	0
Korea	855	1,725	1,177	1,124	1,274	−36.2	−11.8
Thailand	25.81	54.22	36.98	37.15	42.99	−36.0	−13.6
Philippines	26.33	42.16	38.85	40.46	49.25	−33.0	−17.8
Indonesia	2,393	12,900	9,322	7,300	9,370	−73.8	−22.1

[a] Exchange rates on 23 January 1997, 23 January 1998, 25 January 1999, 24 January 2000, and 22 January 2001, as reported in *Far Eastern Economic Review*.
[b] Percentage change between 30 June 1999 and 8 May 1998, dollars per local currency unit, as calculated in Goldstein 1998, 2.
[c] Percentage change between 24 January 2000 and 22 January 2001, dollars per local currency unit.

Table 7.2. Economic Growth

	Annual Change in Real GDP				
	1991–96[a]	1997	1998	1999	2000
Singapore	8.4	8.5	0.1	5.9	9.9
Hong Kong	5.2	5.0	−5.3	3.0	10.5
Taiwan[b]	6.6	6.9	4.3	5.6	6.4
Malaysia	8.9	7.3	−7.4	5.8	8.5
Korea	7.4	5.0	−6.7	10.9	8.8
Thailand	8.2	−1.4	−10.8	4.2	4.3
Philippines	2.7	5.2	−0.6	3.4	4.0
Indonesia	6.0	5.0	−13.2	0.9	4.8

Sources: Montes 1998, 4; Goldstein 1998, 3; Directorate-General of Budget, Accounting and Statistics (Taiwan), *Monthly Bulletin of Statistics*; Hong Kong Census and Statistics Department, national accounts data (www.info.gov.hk/censtatd/); Monetary Authority of Singapore, *Economics Department Quarterly Bulletin*; National Statistical Office (Korea), national accounts data (www.nso.go.kr); Bank Negara Malaysia, *Annual Report*; Bank of Thailand, national accounts data (www.bot.or.th); Bangko Sentral ng Pilipinas, national accounts data (www.bsp.gov.ph).
[a] Average annual growth (Taiwan, 1992–96; Hong Kong, 1992–96; Korea, 1993–96).
[b] GNP.

ments of all the crisis countries also experienced some kind of domestic political pressure. Again, Malaysia's government was least affected. Despite a very public rift within the ruling party and a decline in electoral support (a general election was held in 1999), it was the only incumbent government of 1997 that remained in power in 2000.

NATIONAL RESPONSES AND NATIONAL INSTITUTIONS

These main background constraints against which national responses to the crisis took place are also a measure of how sustainable, or costly, national responses to the crisis were. In some cases the costs were due to policy priorities not related to the governing capacity of state organizations. Hong Kong's recession in 1998, for example, was due to its determination to defend its currency peg, even if doing so entailed very high interest rates in an exceptionally interest-sensitive economy (Lim 1999). Other aspects of national strategies since 1997 are related to the nature of state organizations and their capacity to implement policy in a consistent and disciplined way.

Indonesia

Indonesia was distinguished by the depth of its crisis and the ambition of its reform agenda. From mid-1998, with a new face in power, the process toward democratization under way, and an urgent need for the resumption of external lending,[2] the government adopted a series of reforms and crisis management strategies that were largely in line with the recommendations of the Washington agencies.[3] Domestic reformers of various persuasions were active in Indonesia, but the IMF and the World Bank were central to the design and implementation of policy changes until mid-2000, after which Indonesia's relationship with these agencies became more conflictual.

Perhaps the most striking change in Indonesia's financial system since 1997 is the reversion to a largely government-owned banking system. As described in Chapter 3, the large private banks were so badly affected by the crisis that they were all either taken over by the government or recapitalized, mostly with government funds that were converted to equity. The reform agenda envisages that these banks will return to private ownership and that the original state-owned banks will, in their merged forms, be privatized. The privatization of state-owned banks lies in the distant future, however. The return to full private ownership of the banks taken over or recapitalized with government funds is also unlikely to occur rapidly, although moves toward this end did begin in 2000. Foreign investors have not rushed to take over Indonesian banks, despite new legislation ending restrictions on foreign ownership. The government's sale, in May 2000, of a 22.5 percent stake in what had been the largest private bank in Indonesia, Liem Sioe Liong's Bank Central Asia, did not attract much foreign investment interest (McLeod 2000, 24–26).

2. A total of only $3 billion in IMF funds was actually released in the first six months of Indonesia's crisis.
3. The convoluted processes of Indonesia's crisis management, bank nationalizations, corporate debt restructuring, and post-crisis reform are described in Haggard 2000, 65–72, 171–78; and Hamilton-Hart 2000a.

Similarly, despite the promulgation of a more pro-creditor bankruptcy code and the establishment of a new court to facilitate it, little corporate restructuring resulted from these and other efforts to deal with the corporate debt problem. As of October 2000 the main task force coordinating foreign debt restructuring had restructured only $5.2 billion of an estimated $68.2 billion in foreign corporate debt (*Business Times*, 24 October 2000). The government agency responsible for managing most of the banking system's bad loans, the Indonesian Bank Restructuring Agency (IBRA), had restructured only a small proportion of the loans transferred to it, and its sales of seized collateral and corporate assets were modest. Again, foreign investor interest in acquiring these assets has been low, although a stake in what had been Indonesia's second largest conglomerate, Astra, was sold to a foreign consortium of mainly Singaporean investors in early 2000 (Fane 2000, 41–42). On the whole, however, foreign equity holdings in Indonesian companies have not risen much, if at all.

Thus, in two respects at least, Indonesia's reforms have failed to bring about a more liberal economy: private ownership of the corporate and banking sectors is lower, not higher, and foreign ownership has not increased decisively. Indonesia is still committed to a policy framework that will provide for this shift, and it may occur eventually. In the meantime, there are several reasons why liberalizing reform has been thwarted. The most obvious is simply the extent of the problems in the Indonesian economy, corporate sector, and banking system, coupled with tremendous political upheaval and violent conflict in many areas of the country (Manning and Diermen 2000). In addition, administrative disarray, corruption, and a governing apparatus that continues to rely on informal practices and personal accommodation have affected Indonesia's reforms. Actual or suspected cases of undue influence, corruption, or confusion in the court system, for example, have undermined attempts to use the legal system to recover debt or force corporate restructuring. The single largest creditor to find the process costly and unproductive has been the government's own bank restructuring agency, IBRA, which has won only a handful of its court cases (Fane 2000, 35–37). To the extent that large debtors are being forced to compensate the government for bailout funds, the means employed continue to be the old ones: personalized negotiations, political threats, and individual deals. Partly in consequence, the process has not been particularly effective. Continuing contention in 2000 over the value of assets pledged by bankers in 1998 reinforced earlier suspicions that these deals either overvalued the pledged assets or, because the companies remained under the effective control of the original owners, left the transferred assets open to being plundered (*Business Times*, 24 August 2000).

The central bank was a focus for institutional reform from 1998 onward, and a new Central Bank Act passed in 1999 greatly enhanced its legal independence. Drafted with the help of foreign advisers and approved by the IMF, the act has had some counterproductive results, dramatically illustrated by the arrest and detention of the central bank's governor in mid-2000. The governor had been accused of involvement in a high-profile scandal that surfaced in 1999, during the course of British-owned Standard Chartered Bank's attempt to purchase Bank Bali, a medium-sized Indonesian bank. The scandal revolved around inducements paid by Bank Bali to secure payment of interbank debts due to it and guaranteed by the central bank. The affair implicated individuals connected with the then ruling Golkar Party, government ministers, IBRA, and the central bank (Booth 1999, 5–6). When the attorney general announced that the central bank's governor was a suspect and detained him in June 2000, his arrest was a major crisis for the central bank. The government was unable to dismiss him because, under the new act, the governor can be removed only after being convicted of a crime. Given Indonesia's notoriously corrupt and unreliable court system—which, despite being another major focus for post-crisis reforms, had seen its profile rather than its integrity increase—this law presented a major obstacle to reforming the central bank in a rule-abiding way. In early 2001 the governor actually returned to active duty at the central bank. The unresolved allegations of serious fraud and manipulation involving the central bank justify major changes to the organization, but in this case, elements of the reform program added to the inherent difficulty of the task.

Other reform strategies launched since 1998 have likewise had some perverse effects. New levels of transparency and accountability probably reduced the scale of corruption, but the routines and relational ties that sustain it changed very little. The reliance on informal processes and funding sources by New Order government organizations meant that as post-crisis political change and institutional reforms closed off some of these channels, many parts of the bureaucracy became less and less functional in any sense of the term. As a spokesman for President Abdurrahman Wahid reflected, basic policy implementation as well as reform was stymied by a bureaucratic and military apparatus that had in many cases just "stopped working" (Wimar Witoelar, seminar, Australian National University, Canberra, 23 October 2000).

Overall, the crisis forced Indonesia to adopt a set of reforms that from mid-1998 to mid-2000 largely corresponded with the preferences of actors such as the IMF, thus ruling out responses such as the imposition of Malaysian-style capital controls. It is important not to exaggerate the IMF's influence, however. Even in the absence of conditionality, capital controls would not have been a viable policy option, for, unlike Malaysia, Indonesia did not have the organizational resources to implement them. Even with IMF support and outside technical assistance, it took the central bank two years to introduce more systematic capital-account monitoring—and enforcement of the new reporting requirements was problematic (*Business Times*, 11 October 2000). If reforms are measured by results rather than intent, any alleged triumph for "neoliberalism" or the IMF has been a limited one indeed. Indonesia is still in the process of dramatic and multifaceted change, but it has not acquired a more liberal economy or a more effective set of governing institutions than before the crisis.

Singapore

Singapore's response to the crisis was also ambiguous, involving selective liberalization and active government stewardship of the economy. The comparatively healthy position of Singapore banks despite regional exposure meant that although their profits declined temporarily, they did not need any support. Given also the government's strong fiscal position and large foreign reserves, Singapore was not under anything like the same pressure as other countries in the region. Singapore did, nevertheless, respond to the crisis by stepping up several reforms, mostly in the financial sector.

Financial policy had been under review since the middle of 1997. As at various times in the past, there had been calls from the private and foreign sectors to open up the management of government-controlled funds and to relax financial-sector regulatory controls. A review panel of four senior civil servants and Deputy Prime Minister Lee Hsien Loong was set up in 1997 to look at ways to ensure the competitiveness of the industry. Concurrently, a mixed industry-government body, the Banking and Finance Subcommittee, was considering policy options as part of a broader survey of Singapore's competitiveness. This group recommended major cutbacks in government control in the financial sector, including allowing pension funds to be invested privately (*Business Times*, 3 February 1998).

While these processes were in train, the currency and financial crises in the region were deepening. Singapore took the opportunity to market itself as a financial center that conformed to international standards: free of cronyism and transparent, under a government that would support the financial industry and its priorities. Lee Hsien Loong took over the chairmanship of the de facto central-bank and financial-sector regulator, the Monetary Authority of Singapore, and announced that the MAS would have a promotional role rather than the restrictive regulatory stance it had been known (and criticized) for in the past. Foreign banks and financial firms have been granted greater access to the domestic market and enhanced incentives to locate fund management activity in Singapore (Chia 1998; Lim 1999). Government-linked companies have again been pressed into service to support financial market development, this time through increased activity on the local bond market, aimed at increasing its attractiveness to foreign investors.

The government simultaneously called for greater transparency and improved accounting standards in the corporate sector. Although it maintained a tight rein on certain types of information (Rodan 2000), levels of disclosure increased in both company annual reports and official reports on the financial industry. An overhaul of the banking law imposed a new requirement on Singapore banks to divest their significant holdings of nonfinancial assets over the next years. Despite talk of a change in regulatory style, the MAS was still ready to intervene in cases of suspected irregularity involving the financial industry. For example, in conjunction with an investigation by the MAS and another government agency, a large local bank suspected of withholding information from the public stopped all initial public offering activity pending the outcome of inquiries. All bank staff involved were suspended and had their passports impounded, and the bank appointed an international accounting firm to investigate the affair—and report to a former top MAS official (*Business Times*, 29 August 2000; *Straits Times*, 30 and 31 August 2000). The MAS was also studying ways to increase corporate disclosure requirements, tighten licensing of fund managers, and impose registration and examination requirements on private bankers (*Business Times*, 1 and 2 September 2000; *Straits Times*, 5 September 2000).

Official influence continued at high levels in many other areas as well. Selective tax incentives were still being used to encourage the financial industry, and the government's own venture capital and industrial policy initiatives had their funding increased. Probably the largest initiative was a new $10 billion Developmental Investment Fund, to operate under the supervision of the Finance Ministry (*Straits Times*, 23 February 2000). In addition, the science and technology sector was set to receive a total of $13 billion through various government schemes over the period 1999 to 2005 (*Business Times*, 26 October 2000).

The government's outward investment policy continued to involve a range of government agencies and companies in developing the external wing of the Singapore economy. Although the regional crisis had a severe impact on some earlier investments in Asia, the retreat from regionalization was limited. Some government-linked companies capitalized on the crisis by investing in banks and other assets in the region, particularly in the Philippines, Thailand, and Hong Kong. Outward investment moves served both foreign policy and domestic objectives. With regard to a $400 million loan scheme to support Singapore investments in Indonesia, the Economic Development Board said that by encouraging such investments, Singapore "could be catalyst and facilitator for Indonesia's economy recovery." The scheme had been part of a $1.2 billion investment package offered to the new Indonesian government by the Singapore prime minister during a visit to Jakarta in January (*Business Times*, 19 February 2000). Talks about using some of this package to acquire assets held by the Indonesian Bank Restructuring Agency were initiated shortly afterward, led by the government holding companies (*Business Times*, 22 February 2000). Subsequent Singapore government-linked investments in IBRA-held assets included a share in Astra and the purchase of the main Bank Central Asia building in Jakarta (*Business Times*, 5 September 2000).

Overall, although Singapore faced some setbacks with regard to particular initiatives, its policies since 1998 have largely reflected domestic priorities and resources, including the political and organizational resources of the government. Changes in prudential standards have drawn Singapore closer to Anglo-American norms, but only because the government already possessed regulatory organizations capable of enforcing these standards. Singapore continues to show a great deal of concern with its image in the eyes of foreign investors and has adjusted financial policy in ways that allow foreign players greater market access and tax incentives. Singapore's policy choices, however, have been implemented from a position of financial strength and have been combined with strongly interventionist financing schemes and industrial policy ventures. As in the past, "openness to external capital flows and world market forces has been possible and beneficial only because the government exerts considerable control over the domestic economy and polity, controls that it can exercise if necessary to counterbalance external shocks," writes Linda Lim (1999, 113).

Malaysia

Malaysia's response to the crisis overtly rejected certain international orthodoxies. From September 1997, Prime Minister Mahathir waged a very public war of words against currency-market speculators, calling for international regulation of currency trading (Mahathir 1998). Then, in September 1998, the government introduced a package of regulations that fixed the value of the ringgit against the U.S. dollar, restricted the convertibility of the ringgit, banned offshore ringgit-denominated bank transactions, and closed down the large parallel market in Malaysian stocks that traded in Singapore. Faced with a contracting economy, a collapsing stock market, and a continuing steep decline in the value of the ringgit, the government had no viable alternative if it wanted to pursue more expansionary policy (Athukorala 2000). It had earlier adopted a "virtual IMF" program of increased interest rates and fiscal cuts, but these measures did not arrest the decline in the Malaysian currency and economy.

The capital-control elements of the September regulations were the most controversial, and these were eased in early 1999 when the prohibition on portfolio outflows was replaced with a tax, which was partially lifted in September that year and further relaxed in October 2000, before being abandoned in 2001.[4] Many commentators viewed the controls as unnecessary and costly in terms of the damage inflicted on Malaysia's reputation as an investment site and its long-term growth prospects. For example, in Nobel Prize–winner Merton Miller's judgment, "What did Malaysia's experiment with controls actually accomplish? The most favourable answer for Malaysia is nothing. . . . Malaysia's flirtation with currency controls thus must be written off as a failure, and one whose costs will be borne by the Malaysian people for many years to come" (qtd. in Business Times, 12 July 1999; see also Haggard 2000, 85). Yet even as these assessments were being made, Malaysia was already recovering as fast as any of its neighbors (Government of Malaysia 1999). One can argue that Malaysia should have recovered faster because its pre-crisis macroeconomic fundamentals, such as foreign debt, were better. Yet, Malaysia was peculiarly vulnerable because of its level and rate of financial-market

4. Other elements of the September 1998 package were very controversial in Singapore, which was the primary target of regulations governing offshore ringgit accounts and the trade in Malaysian stocks. See Haggard 2000, 73–85. The issue of what to do with the Singapore-traded stocks was eventually resolved, after much controversy, in a way that allowed investors in the parallel Singapore market to sell down their holdings gradually.

development: stock market capitalization, for example, had peaked at an extraordinary 339 percent of GNP in 1996, and the corporate sector carried very high levels of debt, largely because of the privatization policies of the preceding decade. Most negative assessments of Malaysia's capital controls came from outside the country; businesses operating in Malaysia have not, in general, opposed the controls, and many have benefited from them because of the lower interest rates and currency stability they brought.[5] Two years after their imposition, most detailed analyses conclude, the controls did not have a harmful effect on the economy or investor confidence (Athukorala 2000).[6] To the extent that they promoted faster-than-expected recovery and prevented the bad debt problem from ballooning, they would also have reduced the public costs of crisis management (Macquarie Bank 1999, 13).

In addition to its capital-account moves, Malaysia's response to the crisis involved a comprehensive bank recapitalization and debt restructuring program, forced mergers among banks and finance companies, and several rescues of large companies. Overall, the management and restructuring of the financial sector, largely under the auspices of the central bank, proceeded rapidly and successfully: the public costs of rescue were not as large as in Indonesia, Thailand, or Korea, and the financial system as of 2000 was much stronger in terms of capital-adequacy ratios (which were above international standards) and nonperforming loans (NPLs). In contrast, crisis management in the nonfinancial corporate sector did involve some substantial bailouts of private actors.

Problems in the financial sector began to be addressed in early 1998, when Bank Negara forced some consolidation among finance companies. Later that year, two important agencies were established for crisis management. One, Danaharta, was to manage the NPLs of financial institutions. It rapidly removed most bad debts from the banking system, and in a notable contrast with its Indonesian counterpart it acquired these debts at fair market value as assessed by independent auditors. Banks were not compelled to sell these impaired assets but were required to mark down their value. The banks that did sell loans to Danaharta accepted discounts that ranged between zero (on RM 11.6 million acquired from Citibank) and 85 percent (on RM 1.76 billion acquired from Bank Bumiputera). The average discount on NPLs sold to Danaharta was 55 percent (Danaharta 2000). By the end of August 2000, Danaharta had restructured and sold RM 21.6 billion of its assets, 46 percent of its portfolio (*Business Times*, 28 October 2000).

As a result of being required to sell or mark down NPLs, several banks required recapitalization. To this end, the second agency the government set up was a "special purpose vehicle" known as Danamodal to inject capital into financial institutions; in return, Danamodal appointed representatives to the boards of firms

---

5. See, e.g., Macquarie Bank 1999, 15; *Asian Wall Street Journal*, 24 February and 30 August 1999.
6. See also details on investment inflows, foreign reserves, and bond spreads in BNM, *Monthly Bulletin of Statistics*; *Business Times*, 10 February and 16 July 1999; Government of Malaysia 1999, 18, 45.

receiving funds and, depending on the terms of the funds received, acquired equity in some of the banks. It injected a total of RM 7.1 billion into ten institutions and had recovered 70 percent of this amount by the end of 2001 (Bank Negara Malaysia, *Annual Report* 2001). In contrast to Danaharta, which had more independent operational status, Danamodal was closely tied to Bank Negara. Also under the auspices of Bank Negara a Corporate Debt Restructuring Committee (CDRC) was established in July 1998 to facilitate the restructuring of debt owed by viable companies. The committee was chaired by a former Bank Negara official and included representatives from commercial banks, the finance ministry, Bank Negara (which also supplied its secretariat), and professionals from accounting and legal firms. At the end of September 2000 the CDRC had received seventy-one applications from companies (or creditors) regarding total debts of RM 45.9 billion, it had restructured the debts of thirty companies amounting to RM 24 billion, rejected those of nineteen companies on the grounds that they were not viable, and transferred those of another nine to Danaharta.[7] Taking into account these withdrawals, the outstanding value of debts to be resolved was RM 16 billion.

The final element in Malaysia's post-crisis management of the financial sector was a major program of consolidation among financial institutions. After failing to get much of a response to its calls for voluntary mergers, Bank Negara shocked local actors by announcing in July 1999 that the twenty-one domestic banks, twenty-five finance companies, and twelve merchant banks would merge into six bank-based groups, with merger plans to be submitted by the end of September. Apart from relatively smooth progress toward merger by two Chinese banks (Southern and Ban Hin Lee), both with healthy balance sheets (*Business Times*, 24 September 1999), the merger plan immediately prompted resistance from several bankers who stood to lose their banks. Among these were the formerly favored Rashid Hussain and Azman Hashim, who pressed to retain control of their banks. As part of his effort to do so, Rashid Hussain redeemed RM 500 million in bonds issued to Danamodal ahead of schedule. Azman Hashim also accelerated repayments to Danamodal and reportedly made a tearful plea to Mahathir (*Business Times*, 8 October 1999, 1 February 2000). BNM later modified its approach, announcing increased capital requirements for bank-based groups and leaving the choice of merger partners to the bankers themselves. Ten banks emerged as "anchor" banks to lead financial groups each consisting of one commercial bank, one merchant bank, and one finance company. By the end of 2000 only a few proposed mergers remained problematic: fifty of fifty-four financial institutions, accounting for 94 percent of the total assets of the domestic banking sector, had been consolidated into ten banking groups (Bank Negara Malaysia press release, 31 December 2000).

7. Details of CDRC operations are based on Bank Negara Malaysia, "Corporate Debt Restructuring Committee" (www.bnm.gov.my).

In comparative terms, Danaharta, Danamodal, and the CDRC performed well, supporting an effective banking-sector reform program.[8] The major unresolved bad debt problems are associated with loans made by one finance company and two commercial banks (discussed in Chapter 5): Bank Bumiputera and Sime Bank, now merged into Bumiputera-Commerce Bank and RHB Bank. Some of their NPLs were bought, at a discount, by Danaharta, which put a further RM 26 billion in their acknowledged NPLs "under management" but did not purchase them (Danaharta 2000, app. 1). These debts are a major contingent liability for the public sector.

Malaysia's response to the crisis involved a sharp increase in the government's other contingent liabilities, debts, economic assets, and distribution of privilege to private actors. Government spending switched to become countercyclical in mid-1998, and in a reversal of its pre-crisis fiscal position the government planned for budget deficits through 2001. In another reversal, several firms and services privatized in the decade before 1997 were renationalized when their private owners ran into problems caused by excessive debt. Others received privileges to help them service debts (Haggard 2000, 162–71) that were in many cases very large, prompting criticism from many domestic actors. Total contingent liabilities of the Malaysian Treasury rose sharply to RM 48 billion, mostly in the form of guarantees for loans to eight firms, according to the 1999 auditor general's report (*Business Times*, 30 October 2000). Small and medium businesses received some support: loan facilities under BNM supervision increased to around RM 3.1 billion.[9]

The most basic precondition for Malaysia's post-crisis initiatives was access to finance. To fund its crisis management and recovery program it tapped the resources of the central pension fund, rounded up U.S.$1.35 billion in pledged financing from foreign banks operating in Malaysia, and gained pledges for a further U.S.$6 billion from the Japanese government and two Japanese banks (Government of Malaysia 1999; *Business Times*, 12 January 1999). A further precondition was political control of the economic bureaucracy, including the central bank. The idea for capital controls originated in the political sphere. Bank Negara was believed to have been given two weeks to draft a set of capital-control measures, a request that followed months of conflict between Mahathir and the central bank and precipitated the resignation of its governor and deputy governor (*Business Times*, 29 August 1998).

Although the major policy initiatives were set politically, Malaysia's response to the crisis drew considerably upon organizational resources. Access to the financial resources of the government-controlled pension fund was possible only because Malaysia, unlike many developing countries, had been able to run this fund sus-

8. This was the assessment of the Bank for International Settlements, reported in the *Asian Wall Street Journal*, 6 June 2000. See also the views of an independent consultant reported in the *Jakarta Post*, 4 and 5 May 2000; and Haggard 2000, 162.
9. See Bank Negara Malaysia, "BNM-Administered Special Funds" (www.bnm.gov.my); and *Business Times*. 3 April and 15 May 2000.

tainably over the preceding decades. The successful enforcement (largely by the central bank) of capital controls in 1998 called upon an extensive administrative infrastructure that was already functioning (see Chapter 6). It is also possible that, as argued by Mahathir, Bank Negara's ability to implement the controls was derived from the experience gained during its period as an active foreign exchange trader between 1985 and 1993 (*Business Times*, 25 August 2000). The main architect of the controls was the official who had been in charge of currency trading at the central bank; he returned briefly as an adviser when the controls were introduced. The other crisis management agencies drew heavily on the central bank's organizational resources, and in addition a steering committee chaired by the governor of Bank Negara coordinated and monitored the whole bank and corporate debt-restructuring process.

While Danamodal and the CDRC remained under Bank Negara, Danaharta developed an independent organizational base. Its annual report for 1999 and operational report to mid-2000 form a remarkable contrast with the reports issued by the Indonesian restructuring agency. Danaharta's annual report shows a concern with organizational identity in its visual representation of the agency's mission, the biographical information it gives for directors and senior management, and its attention to organizational structure and staff. Although unverifiable by an outsider, the operational information in its reports is also scrupulous in its attention to detail, clear delineation of categories, and transparency as regards institution-by-institution data, including the names of those appointed as company administrators. Its Indonesian counterpart, in contrast, did not have the organizational capacity (or inclination) for this kind of record-keeping, was not unified in an effective hierarchical structure internally, and devolved many tasks to a team of foreign merchant bankers.

Malaysia's response to the crisis demonstrated flexibility and willingness to adjust policy on the basis of changing conditions or new information. As noted, the capital controls were progressively modified. Their introduction also showed a certain pragmatism on the part of Mahathir. He later revealed that such controls had not been his preferred option, which was to offset the effects of devaluation by doubling domestic incomes and prices. Fortunately, that idea was rejected: "My colleagues [on the National Economic Action Council] shot down the plan" (qtd. in *Business Times*, 3 May 2000).

Doubts remain, of course, about the long-term sustainability of Malaysia's response to the crisis. For example, using pension-fund share purchases to prop up the stock exchange generated anxiety about the safety of these investments. Both the pension fund and the government's main holding company, Khazanah Nasional, were already significant stock market investors before the crisis, however, and the dramatic decline in the main index had caused them paper losses to the value of more than half their portfolios. Purchases since September 1998 have helped drive up the stock index and, in consequence, the market value of the public assets that these institutions control (*Business Times*, 9 March and 14 September 1999).

There is also some question over whether Malaysia's political and administrative institutions decayed over the crisis period. In particular, the apparently instrumental use of the court system to deal with the former minister of finance and deputy prime minister, Anwar Ibrahim, the ousting of those identified as Anwar supporters from government and corporate positions, and the privileges conferred on politically favored entrepreneurs have all been taken to indicate a decline in the integrity of government. The return of Daim Zainuddin as finance minister from 1998 to mid-2001 again put one of the country's wealthiest entrepreneurs into a prime decision-making position, able to influence his own commercial interests and those of his protégés. But these tendencies are not new in the Malaysian context, and it is too early to say whether they will evolve into a decisively more patronage-based system of government or less coherence in bureaucratic organizations.

The central bank itself does not seem to have suffered as an organization. The removal of its governor and deputy governor because of their opposition to the government policy and support for Anwar simply confirms the intolerance of dissident figures in Malaysian state organizations—not a new development. The governor who took over in September 1998 was subject to allegations of improper conduct and had had little relevant experience; however, he was replaced by the central bank's deputy governor, who had been with Bank Negara for fifteen years. Her appointment was welcomed by both foreign and domestic commentators and industry actors, who regarded her as a professional, highly qualified official (*Star*, 22 April 2000; *Business Times*, 24 April 2000; *Asian Wall Street Journal*, 25 April 2000).

The demonstrated effectiveness of the central bank since 1998 also confirms the depth of its organizational capacities. It administered or oversaw the restructuring program for the financial sector with reasonable efficiency and considerable determination. Although the preferences of some bankers were partially accommodated in the revised merger plan, it was plain that many were not happy. According to one banker, "We were holed up in a room at Bank Negara and were told that we could not leave until agreement was reached. We were threatened, we were coerced and we were arm-twisted. And we argued until the last minute" (qtd. in *Business Times*, 2 September 2000). Bank Negara's active promotion of disclosure standards in the banking sector even saw the central bank use its website to host the financial accounts of commercial and merchant banks—a temporary measure, it explained, "until the banking institutions' associations establish a proper website for this and other purposes."[10]

Problems of retaining staff may have been temporarily reduced by the crisis, but salaries remained below market rates. Bank Negara sent out a memo to former staff offering to rehire them, but the salaries offered reportedly would have entailed pay cuts of 50 percent for some. Reentry was subject to a six-month waiting time between serving in a financial institution supervised by Bank Negara and return-

---

10. Bank Negara Malaysia, "Banking Institutions Published Accounts for 1999 and 2000" (www.bnm.gov.my).

ing to the central bank (*Straits Times*, 28 July 2000). Lateral entry to some senior positions, which began in the 1980s, has continued, along with efforts at socialization. Bank Negara revised its induction program for new senior executives with the aim of "helping them integrate into the work culture of the Bank." It also introduced a mentoring program to provide a support system for new executives (Bank Negara Malaysia, *Annual Report* 1998, 197). For the time being, although the potential for a slide toward a more patrimonial political system and less rationalized state organizations definitely exists, both state and central banks in Malaysia show more signs of continuity than of change.

Other Countries

The countries under IMF programs were effectively barred from pursuing a Malaysian-style response to the crisis. It is not much of an exaggeration to say with Dani Rodrik (1999, 6) that the conditions attached to Korea's international rescue package, covering its labor market, trade policy, capital account, and government-business relations, "entail a remolding of the Korean economy in the image of a Washington economist's idea of a free-market economy" (see also Feldstein 1998, 26). The Philippines' graduation from IMF and World Bank lending programs at the time the crisis broke was short-lived, and recourse to these agencies ruled out major deviations from the country's program of financial liberalization.

Thailand had little choice but to accept the $17 billion in rescue funds coordinated by the IMF and in the short run to comply with the conditions attached. Although the fund reversed its initial directive on contractionary fiscal policy, it maintained pressure for a range of policy and institutional reforms: privatization, increased access for foreign investors, new laws on bankruptcy and foreclosure, and other efforts to provide Thailand with what it was deemed to have lacked prior to the crisis—good governance. These reforms were drawn up and implemented with the close involvement of personnel from international agencies such as the IMF and large numbers of foreign consultants. A local analyst could fairly write that Washington was now a player in Thai politics (Baker 1999, 20).

Beneath this apparent conformity, however, practice has been more mixed. A strong current of localism and opposition to both the economic policy and "governance" aspects of Thailand's official reform program suggest that its political foundations are not necessarily secure (Baker 1999; Pasuk 1999). Cleaner government may be the result of constitutional reform aimed at reducing political corruption. On the one hand, a newly vigorous antigraft agency, headed by a respected retired official, has scored several wins in action against corruption and against politicians who failed to declare assets (*Straits Times*, 14 October 2000). On the other hand, corrupt practices remain pervasive in both politics and the bureaucracy. Further, while there was some readiness to investigate the organizational and political deficiencies that lay behind the central bank's failings before the crisis (Nukul Commission 1998), some of those accused of wrongdoing remain in positions of authority. For example, the official in charge of the central bank's case against other officials and bankers not only confronted legal teams with better resources but also operated in an organization where an assistant governor and the deputy governor faced criminal charges over their involvement with a finance company. Neither had resigned (*Nation*, 4 July 2000). In another case, a banker charged by the central bank with illegal loan approval was appointed as chairman of the Office of the Auditor General, responsible for auditing the central bank (*Business Times*, 6 July 2000). The central bank's new governor since the crisis has also been controversial. He came to the bank with a reputation for correct behavior as a senior civil servant, one who had taken action against allegedly corrupt politicians, Yet he was embroiled in a series of very public disputes with the government, which led to his removal in 2001 (*Business Times*, 10 April and 20 July 2000, 30 May 2001).

Overall, the capacities and attributes of state organizations in Southeast Asia have not become more similar as a result of the crisis. Malaysia and Singapore have changed very little. To the extent that Singapore's highly disciplined state apparatus and Malaysia's more heterogeneous one are changing, they are doing so in ways that reflect the continuation of pre-crisis changes in the identity of their governing elites. Definite processes of change are under way in Indonesia and Thailand. Reforms in Indonesia, however, have not gone according to anyone's plan, and the direction of change has not been toward greater rationalization in administrative agencies. In the Philippines, corruption scandals involving President Joseph Estrada during 2000 led to his impeachment and paved the way for members of the old political elite to replace him in a manner that was, arguably, unconstitutional. The country remains perched between consolidating the anti-corruption reforms of the 1990s and sliding toward political disarray.

Across the region, post-crisis reforms have varied in intent and in practice. The variation was partly due to differences in the initial set of economic pressures that each government faced. In addition, however, the choice and implementation of national reform strategies reflected each government's underlying administrative resources, as well as more obvious political endowments and constraints. Financial policies in both Singapore and Malaysia, though differing in content, involved government agencies in active implementation roles and allowed each government to realize independent national objectives. Without coherent, capable, and reasonably depersonalized state organizations, these policy initiatives would have had very little success. In contrast, Thailand, Indonesia, and the Philippines continued to face several obstacles to realizing greater control over their domestic economies. As long as their administrative resources remain limited, many of their efforts at financial sector management are likely to be ineffective or costly.

The implications of low governing capacity, however, are not registered just at the national level. The attributes and capacities of domestic state organizations can have international repercussions, particularly at the regional level.

8.

Building a New Asia

Ideas and initiatives for regional cooperation in Asia gained momentum after the financial crises of 1997 and 1998. In the words of one regional leader, it was time for a "New Deal for Asia"—time to build an Asia that would be more assertive, cooperative, and influential (Mahathir 1999). Any such new Asia will be built by both old and new states in the region. Although private firms have propelled economic integration, only governments can supply the kind of cooperation that many are now calling for. In dealing with the effects of economic integration and capital mobility, central banks and other state organizations are the prime movers behind most international institutions that aim to promote financial stability at the global level. As the demand for regional institutions to complement these global structures grows, regional states and central banks will be called upon to play key roles in creating and maintaining such institutions.

Because the characteristics and capacities of state organizations shape the cooperative structures they build, the scope and nature of regional cooperation is likely to be colored by the nature of the states in Asia. The regional cooperation agenda includes a recent upsurge in initiatives to develop regional solutions to the problems of managing money and finance. What are the prospects for these initiatives? The wide variation in the governing capacity of Asian states may be a serious obstacle to certain types of cooperation. Although an uneven distribution of governing capacity does not preclude economic integration or largely symbolic moves to bring regional countries closer together in shows of unity, it does make cooperative management of the side effects of economic integration difficult.

CONSTRUCTING AN ASIAN REGION: IDEAS AND INITIATIVES

Extreme financial instability followed by severe economic downturns in many emerging markets in the late 1990s highlighted the need for governments to play prudential and crisis-management roles in the financial system. Even financial industry publications conceded that international capitalism was "red in tooth and claw" and that untrammeled financial flows could be hugely destructive (*Euromoney*, September 1998). The world's major governments responded to the crises by stepping up cooperative efforts to promote financial stability. After an initial flurry of activity to develop a "new financial architecture," however, it soon appeared that the new architecture would be a minimal departure from the old one (Kahler 2000; Eichengreen 2000). The international organization that was the focus of efforts to formulate and implement the new financial architecture, the International Monetary Fund, soon took up its pre-crisis move to add capital-account liberalization to its list of official goals.[1]

Many countries in Asia were dissatisfied with the process of international financial reform and crisis management centered on the IMF. Some resented the way the IMF and the United States had responded to the crisis in Asia, believing the conditions attached to IMF lending to be inappropriate and the American opposition to a 1997 Japanese proposal for a regional support facility, dubbed an Asian Monetary Fund (AMF), to be ill-judged (Higgott 1998). Some countries in Asia also disagreed with the content of the emerging international regime governing finance, and there was a widespread perception that the process had been unduly dominated by the United States and Europe. It seemed to confirm a more general pattern identified in Charles Morrison's introduction to a study of East Asia (defined as the countries of the western Pacific) that countries in the region "have not been major actors in shaping the institutions and rules of the international system. They often lack the weight and status in international organizations they should have based on population or economic size. . . . Where they have representation and status, they are rarely demandeurs or agenda-setters." A desire to rectify this lack of influence in international settings was coupled with an increasing sense of regional identity: "A lasting effect of the Asian economic crisis and the Western triumphalism associated with it was to help bring East Asian countries, including Japan, closer together" (Morrison 2001, 1, 7).

This assessment resonates with recent statements by many actors in Asia, including many of the region's central bankers. The voice of the Malaysian prime minister remains unique in its pitch, but elements of the same message—Asia needs to speak more loudly and do more to address shared problems—can be found in statements by policymakers across the region. For example, the governor of the Philippines' central bank maintained that increased economic integration and political cohesion in Asia had led to "a serious determination to establish regional institutions geared to look after Asia's needs." Regional cooperation after the crisis, he said, intensified because of a desire for "a uniquely Asian institution that will have a focused mandate and will be responsive to the region's needs."[2] The aim is not to replace global cooperative mechanisms with regional ones. Rather, the desirability of establishing regional institutions is predicated on the view that global institutions sometimes lack the focus to respond in a timely and appropriate way to the particular needs of the region. The solution is to develop complementary

1. See the managing director's statement to the executive board of the IMF, reported in *IMF Survey* 28 (10 May 1999): 143–44.
2. See "Some Thoughts on the Prospects for Asian Economic Cooperation," speech by Rafael Buenaventura, governor of Bangko Sentralng Pilipunas, to the First International Conference of Asian Political Parties, Manila, 19 September 2000 (www.bsp.gov.ph).

regional mechanisms and to present the region's interests more forcefully at the global level.[3]

Before 1997, cooperative bodies in the region had very modest agendas, and most existed on either a subregional, Southeast Asian basis or extended to take in the entire pan-Pacific area. Hence, the most successful regional organization, ASEAN (the Association of Southeast Asian Nations, established in 1967), involved Southeast Asia only; and the most visible institution to bring together a wider set of regional countries was APEC (Asia-Pacific Economic Cooperation, established in 1989), which by the late 1990s comprised no fewer than twenty-one countries on both sides of the Pacific. A distinctly Asian group did exist in the East Asian Economic Caucus (EAEC), the product of a 1990 Malaysian proposal for intra-Asian cooperation, but it remained a controversial and nebulous dialogue forum only.

Although no encompassing organization fully united the region, quite a number of low-profile, special-purpose bodies brought together various combinations of Asian countries. Organizations dealing with some aspect of finance, from the provision of financial resources to collaboration among central banks, date from the late 1950s (Katzenstein et al. 2000, 137–45). In 1991, cooperation among regional central banks was raised to a new level when, as the result of a Japanese proposal, eleven countries of the western Pacific, including Australia and New Zealand, formed the Executives' Meeting of East Asia Pacific central banks (EMEAP). Besides holding regular meetings, members of this group established a network of currency-support agreements in the mid-1990s (Yam 1997). Asian countries also worked together in regular Asia-Europe Meeting (ASEM) dialogues. As an interregional process, ASEM "required its East Asian side to organize and coordinate, and thus became an incubator for broader East Asian regional cooperation" (Morrison 2001, 8). None of these organizations actually did very much, but along with the subregional and pan-Pacific bodies, they show that countries in Asia have been engaged in various cooperative efforts for quite some time.

Since 1997, specifically Asian initiatives have dominated the cooperation agenda. These initiatives are diverse, comprising a range of private, official, and quasi-official conferences and dialogues on various issues of common concern, from human security to the "future of Asia" and monetary cooperation. After failing to realize its proposal for an Asian Monetary Fund, Japan did launch a large aid plan for crisis-affected Asia, under which $48 billion had been committed by early 1999 (Masuyama 2000, 243–46). The ASEM process has continued to provide Asian countries with an opportunity to organize regionally and to discuss regional cooperation. For example, Thailand and China used the occasion of the 2001 ASEM finance ministers' meeting to endorse regional cooperation in Asia,

---

3. See, e.g., "Globalization and Regional Cooperation in Asia," speech by Hayami Masaru, governor of the Bank of Japan, to the Asian Pacific Bankers Club, 17 March 2001 (www.boj.or.jp).

and Korea took the same opportunity to express its dissatisfaction with the global-level international financial reform process.[4]

The main institutional locus for cooperation among Asian countries is the series of meetings being held by "ASEAN + 3": Japan, China, and Korea have joined the ASEAN countries at the summit level (the first summit meeting occurred in 1999) as well at the officials' and ministers' level. Chinese Prime Minister Zhu Rongji has said that the ASEAN + 3 mechanism could serve as a means to "gradually establish a framework for regional financial, trade and investment cooperation, and furthermore to realize still greater regional economic integration in a step by step manner" (qtd. in *International Herald Tribune*, 27 November 2000). ASEAN + 3 has embarked on some substantive cooperation projects. For example, at their third meeting in May 2001, the ASEAN + 3 economic ministers announced six projects for cooperation in the area of information technology.[5] That month, the finance ministers' meeting endorsed regional cooperation, affirming that "we will continue to hold policy dialogues and regional cooperation activities, particularly in the areas of regional self-help and support mechanisms, international financial reform and short-term capital flows monitoring." The group has welcomed Japan's provision of technical support (through the ASEAN secretariat) for monitoring short-term capital flows.

The most visible cooperative outcome associated with ASEAN + 3 meetings is a set of regional currency-swap agreements. The plan to establish such support facilities, known as the Chiang Mai Initiative, was announced by the ASEAN + 3 finance ministers in May 2000. A year later, it resulted in three bilateral swap deals between Japan and Korea, Thailand, and Malaysia. Total support committed under these swaps came to $6 billion ($1 billion to Malaysia, $2 billion to Korea, $3 billion to Thailand),[6] and similar pacts were being negotiated with the Philippines and China. These agreements added to pre-crisis swap and repurchase agreements involving regional countries, as well as an intra-ASEAN swap facility established in 1977 and involving $1 billion as of November 2000. While adding some substance to ideas for greater regional self-reliance, these agreements did not mark a move to break away from multilateral crisis management rules: Japan succeeded in linking all but 10 percent of these facilities to IMF conditionality, a stipulation that Malaysia in particular had opposed (*Business Times*, 7 March and 21 April 2001).

Other kinds of cooperation remain ideas rather than initiatives. One of the most ambitious is the idea of currency cooperation, whether for greater use of the yen, monetary union, or even a common currency. In early 1999, Miyazawa

---

4. Speeches by the finance ministers are available through the Japanese Ministry of Finance website (www.mof.jo.jp/english/asem).
5. Press statements from ASEAN + 3 meetings are available through the ASEAN secretariat (www.ASEAN.or.id/news/3aem_cjk.htm; and www.ASEAN.or.id/economic/jms_as+3fmm.htm).
6. Malaysia and Japan already had a $2.5 billion agreement in place under Japan's crisis-related aid package for Asia.

Kiichi, then Japanese finance minister, suggested that Asia adopt a currency basket based on the yen, the dollar, and the euro (*Asian Wall Street Journal*, 18 January 1999), a proposal that Japanese Ministry of Finance officials have since promoted in public speeches on regional cooperation in Asia. Many policymakers in Japan have called for increasing the use of the yen as an international currency, and the Japanese government has taken up that idea in an official inquiry (CFEOT 1999). Suggestions for various forms of currency cooperation, including a common currency, have been raised as future possibilities by the secretary-general of ASEAN, policymakers in Japan and Taiwan, the financial secretary of Hong Kong, the governor of the Hong Kong Monetary Authority, the governor of the Philippine central bank, and (while he was in office) Philippine President Estrada. The December 1998 ASEAN action plan included a feasibility study of an ASEAN currency, and Malaysia later sponsored a forum on monetary union (Castellano 2000, 3). Overall, even though there is no serious support for a common Asian currency in the near term, it is significant that the idea has become thinkable. Together with the actual initiatives on the cooperation agenda, it points to the existence of a widespread desire to construct more substantive regional institutions in Asia.

PROSPECTS FOR THE NEW ASIA: REGIONAL REPERCUSSIONS OF NATIONAL INSTITUTIONS

Although initiatives to create regional institutions in Asia are unlikely to subside in the immediate future, what they will actually lead to is unclear. There are real incentives for monetary and financial cooperation, and the political obstacles to such cooperation are probably not prohibitive. The governing capacity of regional states, however—their ability to implement policy consistently—is likely to be an important influence on the kind of cooperation that does take place. Asia is made up of states with widely varying levels of governing capacity, and this diversity will affect both the demand for and feasibility of particular types of cooperation.

As suggested by the number of cooperative schemes that have been launched, there is considerable demand for intra-Asian cooperation. Even before the crisis, several analyses argued that shared interests, on some issues set countries in the region apart from Europe and North America and thus created incentives for their cooperation (Stubbs 1998). The perception of potential gains has clearly risen in recent years. The economic preconditions for a shared regional currency probably do not exist, given the current level of economic diversity, but subregional arrangements may well make sense.[7] Reducing the overwhelming reliance on the U.S. dollar in currency baskets, international transactions, and reserve holdings could

7. This paragraph draws on analyses in Kwan 1996; Yam 1997; Kusukawa 1999; Brouwer 2000; Chalongphob 2000; Kawai and Akiyama 2001; Kawai and Takagi 2001.

also yield benefits, although doing so depends on the development of stable, liquid, and attractive markets for yen- and euro-denominated financial assets. There is also scope for many other kinds of monetary and financial cooperation, such as capital-account monitoring, currency swaps and regional support facilities, information exchange, and the promotion of regulatory standards both in regional settings and at the global level.

The demonstrated potential for short-term capital flows to be volatile and destabilizing means that countries in the region have a particular incentive to develop mechanisms to ensure a degree of insulation from such flows: capital-account monitoring, technical and diplomatic support for introducing controls on short-term capital flows, and the promotion of longer-term sources of finance. As noted by Joseph Yam, the governor of the Hong Kong Monetary Authority, improving the region's self-sufficiency in long-term finance could reduce its vulnerability to currency destabilization and speculative pressures; by improving regional financial markets, Asia could avoid channeling a large part of its savings to developed countries. In 1997, he said, 80 percent of total Asian foreign exchange reserves of about $600 billion were invested in North America and Europe, which meant that "Asia is financing much of the budget deficits of developed economies, particularly the United States, but has to try hard to attract money back into the region through foreign investments. . . . Some have even gone as far as to say that the Asian economies are providing the funding to hedge funds in non-Asian centres to play havoc with their currencies and financial markets" (Yam 1997).[8]

Despite such incentives, few people expect the path to higher levels of regional cooperation to be a smooth one. When compared with those in Europe, political rivalries and suspicion, particularly between Japan and China, are more intense. Strategic uncertainties are higher, and the influence exercised by the United States is a factor that has militated against intraregional cooperation in Asia. Still, although such considerations mean that there are real political obstacles, it is important not to exaggerate them. Portraits of the region that present it as entirely lacking any institutional infrastructure and riven by distrust are misleading. The degree of economic interdependence that exists, together with the proliferation of initiatives for cooperation, makes it unreasonable to assert that governments in the region are wholly concerned with maximizing their independence. In many respects their openness to international flows of goods, money, and people means that they have already given up control over some economic management levers. On most of the issues of monetary and financial cooperation described above, regional cooperation holds out to several governments the

8. Recent moves to develop regional bond markets and close the gap between ratings on Asian bonds and the needs of local institutional investors have been explicitly related to these concerns. See "Governor's Statement," address by Norman Chan to the 34th Asian Development Bank Annual Meeting, Honolulu, 9–11 May 2001 (www.info.gov.hk/hkma/speeches/speechs/norman/20010510e.htm).

prospect of increasing rather than giving up control over their economies and financial systems.

Where the incentives to cooperate exist, rivalry or strategic uncertainty should not preclude regional countries from developing ways of surmounting the obstacles. What is likely to affect the emergence of regional institutions is the nature of regional states and their capacity to implement declared policy in a consistent way.[9] State organizations and central banks vary considerably in their structures, routines, and norms, with the result that some of them are more able to implement policy consistently than others. This uneven distribution of governing capacity among the countries of Asia has repercussions at the regional level, making some kinds of cooperation particularly difficult.

Part of the difficulty is related to the way governing capacity affects the demand for cooperation. As shown in previous chapters, states with higher levels of governing capacity are better able to maintain national policy goals under conditions of capital mobility than are states with lower levels of governing capacity. This means that the demand for cooperation, which occurs only when governments are not able to realize goals unilaterally, can vary according a state's level of governing capacity: states with higher levels of governing capacity have less interest in some kinds of cooperation because they are more able to take care of themselves. States such as Singapore, for example, do not need any help to monitor their capital accounts.

A second difficulty arises because low levels of governing capacity can make meaningful cooperation almost impossible on issues that require ongoing domestic implementation. Such issues include many of the financial management tasks that are the subject of international and regional initiatives to promote financial stability and manage crises when they do occur. For example, regulating the activities of highly leveraged institutional investment funds (commonly known as hedge funds) requires more than agreement on a set of common standards; it also requires that national agencies then enforce these standards on players within their jurisdiction. Implementing this kind of regulatory policy demands administrative expertise, coherence, and discipline of a sort that some regional states simply do not have.

It is clear why a government such as Indonesia's should be a poor cooperator on many of the goals associated with efforts to promote financial stability. Not only are implementation problems at the domestic level likely to undermine the effectiveness of agreements that are made; they also make concrete agreements less likely in the first place. The low credibility of its commitments on issues that require disciplined implementation will make potential partners wary about Indonesia's ability to deliver on its promises. Thus coordinated policies to prevent

9. Other analyses that identify domestic governing systems as important determinants of regional cooperation and integration are Crouch 1984; Dauvergne 1997; and Katzenstein 1997.

foreign investors from playing one country off against another would be virtually impossible "where vested interests exercise substantial influence on government decisions not only at the level of policy formulation but also at the level of implementation," as Harold Crouch puts it (1984, 99). Given the technical nature of many potential cooperative tasks, creaky administrative machinery can fail even in the absence of nepotistic intervention. With unreliable partners, other states in the region are likely to be concerned that many cooperative initiatives will founder on domestic implementation problems, leaving them with the costs of cooperation but without the benefits. Indeed, growing awareness of domestic regulatory problems since the crisis has led states such as Singapore and Japan to invest in upgrading the administrative capacities of their neighbors in various technical assistance projects.

Although the varying capacities of state organizations and central banks in the region are likely to set limits on the emergence of regional mechanisms to deal with some problems of financial governance, much of the regional cooperation agenda remains viable. Interests are not always shared, but in many cases they are complementary. Even if countries such as Singapore do not need the cooperation of their neighbors to achieve certain regulatory goals, they do have an interest in the stability and prosperity of their region. To a great extent, therefore, governing ineffectiveness in Indonesia is a problem for Singapore, Malaysia, and Japan.

Many types of cooperation need not be hampered by different levels of governing capacity. Diplomatic shows of unity and regional dialogues, for example, do not in themselves require much in the way of domestic governing capacity, because no implementation is required. Regional economic integration can also occur with relatively little implementation at the domestic level: considerable political will may be needed in some cases, but the concrete tasks involved in, for example, tariff liberalization are less administratively demanding than ongoing regulation. Financial transfers and aid can also be distributed with little difficulty to governments with low levels of governing capacity, although if aid is intended to support particular policy goals, the recipient's governing capacity is likely to be an issue.

The proliferation of projects for improving "governance" in Asia since the crisis signals a growing appreciation of the importance of governing capacity for a wide range of outcomes. Current prescriptions for institutional reform, however, have done little to create the kind of government organizations that are disciplined and coherent enough to implement regulatory policy consistently. Not even well-designed, deliberate efforts to reconstruct government organizations will always succeed. The attributes of state organizations in Asia, the product of historical pressures and constraints, are unlikely to change quickly. As this book has shown, state organizations can follow diverse national trajectories within the constraints set by broadly similar historical experiences and challenges. This means that although many governments in the region now face some common structural pressures, they will not necessarily converge on a shared organizational model.

The states and central banks of modern Indonesia, Singapore, and Malaysia all developed on institutional foundations laid down in the nineteenth and early twentieth centuries in response to the political and economic challenges of governing colonial territories. The institutional inheritance with which national leaders worked after independence, however, was not the same in all countries: the colonial organizations themselves had varied, and the circumstances in which the new countries emerged had drastic consequences for the coherence, strength, and discipline of their governing structures. The slow transition to independence in Malaysia and Singapore meant not only that economic and administrative continuity had been reestablished after World War II, but that significant state-building efforts had strengthened government organizations before independence. The organizational tools at the disposal of Indonesia's new leaders were rudimentary by comparison: few state institutions survived the upheaval of Japanese occupation, followed by a prolonged military struggle against the returning Dutch colonizers, and those that did tended to be the least rationalized parts of the colonial state.

The central banks that operated in these state systems were thus located in very different institutional environments and developed noticeably different internal structures, routines, and norms. These different organizational attributes lent themselves to significantly different styles of policy implementation and, as a result, different national strategies for governing money and finance. Disciplined, hierarchical state organizations in Singapore ensured that declared policy was implemented consistently, making it possible for the government to pursue an ambitious set of financial policies while maintaining overall financial stability and growth. In Indonesia, by contrast, personalized organizations in which informal hierarchies were common and internal rules were routinely broken meant that consistent implementation of regulatory policy was rare; as a result, both interventionist and deregulatory financial policy initiatives proved costly in terms of either financial stability or development. The attributes of Malaysia's state organizations—a mix of formalized, hierarchical meritocracy and systems in which private interests were loosely differentiated from official goals—produced a variegated pattern of policy implementation. Organizations such as the central bank, with more rationalized organizational structures and norms, were able to implement a range of policies consistently when they were free of political interference; other organizations, deliberately set up with fewer internal controls, were more prone to irregular action.

These national histories show that governing highly internationalized economies and financial systems is difficult. It requires an active government role and, therefore, government organizations that are able to implement policy consistently. Of Malaysia's somewhat unorthodox approach to gaining control over its financial system, Mahathir declared, "We may fail of course but we are going to do our damndest to succeed even if all the forces of the rich and powerful are aligned against us" (1998, 135). Governing the financial sector entails a certain contest with the rich and powerful. Malaysia has, fitfully, been able to engage in this contest and succeed. So, more circumspectly and consistently, has Singapore. Standing behind their strategies have been the organizational resources of the state sector: the habits and hierarchies that determine how policy actually gets implemented.

Appendix 1

Table A1.1. Exchange Rates against the U.S. Dollar, 1950–2000

	Singapore (S$)	Malaysia (RM)	Indonesia (Rp.)
1950	3.06	3.06	3.8
1955	3.06	3.06	11.4
1960	3.06	3.06	143
1961	3.04	3.04	270
1962	3.05	3.05	917
1963	3.06	3.06	1,216
1964	3.07	3.07	5,747
1965	3.06	3.06	35
1966	3.07	3.07	143
1967	3.07	3.06	251
1968	3.07	3.06	478
1969	3.08	3.07	547
1970	3.09	3.08	378
1971	3.03	2.89	415
1972	2.81	2.82	415
1973	2.44	2.45	415
1974	2.44	2.31	415
1975	2.37	2.59	415
1976	2.47	2.53	415
1977	2.44	2.36	415
1978	2.27	2.21	625
1979	2.17	2.19	627
1980	2.14	2.22	627
1981	2.11	2.24	644
1982	2.14	2.32	693
1983	2.11	2.34	994
1984	2.13	2.43	1,074
1985	2.20	2.41	1,125
1986	2.18	2.60	1,641
1987	2.11	2.49	1,650
1988	2.01	2.71	1,731
1989	1.95	2.70	1,795

Table A1.1. (*Continued*)

	Singapore (S$)	Malaysia (RM)	Indonesia (Rp.)
1990	1.81	2.70	1,901
1991	1.73	2.72	1,992
1992	1.63	2.61	2,062
1993	1.62	2.70	2,110
1994	1.53	2.56	2,200
1995	1.42	2.54	2,308
1996	1.41	2.53	2,383
1997	1.48	3.89	4,650
1998	1.67	3.80	8,025
1999	1.69	3.80	7,120
2000	1.72	3.80	9,595

Sources: Emery 1970, 154, 495; Cole and Slade 1996, 20; Bank Indonesia, *Indonesian Financial Statistics* (various issues); BNM 1994, Table A.41; Bank Negara Malaysia, *Quarterly Bulletin* (various issues); Monetary Authority of Singapore, *Annual Report* (various issues); Department of Statistics (Singapore), *Yearbook of Statistics* (various issues).

Notes: End-of-year rates (Malaysia and Indonesia); average for the year (Singapore). Singapore and Malaysia shared their currency until 1967, and the two currencies were exchangeable at par until 1973.

Rates for Indonesia 1960–69 are free market (Hong Kong) rates; others are official or Bank Indonesia rates. The rupiah was revalued in 1965: 1,000 old rupiah = 1 new rupiah.

Appendix 2

Table A2.1. Indicators of Governing Capacity

Country	Revenue[a]	Corruption[b]	Law[c]	Personnel[d]
Singapore	31	9.26	8.57	23 (45)
Japan	23	6.72	8.98	33
Taiwan	24	5.08	8.52	47
Malaysia	26	5.28	6.78	48
Korea	17	4.29	5.35	20
Thailand	19	2.79	6.25	33
Indonesia	17	1.94	3.98	21
Philippines	17	2.77	2.73	18

Sources: REVENUE: International Monetary Fund, *International Financial Statistics*, October 1998; Republic of China, Directorate General of Budget, Accounting, and Statistics, *Quarterly National Economic Trends Taiwan Area*, February 1998. CORRUPTION: Transparency International (www.gwdg.de/rank-95.htm). LAW: La Porta et al. 1998, table 5. PERSONNEL: Department of Statistics (Singapore), *Yearbook of Statistics* 1993; Management and Coordination Agency (Japan), *Japan Statistical Yearbook* 1999; Directorate-General of Budget, Accounting and Statistics (Taiwan), *Monthly Statistical Bulletin* November 1999; Ministry of Government Administration (Korea), *Yearbook of Government Administration* 1992; Department of Statistics (Malaysia), *Yearbook of Statistics* 1990; National Statistical Office (Thailand), *Statistical Yearbook of Thailand* 1993; Biro Pusat Statistik (Indonesia), *Statistik Indonesia* 1990; Department of Labor and Employment (Philippines), *1996 Yearbook of Labor Statistics*. Alternative estimate of public sector employees for Singapore: Burns ed. 1994, 5.

[a] Government revenue as a percentage of GDP, 1991.

[b] Consolidated score on corruption surveys carried out between 1980 and 1994: 10 indicates the perception of totally clean government; 0 is most corrupt.

[c] Rule-of-law index: highest possible score is 10 (rule of law prevails); lowest, 1 (rule of law is absent).

[d] Government employees per 1,000 population, 1990, except Taiwan and Korea (1991). Figures vary enormously according to source. In Singapore, where many core government tasks are delegated to statutory authorities, a broader measure of public-sector personnel puts the number at 45 per 1,000 population.

Appendix 3

Table A3.1. Bank Indonesia Governors

Tenure	Name
1951–58	Sjafruddin Prawiranegara
1958–59	Loekman Hakim
1959–60	Soetikno Slamet
1960–63	Soemarno
1963–66	Jusuf Muda Dalam
1966–73	Radius Prawiro
1973–83	Rachmat Saleh
1983–88	Arifin Siregar
1988–93	Adrianus Mooy
1993–98	Soedradjad Djiwandono
1998–	Syaril Sabirin

Table A3.2. Bank Indonesia Managing Directors

	Total	5 Years or More
1953–58	5	5 (100%)
1958–66	18	11 (61%)
1966–68	15	7 (47%)
1968–93	24	21 (87.5%)

Source: Rahardjo 1995, 127, 269–70.

Table A3.3. Bank Indonesia Personnel

	Total	Head Office (%)	Level (%)			
			I	II	III	IV
1953	1,338	59	1	14	50	35
1989	7,998	57				
1993	7,845	56	1	6	32	48
1997	6,374	52				

Sources: Rahardjo 1995, 94, 272; Bank Indonesia, *Report for the Financial Year* (various issues).
Note: Categorization of personnel by level shows the distribution of total staff across categories denoting position and/or function, with level I being the most senior. In 1993, the categories were *Utama* (divisional heads, their deputies and assistants), *Madya* (departmental heads and deputies), *Muda* (section heads and deputies), and *Pertama* (clerks, typists, cashiers, and security guards).

Appendix 4

Table A4.1. Monetary Authority of Singapore: Number of Staff

Year	Total
1971	112
1975	322
1980	417
1981	503
1982	369
1985	430
1990	499
1995	506
1997	549

Sources: Monetary Authority of Singapore, *Annual Report* (various issues); *Far Eastern Economic Review*, 3 April 1981.
Note: Figures refer to staff strength at March each year except 1971 (January) and 1981 (peak for the year).

Table A4.2. Monetary Authority of Singapore: Continuity of Senior Personnel

Year	Total	5+[a]	Managers[b]	5+
1975	42	6 (14%)	5	4 (80%)
1980	38	27 (71%)	11	9 (82%)
1982	39	6 (15%)	10	4 (40%)
1986	51	16 (31%)	12	6 (50%)
1997	71	54 (76%)	10	10 (100%)

Note: The table understates continuity, since only relatively senior people are listed in the *Government Directory*.
[a] 5+ refers to the number listed in the *Government Directory* five years previously.
[b] Managers are heads of departments or divisions.

Appendix 5

Table A5.1. Bank Negara Malaysia Governors

Tenure	Name
1959–62	W. H. Wilcock (Tan Sri)
1962–80	Ismail b. Mohamed Ali (Tun)
1980–85	Abdul Aziz b. Hj. Taha (Tan Sri)
1985–94	Jaffar b. Hussein (Tan Sri Dato')
1994–98	Ahmad b. Mohd Don (Tan Sri)
1998–2000	Ali Abdul Hassan b. Sulaiman (Tan Sri Dato' Seri)
2000–	Zeti Akhtar Aziz (Datuk Dr.)

Table A5.2. Bank Negara Malaysia Personnel

Year	Staff	HQ[a]	20+[b]	Retirees
1959	46	3	—[c]	—
1960	114	—	—	—
1965	293	—	—	—
1970	666	—	—	—
1975	1,057	804	—	—
1980	1,488	1,108	—	—
1985	1,792	996	6	69[d]
1990	2,710	1,911	70	—
1995	2,865	1,896	124	32
1996	2,425	—	134	29
1997	1,595	—	60	17
1998	1,560	—	28	20

Source: Bank Negara Malaysia *Annual Report* (various issues).
[a] Number at head office (1975 and 1980 include those at mint and staff training center).
[b] Number receiving awards for service of twenty years or more.
[c] —signals data not available.
[d] Of which 8 retired, 61 resigned.

Table A5.3. Bank Negara Malaysia Senior Officers: Continuity and Ethnicity

	Total[a]	5+[b]	Malay[c]
1960	16	—	2
1965	15	5	4
1970	20	6	11
1975	19	2	10
1980	24	7	15
1985	34	8	19
1991	46	17	34[d]
1996	42	16	27[d]

Source: Bank Negara Malaysia *Annual Report* (various issues).
[a] Departmental and branch managers, advisers, secretary, assistant governor, deputy governor, and governor.
[b] Listed in a senior position five years previously.
[c] Considered ethnic Malay on the basis of names.
[d] Possibly 36 (1991) and 29 (1996).

References

Abdullah Ali. 1995. *Liku-Liku Sejarah Perbankan Indonesia*. Jakarta: Grasindo.

Adams, Julia. 1996. "Principals and Agents, Colonialists and Companymen: The Decay of Colonial Control in the Dutch East Indies." *American Sociological Review* 61:12–28.

Allen, George, and Audrey Donnithorne. 1957. *Western Enterprise in Indonesia and Malaya: A Study in Economic Development*. London: Allen & Unwin.

Ammar Siamwalla. 1997a. "Can a Developing Democracy Manage Its Macroeconomy? The Case of Thailand." In *Thailand's Boom and Bust: Collected Papers*, 63–75. Bangkok: Thailand Development Research Institute.

——. 1997b. "The Thai Economy: Fifty Years of Expansion." In *Thailand's Boom and Bust: Collected Papers*, 1–20. Bangkok: Thailand Development Research Institute.

Amyx, Jennifer. 1998. "Banking Policy Breakdown and the Declining Institutional Effectiveness of Japan's Ministry of Finance: Unintended Consequences of Network Relations." Ph.D. dissertation, Stanford University.

Anderson, Benedict. 1966. "Japan: 'The Light of Asia.'" In *Southeast Asia in World War II: Four Essays*, edited by Josef Silverstein, 13–50. Monograph Series 7. New Haven: Yale University Southeast Asia Studies.

——. 1972. *Java in a Time of Revolution: Occupation and Resistance, 1944–1946*. Ithaca: Cornell University Press.

——. 1990. *Language and Power: Exploring Political Cultures in Indonesia*. Ithaca: Cornell University Press.

——. 1998. *The Spectre of Comparisons: Nationalism, Southeast Asia, and the World*. London: Verso.

Anspach, Ralph. 1969. "Indonesia." In *Underdevelopment and Economic Nationalism in Southeast Asia*, by Frank Golay, Ralph Anspach, M. Ruth Pfanner, and Eliezer Ayal, 111–201. Ithaca: Cornell University Press.

Aoki, Masahiko, and Hugh Patrick, eds. 1994. *The Japanese Main Bank System: Its Relevance for Developing and Transforming Economies*. Oxford: Oxford University Press.

Apter, Andrew. 1999. "The Subvention of Tradition: A Genealogy of the Nigerian Durbar." In *State/Culture: State Formation after the Cultural Turn*, edited by George Steinmetz, 213–52. Ithaca: Cornell University Press.

Arndt, H. W. 1984. *The Indonesian Economy: Collected Papers*. Singapore: Chopmen.

Arndt, H. W., and Njoman Suwidjana. 1982. "The Jakarta Dollar Market." *Bulletin of Indonesian Economic Studies* 18 (2):35–64.

Asher, Mukul. 1994. *Social Security in Malaysia and Singapore: Practices, Issues, and Reform Directions*. Kuala Lumpur: ISIS.

——. 1999. "Tax Reform in Singapore." Working Paper 91, Asia Research Centre, Murdoch University, Perth.

Athukorala, Prema-Chandra. 2000. "The Malaysian Experiment." In *Reform and Recovery in East Asia: The Role of the State and Economic Enterprise*, edited by Peter Drysdale, 169–90. London: Routledge.

Azhari Zahri. 1965. "Public Control and Planning in Indonesia." Ph.D. dissertation, Indiana University.

Backman, Michael. 1999. *Asian Eclipse: Exposing the Dark Side of Business in Asia*. Singapore: Wiley.

Baker, Chris. 1999. "Politics of Crisis: Failure, Reform, and Division." Paper presented to the National Thai Studies Centre and APSEM Thailand Update Conference, Australian National University, Canberra, 21 April 1999.

Baker, Dean, Gerald Epstein, and Robert Pollin, eds. 1998. *Globalization and Progressive Economic Policy*. Cambridge: Cambridge University Press.

Bank Indonesia. 1994. *Peraturan Disiplin Pegawai Bank Indonesia*. Jakarta: Bank Indonesia.

Bank of Thailand. 1992. *50 Years of the Bank of Thailand*. Bangkok: Bank of Thailand.

Bapindo (Bank Pembangunan Indonesia). 1980. *20 Tahun Bapindo*. Jakarta: Bapindo.

———. 1985. *25 Tahun Bapindo*. Jakarta: Bapindo.

———. 1990. *30 Tahun Bapindo*. Jakarta: Bapindo.

Barnett, Michael, and Martha Finnemore. 1999. "The Politics, Power, and Pathologies of International Organizations." *International Organization* 53:699–732.

Barret-Kriegel, Blandine. 1989. *L'Etat et les esclaves*. Paris: Payot.

BCE (BMFL Committee of Enquiry). 1986. *Final Report*. Kuala Lumpur: Bank Bumiputera Malaysia.

Bell, Hesketh. 1928. *Foreign Colonial Administration in the Far East*. London: Edward Arnold.

Bello, Walden. 1998. "East Asia: On the Eve of the Great Transformation?" *Review of International Political Economy* 5:424–44.

Benda, Harry. 1966. "The Pattern of Administrative Reform in the Closing Years of Dutch Rule in Indonesia." *Journal of Asian Studies* 25:589–605.

Berg, N. P. van den. 1996. *Currency and the Economy of Netherlands India, 1870–95*. Singapore: ISEAS; Canberra: RSPAS, Australian National University.

Berger, Suzanne, and Ronald Dore, eds. 1996. *National Diversity and Global Capitalism*. Ithaca: Cornell University Press.

Bhagwati, Jagdish. 1998. "The Capital Myth: The Difference between Trade in Widgets and Dollars." *Foreign Affairs* 77 (3):7–12.

BNM (Bank Negara Malaysia). 1971. "Senior Officers' Seminar." Port Dickson, Malaysia, 1–2 May 1971. Mimeo.

———. 1981a. "Course Specifications of the Officers' Training Programme." Revised 31 July 1981. Mimeo.

———. 1981b. "LENS Seminar on Achieving Organizational Objectives through Effective Communication and Teamwork." 12–13 December 1981. Mimeo.

———. 1989. *Central Banking in an Era of Change: Landmark Speeches: 1959–1988*. Kuala Lumpur: BNM.

———. 1994. *Money and Banking in Malaysia*. 4th ed. Kuala Lumpur: BNM.

Booth, Anne. 1990. "The Evolution of Fiscal Policy and the Role of Government in the Colonial Economy." In *Indonesian Economic History in the Dutch Colonial Era*, edited by Anne Booth, W. J. O'Malley, and Anna Weidemann, 210–43. Monograph Series 35. New Haven: Yale University Southeast Asia Studies.

——. 1999. "Survey of Recent Developments." *Bulletin of Indonesian Economic Studies* 35 (3):3–38.

Bourdieu, Pierre. 1989. *La Noblesse d'état: Grandes écoles et esprit de corps.* Paris: Minuit.

Bowie, Alasdair. 1991. *Crossing the Industrial Divide: State, Society, and the Politics of Economic Transformation in Malaysia.* New York: Columbia University Press.

Bresnan, John. 1993. *Managing Indonesia: The Modern Political Economy.* New York: Columbia University Press.

Broad, Robin. 1988. *Unequal Alliance: The World Bank, the International Monetary Fund, and the Philippines.* Berkeley: University of California Press.

Brouwer, Gordon de. 1997. "Interest Parity Conditions as Indicators of Financial Integration in East Asia." Pacific Economic Papers 268, Australia-Japan Research Centre, Australian National University, Canberra.

——. 2000. "Does a Formal Common-Basket Peg in East Asia Make Economic Sense?" Paper presented to Conference on Financial Markets and Policies in East Asia, Australian National University, Canberra, 4–5 September.

Brown, Ian. 1992. *The Creation of the Modern Ministry of Finance in Siam, 1995–1910.* London: Macmillan.

Burns, Peter, ed. 1994. *Asian Civil Service Systems: Improving Efficiency and Productivity.* Singapore: Times Academic Press.

Butcher, John, and Howard Dick, eds. 1993. *The Rise and Fall of Revenue Farming: Business Elites and the Emergence of the Modern State in Southeast Asia.* New York: St. Martin's Press.

Castellano, Mark. 2000. "East Asian Monetary Union: More than Just Talk?" *Japan Economic Institute Report* 12A (24 March 2000).

Cerny, Philip. 1996. "What Next for the State?" In *Globalization: Theory and Practice*, edited by Eleonore Kofman and Gillian Youngs, 123–37. London: Pinter.

CFEOT (Council on Foreign Exchange and Other Transactions). 1999. "Internationalization of the Yen for the 21st Century." 20 April 1999 (www.mof.go.jp/english/if/elb064a.htm).

Chalongphob Sussangkarn. 2000. "A Framework for Regional Monetary Stabilization." *NIRA Review*, Autumn 2000:16–20.

Chan Heng Chee. 1975. "Politics in an Administrative State: Where Has the Politics Gone?" In *Trends in Singapore*, edited by Seah Chee Meow, 51–68. Singapore: ISEAS.

——. 1976. *The Dynamics of One Party Dominance: The PAP at the Grass Roots.* Singapore: Singapore University Press.

Chan, S. K., Chai, T. K., and R. Iau, K. K. 1987. "Report of the Commission of Inquiry on Investigations concerning the Late Mr. Teh Cheang Wang." Report to Parliament, 28 December 1987, Singapore.

Chaudry, Kiren Aziz. 1989. "The Price of Wealth: Business and State in Labor Remittance and Oil Economies." *International Organization* 43:101–45.

Chia Siow Yue. 1998. "The Asian Financial Crisis: Singapore's Experience and Response." *ASEAN Economic Bulletin* 15:297–308.

Chirot, Daniel, and Anthony Reid, eds. 1997. *Essential Outsiders: Chinese and Jews in the Modern Transformation of Southeast Asia and Central Europe.* Seattle: University of Washington Press.

Chiu, Stephen W. K. 1992. "The State and the Financing of Industrialization in East Asia: Historical Origins of Comparative Differences." Ph.D. dissertation, Princeton University.

Christiansen, Peter Munk. 1998. "A Prescription Rejected: Market Solutions to Problems of Public Sector Governance." *Governance* 11:273–95.

Chua Beng-Huat. 1995. *Communitarian Ideology and Democracy in Singapore*. London: Routledge.

Claassen, Emil-Maria. 1992. *Financial Liberalization and Its Impact on Domestic Stabilization Policies: Singapore and Malaysia*. Singapore: ISEAS.

Claessens, Stijn, Simeon Djankov, and Daniela Klingbeil. 1999. "Financial Restructuring in East Asia: Halfway There?" Financial Sector Discussion Paper 3. World Bank, Washington.

Cohen, Benjamin. 1986. *In Whose Interest? International Banking and American Foreign Policy*. New Haven: Yale University Press.

———. 2000. "Taming the Phoenix? Monetary Governance after the Crisis." In *The Asian Financial Crisis and the Architecture of Global Finance*, edited by Gregory Noble and John Ravenhill, 192–212. Cambridge: Cambridge University Press.

Cole, David, and Betty Slade. 1996. *Building a Modern Financial System: The Indonesian Experience*. Cambridge: Cambridge University Press.

———. 1998. "Why Has Indonesia's Financial Crisis Been So Bad?" *Bulletin of Indonesian Economic Studies* 34 (2):61–66.

Collins, James, and Jerry Poras. 1994. *Built to Last: Successful Habits of Visionary Companies*. New York: Harper Business.

Collins, Michael, ed. 1993. *Central Banking in History*. Vol. 1, *Central Bank Functions*. Aldershot: Edward Elgar.

Commissioners' Report. 1955. *Report of a Commission to Enquire into Matters Affecting the Integrity of the Public Services*. Kuala Lumpur: Government Press.

Committee to Promote Enterprise Overseas. 1993a. *Interim Report*. Singapore: SNP.

———. 1993b. *Final Report*. Singapore: Ministry of Finance.

Conant, Charles. 1927. *A History of Modern Banks of Issue*. New York: Putnam.

Cooper, Richard. 1968. *The Economics of Interdependence: Economic Policy in the Atlantic Community*. New York: McGraw-Hill.

Credit Lyonnais Securities. 1996. "The Indonesian Banking Sector: Rise and Shine." 19 November 1996, Jakarta.

Crouch, Harold. 1984. *Domestic Political Structures and Regional Economic Cooperation*. Singapore: ISEAS.

———. 1988 [1978]. *The Army and Politics in Indonesia*. Rev. ed. Ithaca: Cornell University Press.

———. 1996. *Government and Society in Malaysia*. St. Leonards, New South Wales: Allen & Unwin.

Danaharta. 2000. "Operations Report: Six Months Ended 30 June 2000." Kuala Lumpur.

Dauvergne, Peter. 1997. *Shadows in the Forest: Japan and the Politics of Timber in Southeast Asia*. Cambridge, Mass.: MIT Press.

DBS (Development Bank of Singapore). 1988. "Let Us Be Distinctively DBS: 20 Years of DBS Bank." *Banknotes: House Journal of the DBS Group*, May–June 1988.

DC/ICN. *Data Consult/Indonesian Commercial Newsletter*. Various issues. Jakarta.

De Bree, L. 1928. *Gedenkboek van de Javasche bank, 1828–24*. Weltevredem: G. Kolff.

Department of Statistics (Singapore). N.d. "Foreign Equity Investment in Singapore, 1987–1994."

———. 1995. "The Extent and Pattern of Foreign Investment Activities in Singapore." Occasional Paper Series.

——. 1997. "Foreign Direct Investment Activities of Singapore Companies 1995." Occasional Paper Series.

——. 1998. "Singapore's External Debt." Occasional Paper Series.

DFAT (Department of Foreign Affairs and Trade). 1995. *Overseas Chinese Business Networks in Asia*. Canberra: East Asia Analytic Unit, DFAT.

Diaz-Alejandro, Carlos. 1985. "Good-bye Financial Repression, Hello Financial Crash." *Journal of Development Economics* 19:1–24.

Diehl, F. W. 1993. "Revenue Farming and Colonial Finances in the Netherlands East Indies." In *The Rise and Fall of Revenue Farming: Business Elites and the Emergence of the Modern State in Southeast Asia*, edited by John Butcher and Howard Dick, 196–232. New York: St. Martin's Press.

Doh Joon Chien. 1985. *Tan Sri Ahmad Noordin: Kampung Boy to Auditor-General*. Petaling Jaya: Pelanduk.

Doner, Richard. 1997. "Japan in East Asia: Institutions and Regional Leadership." In *Network Power: Japan and Asia*, edited by Peter Katzenstein and Takashi Shiraishi, 197–223. Ithaca: Cornell University Press.

EDB (Economic Development Board). 1991. *Singapore Economic Development Board: Thirty Years of Economic Development*. Singapore: EDB.

Eichengreen, Barry. 2000. "The International Monetary Fund in the Wake of the Asian Crisis." In *The Asian Financial Crisis and the Architecture of Global Finance*, edited by Gregory Noble and John Ravenhill, 170–91. Cambridge: Cambridge University Press.

Emerson, Rupert. 1964 [1937]. *Malaysia: A Study in Direct and Indirect Rule*. Kuala Lumpur: University of Malaya Press.

Emery, Robert. 1970. *The Financial Institutions of Southeast Asia: a Country-by-Country Study*. New York: Praeger.

Emmerson, Donald 1978. "The Bureaucracy in Political Context: Weakness in Strength." In *Political Power and Communications in Indonesia*, edited by Karl Jackson and Lucien Pye, 82–135. Berkeley: University of California Press.

Eng, Pierre van der. 1996. Introduction to *Currency and the Economy of Netherlands India, 1870–95*, by N. P. van den Berg, vii–xxvi. Singapore: ISEAS; Canberra: RSPAS, Australian National University.

EPU-ISIS (Economic Planning Unit–Institute of Strategic and International Studies). 1991. Discussion paper on growth triangles. Mimeo.

Esman, Milton. 1972. *Administration and Development in Malaysia: Institution Building and Reform in a Plural Society*. Ithaca: Cornell University Press.

——. 1994. *Ethnic Politics*. Ithaca: Cornell University Press.

Evans, Peter. 1995. *Embedded Autonomy: States and Industrial Transformation*. Princeton: Princeton University Press.

Evans, Peter, and James Rausch. 1999. "Bureaucracy and Growth: A Cross-National Analysis of the Effects of 'Weberian' State Structures on Economic Growth." *American Sociological Review* 64:748–65.

Evers, Hans-Dieter. 1987. "The Bureaucratization of Southeast Asia." *Comparative Studies in Society and History* 29:666–85.

Fane, George. 1994. "The Sequencing of Economic Deregulation in Indonesia." In *Indonesia Assessment 1994: Finance as a Key Sector in Indonesia's Development*, edited by Ross McLeod, 101–18. Singapore: ISEAS; Canberra: Australian National University.

———. 2000. "Survey of Recent Developments." *Bulletin of Indonesian Economic Studies* 36 (1):13–44.

Federation of Malaya. 1956a. *Malayanisation of the Public Service: A Statement of Policy.* Kuala Lumpur: Government Press.

———. 1956b. *Report of the Committee on Malayanisation of the Public Service.* Kuala Lumpur: Government Press.

Feith, Herbert. 1962. *The Decline of Constitutional Democracy in Indonesia.* Ithaca: Cornell University Press.

Feldstein, Martin. 1998. "Refocusing the IMF." *Foreign Affairs* 77 (2):20–33.

Fokkens, F. 1992. "The Power of Money-Lenders in Java." In *Chinese Economic Activity in Netherlands India: Selected Translations from the Dutch,* edited by M. R. Fernando and David Bulbeck, 43–57. Singapore: ISEAS; Canberra: RSPAS, Australian National University.

Fry, Maxwell. 1995. *Money, Interest, and Banking in Economic Development.* 2d ed. Baltimore: Johns Hopkins University Press.

Furnivall, John. 1939. *Netherlands India: A Study of Plural Economy.* Cambridge: Cambridge University Press.

Gale, Bruce. 1981. *Politics and Public Enterprise in Malaysia.* Singapore: Eastern Universities Press.

Geddes, Barbara. 1994. *Politician's Dilemma: Building State Capacity in Latin America.* Berkeley: University of California Press.

Gill, Ranjit. 1985. *George Tan: The Carrian Saga.* Petaling Jaya: Pelanduk.

———. 1987. *Khoo Teck Puat: Tycoon on a Tightrope.* Singapore: Sterling Corporate Services.

Gilmour, Andrew. 1974. *An Eastern Cadet's Anecdotage.* Singapore: University Education Press.

Glassburner, Bruce. 1971. "Economic Policy-Making in Indonesia, 1950–1957." In *The Economy of Indonesia: Selected Readings,* edited by Bruce Glassburner, 70–98. Ithaca: Cornell University Press.

Goldstein, Morris. 1998. *The Asian Financial Crisis: Causes, Cures, and Systemic Implications.* Washington, D.C.: Institute for International Economics.

Gomez, Edmund Terence. 1990. *Politics in Business: UMNO's Corporate Investments.* Kuala Lumpur: Forum.

———. 1994. *Political Business: Corporate Involvement of Malaysian Political Parties.* Townsville: Centre for South-East Asian Studies, James Cook University of North Queensland.

———. 1996. "Electoral Funding of General, State, and Party Elections in Malaysia." *Journal of Contemporary Asia* 26 (1):81–99.

———. 1999. *Chinese Business in Malaysia: Accumulation, Accommodation, and Ascendance.* Richmond, Surrey: Curzon.

Gomez, Edmund T., and Jomo, K. S. 1997. *Malaysia's Political Economy: Politics, Patronage, and Profits.* Cambridge: Cambridge University Press.

Gorski, Philip. 1995. "The Protestant Ethic and the Spirit of Bureaucracy." *American Sociological Review* 60:783–86.

Government of Malaysia. 1999. *White Paper on the Status of the Malaysian Economy.* Parliamentary paper, 6 April 1999, Kuala Lumpur.

Granovetter, Mark. 1985. "Economic Action and Social Structure: The Problem of Embeddedness." *American Journal of Sociology* 91:481–510.

Grenville, Stephen. 1994. "Comments on Professor Wardhana's Paper." In *Indonesia Assessment 1994: Finance as a Key Sector in Indonesia's Development*, edited by Ross McLeod, 94–100. Singapore: ISEAS; Canberra: Australian National University.

Grindle, Merilee. 1980. "Policy Content and Context in Implementation." In *Politics and Policy Implementation in the Third World*, edited by Merilee Grindle, 3–34. Princeton: Princeton University Press.

Gruen, David, and Luke Gower, eds. 1999. *Capital Flows and the International Financial System*. Sydney: Reserve Bank of Australia.

Gullick, J. M. 1958. *Indigenous Political Systems of Western Malaya*. London: Athlone Press.

———. 1992. *Rulers and Residents: Influence and Power in the Malay States, 1870–1920*. Singapore: Oxford University Press.

Haggard, Stephan. 1990. *Pathways from the Periphery: The Politics of Growth in the Newly Industrializing Economies*. Ithaca: Cornell University Press.

———. 2000. *The Political Economy of the Asian Financial Crisis*. Washington, D.C.: Institute for International Economics.

Haggard, Stephan, and Chung H. Lee, eds. 1995. *Financial Systems and Economic Policy in Developing Countries*. Ithaca: Cornell University Press.

Haggard, Stephan, Chung H. Lee, and Sylvia Maxfield, eds. 1993. *The Politics of Finance in Developing Countries*. Ithaca: Cornell University Press.

Hamashita, Takeshi. 1991. "The Asian Network and Silver Circulation." In *Money, Coins, and Commerce: Essays in the Monetary History of Asia and Europe (from Antiquity to Modern Times)*, edited by E. H. G. van Cauwenberghe, 47–54. Louvain, Belgium: Leuven University Press.

———. 1997. "The Intra-Regional System in East Asia in Modern Times." In *Network Power: Japan and Asia*, edited by Peter Katzenstein and Takashi Shiraishi, 113–35. Ithaca: Cornell University Press.

Hamilton-Hart, Natasha. 1999. "States and Capital Mobility: Indonesia, Malaysia, and Singapore in the Asian Region." Ph.D. dissertation, Cornell University.

———. 2000a. "Indonesia: Reforming the Institutions of Financial Governance?" In *The Asian Financial Crisis and the Architecture of Global Finance*, edited by Gregory Noble and John Ravenhill, 108–31. Cambridge: Cambridge University Press.

———. 2000b. "The Singapore State Revisited." *Pacific Review* 13:195–216.

———. 2001. "Anti-Corruption Strategies in Indonesia." *Bulletin of Indonesian Economic Studies* 37 (1):65–82.

Helleiner, Eric. 1994. *States and the Reemergence of Global Finance*. Ithaca: Cornell University Press.

Hellman, Thomas, Kevin Murdock, and Joseph Stiglitz. 1997. "Financial Restraint: Toward a New Paradigm." In *The Role of Government in East Asian Economic Development: Comparative Institutional Analysis*, edited by Masahiko Aoki, Hyung-Ki Kim, and Masahiro Okuno-Fujiwara, 163–207. Oxford: Clarendon Press.

Heng Pek Koon. 1992. "The Chinese Business Elite of Malaysia." In *Southeast Asian Capitalists*, edited by Ruth McVey, 127–44. Ithaca: Cornell University Southeast Asia Program.

Heussler, Robert. 1981. *British Rule in Malaya: The Malayan Civil Service and Its Predecessors, 1867–1942*. Oxford: Clio Press.

Hewison, Kevin. 1989. *Bankers and Bureaucrats: Capital and the Role of the State in Thailand*. New Haven: Yale Center for International and Area Studies.

Higgins, Benjamin. 1957. *Indonesia's Economic Stabilization and Development*. Westport, Conn.: Greenwood Press.

Higgott, Richard. 1998. "The Asian Economic Crisis: A Study in the Politics of Resentment." *New Political Economy* 3:333–56.

Hill, Hal. 1996. *The Indonesian Economy since 1966: Southeast Asia's Emerging Giant*. Cambridge: Cambridge University Press.

Hirschman, Albert. 1970. *Exit, Voice, and Loyalty*. Cambridge: Harvard University Press.

Hirst, Paul, and Graham Thompson. 1996. *Globalization in Question: The International Political Economy and the Possibilities of Governance*. Cambridge: Polity Press.

Ho Rih Hwa. 1991. *Eating Salt: An Autobiography*. Singapore: Times Books International.

Huff, W. G. 1994. *The Economic Growth of Singapore: Trade and Development in the Twentieth Century*. Cambridge: Cambridge University Press.

Huntington, Samuel. 1968. *Political Order in Changing Societies*. New Haven: Yale University Press.

Hutchcroft, Paul. 1998. *Booty Capitalism: The Politics of Banking in the Philippines*. Ithaca: Cornell University Press.

———. 1999. "Neither Dynamo nor Domino: Reforms and Crises in the Philippine Political Economy." In *The Politics of the Asian Economic Crisis*, edited by T. J. Pempel, 163–83. Ithaca: Cornell University Press.

Jayasuriya, Kanishka. 1996. "Legalism and Social Control in Singapore." *South East Asia Research* 4 (1):85–94.

Jesudason, James. 1989. *Ethnicity and the Economy: The State, Chinese Business, and Multinationals in Malaysia*. Singapore: Oxford University Press.

Johnson, Chalmers. 1998. "Economic Crisis in East Asia: The Clash of Capitalisms." *Cambridge Journal of Economics* 22:653–61.

Johnson, Colin. 1998. "Survey of Recent Developments." *Bulletin of Indonesian Economic Studies* 34 (2):3–60.

Jomo, K. S. 1986. *A Question of Class: Capital, the State, and Uneven Development in Malaya*. Singapore: Oxford University Press.

———, ed. 1995. *Privatizing Malaysia: Rents, Rhetoric, Realities*. Boulder, Colo.: Westview Press.

Jones, S. W. 1953. *Public Administration in Malaya*. London: Royal Institute of International Affairs.

Kadushin, Charles. 1995. "Friendship among the French Financial Elite." *American Sociological Review* 60:202–21.

Kahar Bador, A. 1973. "Social Rank, Status-Honour, and Social Class Consciousness amongst the Malays." In *Modernization in South-East Asia*, edited by Hans-Dieter Evers, 132–49. Singapore: Oxford University Press.

Kahin, George. 1989. "In Memoriam: Sjafruddin Prawiranegara (1911–1989)." *Indonesia* 48:101–5.

Kahler, Miles. 2000. "The New International Financial Architecture and Its Limits." In *The Asian Financial Crisis and the Architecture of Global Finance*, edited by Gregory Noble and John Ravenhill, 235–60. Cambridge: Cambridge University Press.

Kanapathy, Vijayakumari, and Ismail Muhd Salleh, eds. 1994. *Malaysian Economy: Selected Issues and Policy Directions*. Kuala Lumpur: ISIS.

Kapstein, Ethan. 1994. *Governing the Global Economy: International Finance and the State*. Cambridge: Harvard University Press.

Katzenstein, Peter, ed. 1978. *Between Power and Plenty: The Foreign Economic Policies of Advanced Industrial States*. Madison: University of Wisconsin Press.

——. 1985. *Small States in World Markets: Industrial Policy in Europe*. Ithaca: Cornell University Press.

——. 1997. "Introduction: Asian Regionalism in Comparative Perspective." In *Network Power: Japan and Asia*, edited by Peter Katzenstein and Takashi Shiraishi, 1–44. Ithaca: Cornell University Press.

Katzenstein, Peter, Natasha Hamilton-Hart, Kozo Kato, and Ming Yue. 2000. *Asian Regionalism*. Ithaca: Cornell University East Asia Program.

Kawai, Masahiro, and Shigeru Akiyama. 2001. "Implications of the Currency Crisis for Exchange Rate Arrangements in Emerging East Asia." Working Paper 2502. World Bank, Washington, D.C.

Kawai, Masahiro, and Shinji Takagi. 2001. "Proposed Strategy for a Regional Exchange Arrangement in Post-Crisis East Asia." Working Paper 2503. World Bank, Washington, D.C.

Khan, Mohsin, and Carmen Reinhart, eds. 1995. "Capital Flows in the APEC Region." Occasional Paper 122. International Monetary Fund, Washington, D.C.

Khasnor, Johan. 1984. *The Emergence of the Modern Malay Administrative Elite*. Kuala Lumpur: Oxford University Press.

Kindleberger, Charles. 1989. *Manias, Panics, and Crashes: A History of Financial Crises*. Rev. ed. New York: Basic Books.

King, Frank. 1987. *The History of the Hongkong and Shanghai Banking Corporation*. Cambridge: Cambridge University Press.

Kirshner, Jonathan. 1998. "Disinflation, Structural Change, and Distribution." *Review of Radical Political Economics* 30 (1):53–89.

Kiser, Edgar, and Joachim Schneider. 1994. "Bureaucracy and Efficiency: An Analysis of Taxation in Early Modern Prussia." *American Sociological Review* 59:187–204.

Klein, Peter. 1991. "Dutch Monetary Policy in the East Indies, 1602–1942: A Case of Changing Continuity." In *Money, Coins, and Commerce: Essays in the Monetary History of Asia and Europe (from Antiquity to Modern Times)*, edited by E. H. G. Van Cauwenberghe, 419–53. Louvain, Belgium: Leuven University Press.

Koh Kheng Lian, David Allan, Mary Hiscock, and Derek Roebuck. 1973. *Credit and Security in Singapore: Legal Problems of Development Finance*. St. Lucia: University of Queensland Press.

Kusukawa, Toru. 1999. "Asian Currency Reform: The Option of a Common Basket Peg." Fuji Research Paper 13, Fuji Research Institute Corporation, Tokyo.

Kwan, C. H. 1996. "A Yen Bloc in Asia." *Journal of the Asia Pacific Economy* 1:1–21.

Laanen, J. T. M. van. 1980. *Money and Banking, 1916–1940*. Vol. 6, *Changing Economy in Indonesia: A Selection of Source Material from the Early 19th Century up to 1940*, edited by P. Creutzberg and J. T. M. van Laanen. The Hague: Martinus Nijhoff.

——. 1990. "Between the Java Bank and the Chinese Moneylender: Banking and Credit in Colonial Indonesia." In *Indonesian Economic History in the Dutch Colonial Era*, edited by Anne Booth, William O'Malley, and Anna Weidemann, 244–66. Monograph Series 35. New Haven: Yale University Southeast Asia Studies.

Lamberte, Mario, Joseph Lim, Rob Vos, Josef Yap, Elizabeth Tan, and Ma. Socorro Zingapan. 1992. *Philippine External Finance: Domestic Resource Mobilization and Development in the 1970s and 1980s*. Makati: Philippine Institute of Development Studies.

La Porta, Rafael, Florencio Lopez-de-Silanes, Andrei Shleifer, and Robert Vishny. 1998. "Law and Finance." *Journal of Political Economy* 106:1113–55.

———. 1999. "The Quality of Government." *Journal of Law, Economics, and Organization* 15:222–79.

Lee, Edwin. 1991. *The British as Rulers: Governing Multiracial Singapore, 1867–1914.* Singapore: Singapore University Press.

Lee Hock Lock. 1981. *Public Policies, Commercial Banks, and Other Deposit Institutions in Malaysia: A Study in Resource Mobilization and Utilization.* Kuala Lumpur: UMBC Publications.

———. 1987. *Central Banking in Malaysia: A Study of the Development of the Financial System and Monetary Management.* Singapore: Butterworths.

Lee Sheng-Yi. 1974. *The Monetary and Banking Development of Malaysia and Singapore.* Singapore: Singapore University Press.

———. 1990. *The Monetary and Banking Development of Singapore and Malaysia.* 3d ed. Singapore: Times Academic Press.

Lee Tsao Yuan and Linda Low. 1990. *Local Entrepreneurship in Singapore: Private and State.* Singapore: Times Academic Press.

Leigh, Michael. 1992. "Politics, Bureaucracy and Business in Malaysia: Realigning the Eternal Triangle." In *The Dynamics of Economic Policy Reform in South-East Asia and the South-West Pacific,* edited by Andrew MacIntyre and Kanishka Jayasuriya, 115–23. Singapore: Oxford University Press.

Lev, Daniel. 1972. "Judicial Institutions and Legal Culture in Indonesia." In *Culture and Politics in Indonesia,* edited by Claire Holt, 246–318. Ithaca: Cornell University Press.

———. 1985. "Colonial Law and the Genesis of the Indonesian State." *Indonesia* 40:54–74.

Lien Ying Chow. 1992. *From Chinese Villager to Singapore Tycoon: My Life Story.* Singapore: Times Books International.

Lim Kit Siang. 1986. *BMF: The Scandal of Scandals.* Petaling Jaya, Malaysia: Democratic Action Party.

———. 1994. *The Bank Negara RM30 Billion Forex Losses Scandal.* Petaling Jaya, Malaysia: Democratic Action Party.

Lim, Linda. 1983. "Singapore's Success: The Myth of the Free Market Economy." *Asian Survey* 23:752–64.

———. 1999. "Free Market Fancies: Hong Kong, Singapore, and the Asian Financial Crisis." In *The Politics of the Asian Economic Crisis,* edited by T. J. Pempel, 101–15. Ithaca: Cornell University Press.

Lindsey, Timothy. 2000. "Black Letter, Black Market, and Bad Faith: Corruption and the Failure of Law Reform." In *Indonesia in Transition: Social Aspects of Reformasi and Crisis,* edited by Chris Manning and Peter van Diermen, 278–92. Singapore: ISEAS.

Lippincott, Donald. 1997. "Saturation Training: Bolstering Capacity in the Indonesian Ministry of Finance." In *Getting Good Government: Capacity Building in the Public Sectors of Developing Countries,* edited by Merilee Grindle, 97–123. Cambridge: Harvard Institute for International Development.

Low, Linda, Toh Mun Heng, Soon Teck Wong, Tan Kong Yam, and Helen Hughes. 1993. *Challenge and Response: Thirty Years of the Economic Development Board.* Singapore: Times Academic Press.

MacDougall, John. 1982. "Patterns of Military Control in the Indonesian Higher Central Bureaucracy." *Indonesia* 33:89–121.

MacIntyre, Andrew. 1991. *Business and Politics in Indonesia*. Sydney: Allen & Unwin.
——. 1993. "The Politics of Finance in Indonesia: Command, Confusion, and Competition." In *The Politics of Finance in Developing Countries*, edited by Stephan Haggard, Chung H. Lee, and Sylvia Maxfield, 123–64. Ithaca: Cornell University Press.
——. 1995. "Ideas and Experts: Indonesian Approaches to Economic and Security Cooperation in the Asia-Pacific Region." *Pacific Review* 8:159–72.
MacKenzie, Compton. 1954. *Realms of Silver: One Hundred Years of Banking in the East*. London: Routledge & Kegan Paul.
Mackie, J. A. C. 1967. *Problems of the Indonesian Inflation*. Ithaca: Cornell University Southeast Asia Program.
——. 1990. "The Indonesian Conglomerates in Regional Perspective." In *Indonesia Assessment 1990*, edited by Hal Hill and Terence Hull, 108–21. Canberra: RSPAS, Australian National University.
——. 1991. "Towkays and Tycoons: The Chinese in Indonesian Economic Life in the 1920s and 1980s." *Indonesia*, special issue ("The Role of the Indonesian Chinese in Shaping Modern Indonesian Life":) 83–96.
——. 1996. "The 1941–1965 Period as an Interlude in the Making of a National Economy: How Should We Interpret It?" In *Historical Foundations of a National Economy in Indonesia*, edited by J. Thomas Lindblad, 331–47. Amsterdam: North-Holland and Netherlands Academy of Arts and Sciences.
Macquarie Bank. 1999. "Regaining Confidence in South-East Asia." November, Macquarie Bank Economic Research, Sydney.
McKinnon, Ronald, and Huw Pill. 1996. "Credible Liberalizations and International Capital Flows: The 'Overborrowing Syndrome.'" In *Financial Deregulation and Integration in East Asia*, edited by Takatoshi Ito and Anne Krueger, 7–50. Chicago: Chicago University Press.
McLeod, Ross. 1997. "Survey of Recent Developments." *Bulletin of Indonesian Economic Studies* 33 (1):3–43.
——. 1998. "Indonesia." In *East asia in Crisis: From Being a Miracle to Needing One?* edited by Ross Garnaut and Ross McLeod, 31–48. London: Routledge.
——. 2000. "Survey of Recent Developments." *Bulletin of Indonesian Economic Studies* 36 (2):5–40.
McVey, Ruth. 1971. "The Post-Revolutionary Transformation of the Indonesian Army: Part I." *Indonesia* 11:131–76.
——. 1972. "The Post-Revolutionary Transformation of the Indonesian Army: Part II." *Indonesia* 12:147–81.
——. 1982 [1977]. "The Beamtenstaat in Indonesia." In *Interpreting Indonesian Politics: Thirteen Contributions to the Debate*, edited by Benedict Anderson and Ruth McVey, 84–91. Ithaca: Cornell University Modern Indonesia Project.
Mahathir Mohamad. 1970. *The Malay Dilemma*. Singapore: Times Books International.
——. 1998. *Currency Turmoil*. Petaling Jaya, Malaysia: Limkokwing Integrated.
——. 1999. *A New Deal for Asia*. Subang Jaya, Malaysia: Pelanduk.
Majidi, Nasyith. 1994. *Megaskandal: Drama Pembobolan dan Kolusi Bapindo*. Bandung: Mizan.
Makepeace, Walter, Gilbert Brooke, and Roland St. J. Braddle, eds. 1921. *One Hundred Years of Singapore*. London: John Murray.
Manning, Chris, and Peter van Diermen, eds. 2000. *Indonesia in Transition: Social Aspects of Reformasi and Crisis*. Singapore: ISEAS.

Mansoor Marican, Y. 1979. "Combating Corruption: The Malaysian Experience." *Asian Survey* 19:597–610.

MAS (Monetary Authority of Singapore). 1981. "Singapore." Paper submitted to the fifth SEACEN banking course: Inspection and Supervision of Financial Institutions, 31 July 1981. Mimeo.

Mason, Edward. 1986. *The Harvard Institute for International Development and Its Antecedents.* Cambridge: Harvard Institute for International Development.

Masuyama, Seiichi. 2000. "The Role of Japan's Direct Investment in Restoring East Asia's Dynamism: Focus on ASEAN." In *Restoring East Asia's Dynamism,* edited by Seiichi Masuyama, Donna Vandenbrink, and Chia Siow Yue, 213–58. Tokyo: Nomura Research Institute; Singapore: ISEAS.

Maxfield, Sylvia. 1997. *Gatekeepers of Growth: The International Political Economy of Central Banking in Developing Countries.* Princeton: Princeton University Press.

MBC (Malaysian Business Council). 1995. "Implications, Entrepreneurship Development, and Strategy for a Reverse Investment Initiative." Paper presented to the Sixth Plenary Meeting of the MBC, 25 July 1995, Kuala Lumpur.

——. 1996. Malaysian Business Council. Kuala Lumpur: ISIS.

Means, Gordon. 1991. *Malaysian Politics: The Second Generation.* Singapore: Oxford University Press.

Mehmet, Ozay. 1986. *Development in Malaysia: Poverty, Wealth, and Trusteeship.* London: Croom Helm.

Migdal, Joel. 1988. *Strong Societies and Weak States: State-Society Relations and State Capabilities in the Third World.* Princeton: Princeton University Press.

Milne, R. S. 1987. "Bumiputera Malaysia Finance: Levels of Corruption in Malaysia." *Asian Journal of Public Administration* 9 (1):56–73.

Milner, Anthony. 1995. *The Invention of Politics in Colonial Malaya: Contesting Nationalism and the Expansion of the Public Sphere.* Cambridge: Cambridge University Press.

Ministry of Finance (Singapore). 1963. *Annual Report of the Division of Commerce and Industry, 1960.* Singapore: Government Printers.

Mitchell, Timothy. 1999. "Society, Economy, and the State Effect." In *State/Culture: State Formation after the Cultural Turn,* edited by George Steinmetz, 76–97. Ithaca: Cornell University Press.

Moertono, Soemarsaid. 1981. *State and Statecraft in Old Java: A Study of the Later Mataram Period, 16th to 19th Century.* Ithaca: Cornell University Modern Indonesia Project.

Montes, Manuel. 1998. *The Currency Crisis in Southeast Asia.* Singapore: ISEAS.

Morgan, Gareth. 1998. *Images of Organization: The Executive Edition.* San Francisco: Sage.

Morrison, Charles. 2001. Introduction to *East Asia and the International System: Report of a Special Study Group to the Trilateral Commission.* New York: Trilateral Commission.

Nasution, Anwar. 1983. *Financial Institutions and Policies in Indonesia.* Singapore: ISEAS.

——. 1992. "The Years of Living Dangerously: The Impacts of Financial Sector Policy Reforms and Increasing Private Sector External Indebtedness in Indonesia." *Indonesian Quarterly* 20:405–37.

Nish, Ian. 1962. "British Mercantile Co-operation in the India-China Trade." *Journal of Southeast Asian History* 3 (2):74–91.

Nishihara, Masashi. 1975. *The Japanese and Sukarno's Indonesia: Tokyo-Jakarta Relations 1951–1966.* Honolulu: University Press of Hawaii.

Noble, Gregory, and John Ravenhill, eds. 2000. *The Asian Financial Crisis and the Architecture of Global Finance*. Cambridge: Cambridge University Press.

Nukul Commission. 1998. *Analysis and Evaluation on Facts behind Thailand's Economic Crisis: The Nukul Commission Report*. Bangkok: Nation Mulitmedia Group.

Oei, Anthony. 1991. *Building a New Niche: The Story of Dr. David B. H. Chew*. Singapore: Heinemann Asia.

Oey Beng To. 1991. *Sejarah Kebijakan Moneter Indonesia: Jilid I (1945–1958)*. Jakarta: Lembaga Pengembangan Perbankan Indonesia.

Ong Hong Cheong. 1996. "Exchange Rate Fluctuations and Macroeconomic Management, 1980–1995: A Malaysian Perspective." Paper presented to the Pacific Economic Outlook/Structure Specialists' Meeting, Osaka, 27–28 September.

Onghokham 1978. "The Inscrutable and the Paranoid: An Investigation into the Sources of the Brodiningrat Affair." In *Southeast Asian Transitions: Approaches through Social History*, edited by Ruth McVey, 112–57. New Haven: Yale University Press.

OUB (Overseas Union Bank). 1974. *25th Anniversary, 1949–1974*. Singapore: OUB.

Owyang, Hsuan. 1996. *The Barefoot Boy from Songwad: The Life of Chi Owyang*. Singapore: Times Books International.

Paix, Catherine. 1993. "The Domestic Bourgeoisie: How Entrepreneurial? How International?" In *Singapore Changes Guard : Social, Political, and Economic Directions in the 1990s*, edited by Garry Rodan, 184–200. New York: St. Martin's Press.

Pangestu, Mari. 1996. *Economic Reform, Deregulation, and Privatization: The Indonesian Experience*. Jakarta: CSIS.

Pasuk Phongpaichit. 1999. "Developing Social Alternatives: Walking Backwards into a Klong." Paper presented to the National Thai Studies Centre and APSEM Thailand Update Conference, Australian National University, Canberra, 21 April.

Pasuk Phongpaichit and Sungsidh Piriyarangsan. 1994. *Corruption and Democracy in Thailand*. Chiang Mai: Silkworm Books.

Patrick, Hugh, and Yung Chul Park, eds. 1994. *The Financial Development of Japan, Korea, and Taiwan: Growth, Repression, and Liberalization*. New York: Oxford University Press.

Pauly, Louis. 1995. "Capital Mobility, State Autonomy, and Political Legitimacy." *Journal of International Affairs* 48:369–88.

———. 1997. *Who Elected the Bankers? Surveillance and Control in the World Economy*. Ithaca: Cornell University Press.

Peebles, Gavin, and Peter Wilson. 1996. *The Singapore Economy*. Cheltenham: Edward Elgar.

Pempel, T. J., ed. 1999. *The Politics of the Asian Economic Crisis*. Ithaca: Cornell University Press.

Pillai, Philip. 1983. *State Enterprise in Singapore: Legal Importation and Development*. Singapore: Singapore University Press.

Pipit Rochijat. 1985. "Am I PKI or Non-PKI?" *Indonesia* 40:37–56.

Powell, Walter, and Paul DiMaggio, eds. 1991. *The New Institutionalism in Organizational Analysis*. Chicago: University of Chicago Press.

Prawiro, Radius. 1998. *Indonesia's Struggle for Economic Development: Pragmatism in Action*. Kuala Lumpur: Oxford University Press.

Pridmore, Fred. 1968. *Coins and Coinage of the Straits Settlements and British Malaya, 1786 to 1951*. London: Spink.

Prince, G. H. A. 1996. "Monetary Policy in Colonial Indonesia and the Position of the Java Bank." In *Historical Foundations of a National Economy in Indonesia*, edited by J. Thomas

Lindblad, 55–70. Amsterdam: North-Holland and Netherlands Academy of Arts and Sciences.

Puthucheary, James J. 1960. *Ownership and Control in the Malayan Economy*. Singapore: Donald Moore for Eastern Universities Press.

Puthucheary, Mavis. 1978. *The Politics of Administration: The Malaysian Experience*. Kuala Lumpur: Oxford University Press.

Quah, Jon S. T. 1978. "Administrative and Legal Measures for Combating Corruption in Singapore." Occasional Paper 34, Department of Political Science, University of Singapore.

——. 1982. "Bureaucratic Corruption in the ASEAN Countries: A Comparative Analysis of Their Anti-Corruption Strategies." *Journal of Southeast Asian Studies* 13 (1): 153–77.

——. 1996. "Public Administration in Singapore: Managing Success in a Multi-Racial City-State." In *Public Administration in the NICs: Challenges and Accomplishments*, edited by Ahmed Shafiqul Huque, Jane C. Y. Lee, and Jermain T. M. Lam, 59–89. New York: St. Martin's Press; London: Macmillan.

Rahardjo, M. Dawam. 1995. *Bank Indonesia Dalam Kilasan Sejarah Bangsa*. Jakarta: LP3ES.

Reinhart, Carmen, and Vincent Reinhart. 1998. "Some Lessons for Policy Makers Who Deal with the Mixed Blessing of Capital Inflows." In *Capital Flows and Financial Crises*, edited by Miles Kahler, 93–127. Ithaca: Cornell University Press.

Rich, Paul, and Richard Stubbs, eds. 1997. *The Counter-Insurgent State: Guerrilla Warfare and State Building in the Twentieth Century*. Basingstoke, Eng.: Macmillan; New York: St. Martin's Press.

Riggs, Fred. 1966. *Thailand: The Modernization of a Bureaucratic Polity*. Honolulu: East-West Center Press.

Rijckeghem, Caroline van, and Beatrice Weder. 1997. "Corruption and the Rate of Temptation: Do Low Wages in the Civil Service Cause Corruption?" Working Paper 97/73, International Monetary Fund, Washington, D.C.

Robison, Richard. 1986. *Indonesia: The Rise of Capital*. Sydney: Asian Studies Association of Australia and Allen & Unwin.

——. 1994. "Organizing the Transition: Indonesian Politics, 1993/94." In *Indonesia Assessment 1994: Finance as a Key Sector in Indonesia's Development*, edited by Ross McLeod, 49–74. Singapore: ISEAS; Canberra: RSPAS, Australian National University.

——. 1998. "Indonesia after Soeharto: More of the Same, Descent into Chaos, or a Shift to Reform?" In *The Fall of Soeharto*, edited by Geoff Forrester and R. J. May, 219–30. Bathurst, New South Wales: Crawford House.

Robison, Richard, Mark Beeson, Kanishka Jayasuriya, and Hyuk-Rae Kim, eds. 2000. *Politics and Markets in the Wake of the Asian Crisis*. London: Routledge.

Rodan, Garry. 1989. *The Political Economy of Singapore's Industrialization: National State and International Capital*. Kuala Lumpur: Forum.

——. 1993a. "Reconstructing Divisions of Labour: Singapore's New Regional Emphasis." In *Pacific Economic Relations in the 1990s: Cooperation or Conflict?* edited by Richard Higgott, Richard Leaver, and John Ravenhill, 223–49. Boulder, Colo.: Lynne Reiner.

——, ed. 1993b. *Singapore Changes Guard: Social, Political and Economic Directions in the 1990s*. New York: St. Martin's Press.

——. 2000. "Asian Crisis, Transparency, and the International Media in Singapore." *Pacific Review* 13:217–42.

Rodrik, Dani. 1998. "Why Do More Open Economies Have Bigger Governments?" *Journal of Political Economy* 106:997–1032.

——. 1999. "Governing the Global Economy: Does One Architectural Style Fit All?" Paper prepared for the Brookings Institution Trade Policy Forum Conference on Governing in a Global Economy, Washington, D.C., April 1999.

Root, Hilton. 1996. *Small Countries, Big Lessons: Governance and the Rise of East Asia.* Hong Kong: Asian Development Bank and Oxford University Press.

Rose-Ackerman, Susan. 1999. *Corruption and Government: Causes, Consequences, and Reform.* Cambridge: Cambridge University Press.

Rush, James. 1990. *Opium to Java: Revenue Farming and Chinese Enterprise in Colonial Indonesia, 1860–1910.* Ithaca: Cornell University Press.

Sadli, Mohammed. 1993. "Recollections of My Career." *Bulletin of Indonesian Economic Studies* 29 (1):35–51.

Salim, Emil. 1997. "Recollections of My Career." *Bulletin of Indonesian Economic Studies* 33 (1):45–74.

Sato, Yuri. 1994. "The Development of Business Groups in Indonesia: 1967–1989." In *Approaching Suharto's Indonesia from the Margins,* edited by Takashi Shiraishi, 101–53. Ithaca: Cornell University Southeast Asia Program.

Schein, Edgar. 1996. *Strategic Pragmatism: The Culture of Singapore's Economic Development Board.* Cambridge, Mass.: MIT Press.

Schwarz, Adam. 1994. *A Nation in Waiting: Indonesia in the 1990s.* Sydney: Allen & Unwin.

Schulze, David. 1990. *Domestic Financial Institutions in Singapore: Public Sector Competition.* Singapore: Times Academic Press.

Scott, James. 1998. *Seeing like a State: How Certain Schemes to Improve the Human Condition Have Failed.* New Haven: Yale University Press.

SEACEN. N.d. "The Scope of Loan Supervision and Examination in Indonesia." Indonesia country paper, SEACEN seminar. Mimeo.

Seah Chee Meow. 1975. "The Singapore Bureaucracy and Issues of Transition." Working Paper 12, Department of Political Science, University of Singapore.

——. 1987. "The Civil Service." In *Government and Politics of Singapore,* edited by Jon S. T. Quah, Chan Heng Chee, and Seah Chee Meow, 92–119. Singapore: Oxford University Press.

Searle, Peter. 1999. *Rent-Seekers or Real Capitalists? The Riddle of Malaysian Capitalism.* St. Leonards, New South Wales: Allen & Unwin.

Seow, Francis. 1997. "The Politics of Judicial Institutions in Singapore." Lecture, Sydney (www.Singapore-window.org/1028judi.htm).

——. 1998. *The Media Enthralled: Singapore Revisited.* Boulder, Colo.: Lynne Reinner.

Shiraishi, Saya. 1997. *Young Heroes: The Indonesian Family in Politics.* Ithaca: Cornell University Southeast Asia Program.

Shiraishi, Takashi. 1990. *An Age in Motion: Popular Radicalism in Java, 1912–1926.* Ithaca: Cornell University Press.

——. 1997a. "Anti-Sinicism in Java's New Order." In *Essential Outsiders: Chinese and Jews in the Modern Transformation of Southeast Asia and Central Europe,* edited by Daniel Chirot and Anthony Reid, 187–207. Seattle: University of Washington Press.

——. 1997b. "Japan and Southeast Asia." In *Network Power: Japan and Asia,* edited by Peter Katzenstein and Takashi Shiraishi, 169–94. Ithaca: Cornell University Press.

Sidel, John. 1998. "Macet Total: Logics of Circulation and Accumulation in the Demise of Indonesia's New Order." *Indonesia* 66:159–94.

——. 1999. *Capital, Coercion, and Crime: Bossism in the Philippines*. Stanford, Calif.: Stanford University Press.

Siew Nim Chee. 1960. "Central Banking in Malaysia." In *Central Banking in South and East Asia*, edited by S. Gethyn Davies, 111–27. Hong Kong: Hong Kong University Press.

Siffin, William. 1966. *The Thai Bureaucracy: Institutional Change and Development*. Honolulu: East-West Center Press.

Silberman, Bernard. 1993. *Cages of Reason: The Rise of the Rational State in France, Japan, the United States, and Great Britain*. Chicago: Chicago University Press.

Simkin, C. G. F. 1970. "Indonesia's Unrecorded Trade." *Bulletin of Indonesian Economic Studies* 6 (1):17–44.

Simmons, Beth. 1994. *Who Adjusts? Domestic Sources of Foreign Economic Policy during the Interwar Years*. Princeton: Princeton University Press.

Singh, Supriya. 1984. *Bank Negara Malaysia: The First Twenty-Five Years, 1959–1984*. Kuala Lumpur: Bank Negara Malaysia.

Singh Bal, P. A. 1960. "The Civil Service of the Straits Settlements, 1819–1867." Academic Exercise, University of Malaya, Singapore.

Sjafruddin Prawiranegara. 1987. "Recollections of My Career." *Bulletin of Indonesian Economic Studies* 23 (3):100–108.

Smith, Theodore. 1971. "Corruption, Tradition, and Change." *Indonesia* 11:21–40.

Soedarpo Sastrosatomo. 1994. "Recollections of My Career." *Bulletin of Indonesian Economic Studies* 30 (1):39–58.

Soetjipto, Adi Andojo. 2000. "Legal Reform and Challenges in Indonesia." In *Indonesia in Transition: Social Aspects of Reformasi and Crisis*, edited by Chris Manning and Peter van Diermen, 269–77. Singapore: ISEAS.

Solnick, Steven. 1998. *Stealing the State: Control and Collapse in Soviet Institutions*. Cambridge: Harvard University Press.

Spalding, William. 1924. *Eastern Exchange Currency and Finance*. 4th ed. London: Pitman.

Strange, Susan. 1996. *The Retreat of the State*. Cambridge: Cambridge University Press.

Stubbs, Richard. 1997. "The Malayan Emergency and the Development of the Malaysian State." In *The Counter-Insurgent State: Guerrilla Warfare and State Building in the Twentieth Century*, edited by Paul Rich and Richard Stubbs, 50–71. Basingstoke, Eng.: Macmillan; New York: St. Martin's Press.

——. 1998. "Asia-Pacific Regionalism versus Globalization: Competing Forms of Capitalism." In *Regionalism and Global Economic Integration: Europe, Asia, and the Americas*, edited by William Coleman and Geoffrey Underhill, 68–80. London: Routledge.

——. 1999. "War and Economic Development: Export-Oriented Industrialization in East and Southeast Asia." *Comparative Politics* 31:337–55.

Sugiyama Shinya and Milagros Guerrero, eds. 1994. *International Commercial Rivalry in Southeast Asia in the Interwar Period*. New Haven: Yale University Press.

Sumitro Djojohadikusumo. 1986. "Recollections of My Career." *Bulletin of Indonesian Economic Studies* 22 (3):27–39.

Suryadinata, Leo. 1995. *Prominent Indonesian Chinese: Biographical Sketches*. Singapore: ISEAS.

Sutherland, Heather. 1979. *The Making of a Bureaucratic Elite: The Colonial Transformation of the Javanese Priyayi*. Singapore: Heinemann Educational Books.

——. 1980. "The Transformation of the Trengganu Legal Order." *Journal of Southeast Asian Studies* 11 (1):1–29.

Sutter, John. 1959. *Indonesia: Politics in a Changing Economy, 1940–1955*. Ithaca: Cornell University Southeast Asia Program.

Swidler, Ann. 1986. "Culture in Action: Symbols and Strategies." *American Sociological Review* 51:273–86.

Tabalujan, Carlo Hein. 1995. *Fifty Years of Business in Indonesia (1945–95)*. Edinburgh: Pentland Press.

Tan Chwee Huat. 1974. "State Enterprise System and Economic Development in Singapore." Ph.D. dissertation, University of Wisconsin.

——. 1996. *Financial Markets and Institutions in Singapore*. 8th ed. Singapore: Singapore University Press.

Tan, D. G. K. 1983–84. "The Singapore Civil Service: A Study of Specialist Administrators in Two Ministries." Academic Exercise, National University of Singapore, Singapore.

Theobald, Robin. 1995. "Globalization and the Resurgence of the Patrimonial State." *International Review of Administrative Sciences* 61:423–32.

Thomas, Kenneth, and Bruce Glassburner. 1965. "Abrogation, Take-over, and Nationalization: The Elimination of Dutch Economic Dominance from the Republic of Indonesia." *Australian Outlook* 19 (2):158–79.

Tilly, Charles. 1985. "War Making and State Making as Organized Crime." In *Bringing the State Back In*, edited by Peter Evans, Dietrich Reuschmeyer, and Theda Skocpol, 169–91. Cambridge: Cambridge University Press.

Tilman, Robert. 1961. "Public Service Commissions in the Federation of Malaya." *Journal of Asian Studies* 20:181–96.

——. 1964. *Bureaucratic Transition in Malaya*. Durham, N.C.: Duke University Press.

Toh Mun Heng and Linda Low, eds. 1993. *Regional Cooperation and Growth Triangles in ASEAN*. Singapore: Times Academic Press.

Tokunaga, Shojiro. 1992. "Japan's FDI Promotion and Intra-Asian Networks." In *Japan's Foreign Investment and Asian Economic Interdependence: Production, Trade, and Financial Systems*, edited by Shojiro Tokunaga, 5–47. Tokyo: University of Tokyo Press.

Tregonning, Kennedy. 1965. *The British in Malaya: The First Forty Years, 1786–1826*. Tucson: University of Arizona Press.

Trocki, Carl. 1990. *Opium and Empire: Chinese Society in Colonial Singapore, 1800–1910*. Ithaca: Cornell University Press.

——. 1992. "Political Structures in the Nineteenth and Early Twentieth Centuries." In *The Cambridge History of Southeast Asia*, edited by Nicholas Tarling, 79–130. Cambridge: Cambridge University Press.

Twang Peck Yang. 1998. *The Chinese Business Elite in Indonesia and the Transition to Independence, 1940–1950*. Kuala Lumpur: Oxford University Press.

Unger, Danny. 1998. *Building Social Capital in Thailand: Fibers, Finance, and Infrastructure*. Cambridge: Cambridge University Press.

UOB (United Overseas Bank). 1985. *Growing with Singapore: United Overseas Bank, 1935–1985*. Singapore: UOB.

Varela, Amelia. 1996. *Administrative Culture and Political Change*. Quezon City: College of Public Administration, University of the Philippines.

Vennewald, Werner. 1994. "Technocrats in the State Enterprise System of Singapore." Working Paper 32, Asia Research Centre, Murdoch University, Perth.

Vleming, J. L. 1992. "The Chinese Business Community in Netherlands India." In *Chinese Economic Activity in Netherlands India: Selected Translations from the Dutch*, edited by M. R. Fernando and David Bulbeck, 90–259. Singapore: ISEAS; Canberra: RSPAS, Australian National University.

Vogel, Steven. 1996. *Freer Markets, More Rules: Regulatory Reform in Advanced Industrial Countries*. Ithaca: Cornell University Press.

Wade, Robert. 1990. *Governing the Market: Economic Theory and the Role of Government in East Asian Industrialization*. Princeton: Princeton University Press.

Wade, Robert, and Frank Veneroso. 1998. "The Gathering World Slump and the Battle over Capital Controls." *New Left Review* 231:13–42.

Wardhana, Ali. 1971. "The Indonesian Banking System: The Central Bank." In *The Economy of Indonesia: Selected Readings*, edited by Bruce Glassburner, 338–58. Ithaca: Cornell University Press.

Warr, Peter, and Bhanupong Nidhiprabha. 1996. *Thailand's Macroeconomic Miracle: Stable Adjustment and Sustained Growth*. Washington, D.C.: World Bank.

Weber, Max. 1978. *Economy and Society*. Berkeley: University of California Press.

Wee Mon-Cheng. 1972. *The Future of the Chinese in Southeast Asia: As Viewed from the Economic Angle*. Singapore: University Education Press.

Wertheim, W. F. 1964. *East-West Parallels: Sociological Approaches to Modern Asia*. The Hague: W. Van Hoeve.

White, Nicholas. 1996. *Business, Government, and the End of Empire: Malaya, 1942–1957*. Kuala Lumpur: Oxford University Press.

Williamson, Oliver. 1975. *Markets and Hierarchies: Analysis and Antitrust Implications*. New York: Free Press.

Willner, Ann. 1970. "The Neotraditional Accommodation to Political Independence: The Case of Indonesia." In *Cases in Comparative Politics: Asia*, edited by Lucien Pye, 242–306. Boston: Little, Brown.

Wilson, Dick. 1972. *Solid as a Rock: The First Forty Years of the Oversea-Chinese Banking Corporation*. Singapore: Oversea-Chinese Banking Corporation.

Winters, Jeffrey. 1996. *Power in Motion: Capital Mobility and the Indonesia State*. Ithaca: Cornell University Press.

World Bank. 1983. "Staff Appraisal Report: Indonesia, Bank Pembangunan Indonesia (Bapindo) V, 13 April 1983." Regional Projects Department, East Asia and Pacific Regional Office, World Bank.

——. 1991. "Project Completion Report: Indonesia, Fifth Bank Pembangunan Indonesia (Bapindo) Project, 16 August 1991." Industry and Energy Operations Division, Asia Regional Office, World Bank.

——. 2000. *Combating Corruption in the Philippines*. Report No. 20369-PH, Philippine Country Management Unit, East Asia and Pacific Region, World Bank.

Yam, Joseph. 1997. "Asian Monetary Cooperation." Per Jacobsson Lecture, Hong Kong, 21 September 1997 (www.info.gov.hk.hkma/eng/speeches/speechs/joseph/speech_210997b.htm).

Yamamoto Nobuto. 1997. "Reading and Placing Semaoen's Hikajat Kadiroen: A Thought on Political Discourse and Institutional Politics in Early Indonesian Nationalism." *Keio Journal of Politics* 9:49–79.

Yoshihara Kunio. 1978. *Japanese Investment in Southeast Asia*. Honolulu: University Press of Hawaii.

———. 1988. *The Rise of Ersatz Capitalism in South-East Asia*. Singapore: Oxford University Press.

Zainal Aznam Yusof, Awang Adek Hussin, Ismail Alowi, Lim Chee Sing, and Sukhadave Singh. 1994. "Financial Reform in Malaysia." In *Financial Reform: Theory and Practice*, edited by Gerard Caprio, Izak Atiyas, and James Hanson, 276–320. Cambridge: Cambridge University Press.

Zeti Akhtar Aziz. 1997. "Managing Capital Flows in Malaysia." United Nations University and World Institute for Development Economics Research, Helsinki. Mimeo.

Index

Cornell Studies in Political Economy
A series edited by
Peter J. Katzenstein

Internationalizing China: Domestic Interests and Global Linkages
  by David Zweig

Governments, Markets, and Growth: Financial Systems and the Politics of Industrial Change
  by John Zysman

American Industry in International Competition: Government Policies and Corporate Strategies
  edited by John Zysman and Laura Tyson

Milton Keynes UK
Ingram Content Group UK Ltd.
UKHW050156260324
439865UK00004B/21/J